ARIS AND PHILLIPS HISPANIC CLASSICS

T0369754

GIL VICENTE
Three Discovery Plays

Anthony Lappin

Aris & Phillips is an imprint of Oxbow Books

First published in the United Kingdom in 1997. Reprinted 2016 by
OXBOW BOOKS
10 Hythe Bridge Street, Oxford OX1 2EW

and in the United States by
OXBOW BOOKS
1950 Lawrence Road, Havertown, PA 19083

© Anthony Lappin 1997

Paperback Edition: ISBN 978-0-85668-666-5

A CIP record for this book is available from the British Library

All rights reserved. No part of this book may be reproduced or transmitted in any form
or by any means, electronic or mechanical including photocopying, recording or by any
information storage and retrieval system, without permission from the publisher in writing.

For a complete list of Aris & Phillips titles, please contact:

UNITED KINGDOM	UNITED STATES OF AMERICA
Oxbow Books	Oxbow Books
Telephone (01865) 241249	Telephone (800) 791-9354
Fax (01865) 794449	Fax (610) 853-9146
Email: oxbow@oxbowbooks.com	Email: queries@casemateacademic.com
www.oxbowbooks.com	www.casemateacademic.com/oxbow

Oxbow Books is part of the Casemate Group

Front cover: Bartholemew Diaz on his voyage to the Cape.

Printed and bound by CPI Group (UK) Ltd, Croydon, CR0 4YY

The translator and the publishers gratefully acknowledge the financial assistance of the following institutions in the preparation of this volume

Comissão Nacional dos Descobrimentos

Instituto Camões

and for financial assistance with the translation

Instituto Português da Biblioteca Nacional do Livro

The front cover illustration is a woodcut from
A Historia do muy nobre Vespasiano (1498)

Contents

Acknowledgements.. vi

Auto da Barca do Inferno
    Introduction.. 1
    Text and Translation.. 27
    Notes.. 94

Auto da Índia
    Introduction.. 114
    Text and Translation.. 125
    Notes.. 160

Exortação da Guerra
    Introduction.. 168
    Text and Translation.. 175
    Notes.. 214

Abbreviations & Bibliography.. 221

A brief guide to pronunciation.. 228

Acknowledgements

My thanks are especially due to Professor T. F. Earle who originally suggested this project to me, and has been unfailing in encouragement and suggestions; to the fellows of The Queen's College, Oxford, who, by appointing me as a Laming Junior Research Fellow, enabled me to complete this book in the college's gentlemanly atmosphere; to Dr. Claudia Pazos Alonso, who proof read the text and supplied excellent comments upon every aspect of the book; and, above all, to my wife, Barbara, whose essential contribution has come at all stages of the book's preparation, and it is to her that I dedicate this work.

AJL
Oxford, 1997.

Introduction to the Auto da Barca do Inferno

Life and Works of Gil Vicente

Gil Vicente found remarkable professional success throughout his life. One might conceive of his career as that of a proficient social climber. Born to a goldsmith father, Martim Vicente, in Guimarães, most probably between 1465 and 1470, Gil reached the leading positions in his own trade through royal patronage and, after his death, left his children in advantageous positions at court.[1]

Vicente, in his professional capacity as a goldsmith, was commissioned by Manuel I (r. 1495-1521) in 1503 to produce a monstrance for the monastery of the Jerónimos in Belém with the first gold that Vasco da Gama had brought back from India. The task would seem to have taken Vicente three years.[2] Before 1509, Vicente had entered the service of Queen Lianor, Manuel's sister and widow of John II, as her goldsmith. He continued in this post beyond 1513, although it is not known when he left her service. It was presumably during this period of service that Vicente lived in a house owned by Lianor on the *rua de Jerusalém*, opposite her own palace. At some point before 1526, he moved, probably into the *paços velhos da Alcáçova*, in which Manuel I had resided until 1511, and in which Vicente's children continued to live after their father's death which occurred, most probably, late in 1536.[3]

The early part of Vicente's professional life was not marked out solely by his being goldsmith to the queen. In 1509, Vicente was placed in control of all works carried out in gold or silver for the religious houses of Tomar, Madre de Deus in Xabregas and the hospital of Todolos Santos of

---

1 Guimarães was identified by the genealogist, António de Lima, in his *Nobiliário* as the place of Vicente's birth. This information is likely to be correct, for Vicente's daughter-in-law, Guyomar Tavares, stood as godmother to de Lima's daughter, Maria: Anselmo Braamcamp Freire, *Vida e obras de Gil Vicente, 'trovador, mestre da balança'* (2nd. edn., Lisboa: Novas Edições 'Ocidente', 1944), 46 at n. 74.

2 *Ibid.*, 67-68. Vicente's being both goldsmith and playwright was established by Braamcamp Freire, at 35. The arguments against such an identification have been summarized and satisfactorally dismissed by Gilberto Moura, ed., *Teatro de Gil Vicente: Auto da Índia, Auto da Barca do Inferno, Auto da Barca do Purgatório, Farsa de Inês Pereira*, Biblioteca Ulisséia de autores portugueses, 10 (Lisbon: Ulisséia, s.d.), 10-15.

3 Braamcamp Freire, 77, 121, 48.

Belém.[4] On 21 December 1512, he was elected by the guild of gold and silversmiths as one of the *Casa dos Vinte e Quatro*, according to whose rule he must have been at least forty years old and married.

Following this professional recognition, he was elected as one of the four *procuradores dos mesteres* of Lisbon, an office which allowed him to act as representative in the *Câmara* of the gold, silver and gem masters, and with the right to vote on business concerning the craft guilds or the economic government of the city. A document of 6 October 1513 records Gil Vicente fulfilling his function as *procurador*. In February of the same year, he had been named as one of the two *mestres de balança*, an office in the treasury, which he was awarded during the infancy of the child of the post's former occupant. Fulfilling these varied charges led to his assiduous presence at the court. On 3 August 1517, Vicente sold his position as *mestre de balança* to Diogo Rodrigues, another goldsmith, but in the employ of the Infanta Dona Isabel.[5]

It is perhaps due to Vicente's rôle in administration that few works of *ourivesaria* are actually attributed to him. In her will, Lianor left two chalices upon which he had worked to the monastery of Madre de Deus. Manuel I may have left a large processional cross worked by Vicente to the Jerónimos of Belém.[6]

Vicente married Branca Bezerra around 1490, and had two sons by her: Gaspar and Baldasar. The first son served in Goa under Alfonso de Albuquerque, and was sent in 1512 as part of an embassy to Hidalcão. Gaspar returned from India in 1518, served as a *moço da capela real*, and was probably substituted on his death by his brother, who was still in the post in 1535.[7]

Vicente's second marriage to Melícia Rodrigues gave three children: Paula, Luís and Valéria, born in 1519, 1520 and 1530 respectively. Paula became a lady-in-waiting to the infanta Dona Maria, the daughter of Dom Manuel. Valéria married a nobleman, António de Meneses, and had numerous children. Luís had become a *cavaleyro da casa del Rei* by 1580, and was on sufficiently close terms with the *cronista mor*, Fernão de Pina, to be denounced (along with six others) for having homosexual relations with

---

4   *Ibid.*, 76-77.
5   *Ibid.*, 101-102, 122.
6   *Ibid.*, 23 at n. 18, 70 at n. 152. Care must be taken with such an assertion, however, for in a manuscript held at Lisbon, Biblioteca Nacional, cod. 11352, 'Relação dos bens legados pela Rainha D. Leonor, mulher de D. João II, ao Convento da Madre de Deus em Xabregas', copied around 1537, no mention is made of Vicente with regard to the silver or gold donated to the convent (at f. 2r-2v).
7   *Ibid.*, 99-100.

him to the Évora Inquisition in 1546. The accusation was never acted upon.[8]

Gil Vicente's dramatic career would seem to have begun in 1502 with the *Auto da Visitação*. The plays in this volume are all from the early period of his work, the reign of Dom Manuel. Of these three, only the *Auto da Barca do Inferno* survives in a version printed during Vicente's life-time; texts of the other two plays were only printed long after the playwright's death in the *Copilaçam de todalas obras de Gil Vicente*. The importance, then, of the *Auto da Barca do Inferno* for the edition of any texts from the *Copilaçam* is capital, and it is for this reason that it is the first text to be published in the present volume.

The *Auto de Moralidade*: the first version of the *Auto da Barca do Inferno*

The earliest printed version of the play appeared as a 'folha volante' or chap-book. This small, eight-leaved pamphlet is generally dated, following Carolina de Michaëlis, to 1517 or 1518, since, in the introduction to the work, Vicente's patron, the *rainha velha*, Dona Lianor, is described as *nossa senhora*. Such a title that could only have been applied to her during the period of Dom Manuel's second widowerhood, which lasted from the death of Queen Maria on 17 February 1517 to the king's remarriage, the news of which reached Lisbon in the July of 1518.[9]

The summary of the plot of the play given on the first page of the chap-book sketches out the structure of the play: immediately after the death of their bodies, various souls come to the edge of a river which they have to cross. Those that are damned are taken to Hell on a boat crewed by a demon and his companion; those saved are taken to Heaven on a boat manned by an angel.

Three main strands of influence may be identified in this play. The first, and perhaps most important, is the mediæval tradition of visionary accounts of the judgement of the soul, a tradition which was particularly strong in the Iberian peninsula. In these narratives, a visionary would describe his or her own death, the soul's subsequent escape from the hands of demons thanks to the intervention of angels or saints, its appearance before the judgement-seat of Christ where it might witness the

---

8   *Ibid.*, 318, 329, 121 at n. 288.
9   See I. S. Révah, *Recherches sur les œuvres de Gil Vicente*, I: *Édition critique du premier 'Auto das Barcas'* (Lisbonne: Bibliothèque du Centre d'Histoire du Théâtre Portugais, 1951), 22. Unfortunately, I have been unable to consult Martin Angele, *Gil Vicente: Os Autos das Barcas. 1. Einleitung und Kommentar* (Kassel: Edition Reichenberger, 1995).

judgement of others, and its return to earth to reanimate the visionary's body. The *Vita Theotonii*, written in Portugal in the twelfth century, provides a good example.[10]

A second influence comes from classical texts rediscovered by the Renaissance, in particular Lucian of Samosata's satirical *Dialogues of the Dead*, in which an ironic Charon comments upon the various misdeeds of those he carries across the Styx to Hades.[11]

A final element in the play was provided by the highly popular, moralistic literature which depicted a ship of fools (or sinners) which would carry those embarked upon it to hell, and the ship of penitence, or the Christian life, whose haven would be heaven. Reckert identified Johann Geiler's *Navicula penitentiæ* as a possible source of inspiration for Gil Vicente.[12] The *Navicula* describes the Christian life in terms of an extended allegory upon the figure of a boat.

The title of the play, *Auto de Moralidade*, informs us precisely in what genre we should consider the work. One would expect the *Auto* to have been published with a moralistic intention, its cheap, chap-book format making available to the masses a message which emphasized the importance of fairness and justice rather than hypocritical devotional practice. Gil Vicente presents a satire of Portuguese society through the characters he condemns to hell. A well-known fidalgo or nobleman is damned for his tyrannous and licentious behaviour; a shoemaker for swindling his customers; a Dominican friar for keeping a mistress; a judge and a lawyer for the usual sins of the legal profession; and a usurer, a bawd familiar to the court of Vicente's day, and a man hanged for theft, for their respective sins. A Jew, unaware of the difference between salvation and damnation, asks the devil to let him board without looking for the boat to heaven. He is instructed by the devil to swim behind the

---

10   *Vita Theotonii*, ed. A. Herculano, *Portugaliæ Monumenta Historica: Scriptores I* (Lisbon, 1856), 79-88.

11   E. Asensio, 'Las fuentes de las *Barcas* de Gil Vicente: lógica intelectual e imaginación dramática', *Estudios portugueses* (Paris: Fundação Calouste Gulbenkian-Centro Cultural Português, 1974), 59-77 [reprinted from *Bulletin d'Histoire du Théâtre Portugais*, 4 (1953), 207-37], 60-64.

12   Stephen Reckert, *Gil Vicente: espíritu y letra*, Biblioteca Románica Hispánica, IV, 10 (Madrid: Gredos, 1976), 175-78. Iohannes Geiler, *Navicula Penitentie, per excellentissimum sacre pagine doctorem, Joannem Keyserspergium Argentinensium Concionatorem predicata. A Jacobo Otthero collecta* (1511?). For the possible influence of the *Danza de la Muerte* upon the *Auto*, see Asensio, 65-68, and Celso Lafer, 'O judeu em Gil Vicente', *Gil Vicente e Camões (Dois estudos sobre a cultura portuguesa do século XVI)*, Ensaios, 50 (São Paulo: Ática, 1978), 19-101, at 42.

boat to hell. Only a fool and four crusading knights are welcomed by the angel.

Throughout the play, the dramatic interest of the characters one expects to be damned lies in how they comically seek to justify themselves: the usurer thinks money will solve his predicament; the friar considers the habit of his order sufficient protection; the bawd casts herself as a martyr through her profession. An exception is the Jew, who thinks he is being saved by going to Hell.

In a manner which has common aspects with Erasmianism, but which depended more substantially upon a broader mediæval tradition that emphasized the need for individual conversion,[13] Vicente attacks the belief that the religious practices that accompanied death automatically assured salvation. The magistrate thought confession before death a sufficient act, despite its being incomplete. The noble relied upon his wife's prayers, and the appearances of a 'good' life, but is ridiculed for his tyranny toward the poor. The cobbler expected that the prayers of his confraternity would help him although he had spent the last thirty years committing thefts.[14]

The devotional practices which noble and cobbler espouse, however, were generally seen as efficacious only after the soul had been received into Purgatory, that state in which the soul was purged of the guilt which remained from sins of which it had repented, but for which the person before his or her death had not done penance. Something was, in other words, still due before the spotless soul could see and enjoy the vision of God, that is, the state called 'Heaven'. Purgatory is only mentioned once in the play, and that in the black comedy of the scene of the Hanged Man. It is invoked only to be dismissed, identified with the convict's earthly prison and gallows. Indeed, when the souls arrive at the river, there are only two possibilities painted before them: Heaven or Hell. Purgatory does not feature in the allegorical landscape.[15]

---

13 See Paul Teyssier, 'L'humanisme portugais et l'Europe', in his *Études de littérature et de linguistique* (Paris: Fondation Calouste Gulbenkian, 1990), 1-26, at 10.

14 The cobbler relies upon 'oras dos finados', which would be said not by his family but by a confraternity or other religious order. There were two confraternities of cobblers in Lisbon: São Vicente and Nossa Senhora da Mercê. The latter ran two hospitals. See Maria José Pimenta Ferro Tavares, *Pobreza e morte em Portugal na Idade média* (Lisboa: Presença, 1989), 111, 118. The primary function of confraternities was to pray for their deceased members and benefactors: *Ibid.*, 102.

15 The idea that the river-bank is to be equated with Purgatory is found only in Vicente's later re-working of the overall allegorical scheme in the *Barca do Purgatório*. It is not present in the *Moralidade*, for the introduction on the first page of the chapbook informs the reader that the souls *must* the cross the river in one of the two boats. A sojourn by the banks of Lethe is not envisaged. Gil Vicente was certainly not being an orthodox Catholic in his omission. The Ecumenical Council of Ferrara-Florence in

INTRODUCTION: *AUTO DA BARCA DO INFERNO*

Vicente's simplification of the other-world into a stark, binary opposition sought to increase those anxieties over salvation and damnation which the sacramental practice of confession, the purchase of indulgences and the communal piety of prayers and offerings for the dead strove to assuage. To awaken the fear of hell in its readership is clearly one of the aims of the *Moralidade*, for the knights sing, 'remember, by God, remember, this fearful wharf' (ll. 831-32).

Vicente's antidote to existential anxiety is poised at a psychologically and dramatically key moment. The devil has decided that it is time to set sail, and orders all the damned to push out the boat. The play seems to be coming to an end, and closing with a sombre message, but then the final climax is reached as four crusaders enter singing.

The last scene of the *Moralidade* offers propaganda for a crusade: an unusually lengthy stage-direction announces the arrival of the knights, who have died 'em poder dos Mouros', presumably in captivity in Africa. They are saved because, as this stage-direction informs us, they are 'absolved from all guilt and punishments due for their sins thanks to privileges granted by all the popes of our Holy Mother the Church'. Rather than simply recording useful information on acting and staging, the stage-direction primarily fulfilled the literary aim of reminding the lay reader why those who died fighting the infidel were welcomed into heaven as 'martyres da madre ygreja', martyrs of Mother Church.

The propagandistic aspect to the *Moralidade* is confirmed by the treatment of the Dominican Friar who is summoned to judgement. Founded in the thirteenth-century, the friars were a potent force in the Portugal of Vicente's day, and in numerous plays the writer took the opportunity to criticize them, complaining that the number of vocations that they received drained men away from the important business of the struggle with the Moors. In the *Frágoa de Amor* a friar says, when asked by Cupid why he wants to be transformed into a layman,[16]

1445 had issued a dogmatic teaching on the existence of Purgatory, a statement which revived that of the Council of Lyons in 1275 (see Robert Ombres, OP, 'Images of Healing: the making of the traditions concerning purgatory', *Eastern Churches Review*, 8 (1976), 128-38). Luciana Stegagno Picchio, 'Per una semiologia dell'aldilà: l'idea di purgatorio in Gil Vicente', in *Homenaje a Eugenio Asensio* (Madrid: Gredos, 1988), 447-58, at 457, compares Vicente to Luther because of this omission of Purgatory.

16   *Copilaçam*, f. 155v A.

Porque meu saber nam erra	*because my knowledge does not err*
somos mais frades [n]a terra	*we are too many friars in the land,*
sem conto na Christandade	*uncountable in Christendom,*
sem servirmos nunca en guerra.	*without ever serving in war.*
E aviam mister refundidos	*And at least three quarters of them*
ao menos tres partes delles	*need be recast*
em leygos, & arneses nelles,	*as laymen, and harness put on them,*
& muy bem aprecebidos;	*and have them very well equipped;;*
entam a Mouros co'elles!'	*and then, at the Moors with 'em.*

In the *Moralidade*, the Dominican Friar dances onto the stage with his mistress. He informs the devil that he provided for this woman from the funds of the convent to which he belonged. The devil is surprised, and asks if he had been chastised by his fellows. The Friar's reply is damning, not only of himself, but of the order in general: 'they all do the same thing'. Vicente's satire is not only aimed at the personal morality of the friars. Their disreputable involvement in politics is also alluded to, through Florença, Fray Babriel's mistress. Her name alludes to the city in which the Italian Dominican, Savonarola, had supported the establishment of a democracy, and in the main square of which he had been hanged in May 1498 on the orders of the Borgia pope, Alexander VI (1492-1503).[17]

Furthermore, the dramatic elements of the play reinforce the comparison between the Dominican and the crusaders: the friar comes onto the stage singing, and sings when he approaches the angel's boat. The crusading knights also enter singing, and sing as they go forward to the boat to Heaven. The friar comes armed with sword and buckler; the knights with swords and shields. Yet the friar sings only meaningless syllables, the knights a morally uplifting song; the friar's weapons are for the self-indulgent past-time of fencing, the knights have swords and shields of war.

The moral to be drawn from the contrast could not be clearer. If one were to join the Order of Friars Preachers to save one's soul, one would be in grave danger of losing it. Better, by far, to go on crusade. This certain route to Heaven is pointed out at the very end of the play. The moralist's criticism of over-reliance upon the pious activity of others for one's own spiritual well-being is turned into an apology for militaristic involvement. Communal concern over the welfare of benefactors, friends

---

17   For an account of Savonarola's involvement in Florence and the political forces which led to his execution, see Ferdinand Schevill, *Medieval and Renaissance Florence*, vol. II: *The coming of Humanism and the Age of the Medici* (New York: Harper & Row, 1961), 439-55.

and relatives after death is replaced not by an individual, interior, religious conversion, but by an personal decision to join another communal activity, religious warfare beneath the national flag.

The enthusiasm for crusading that Gil Vicente displays in the *Moralidade* was not without royal approval. Dom Manuel, after a short period of mourning for his deceased wife, announced in the summer of 1517 that he would lead a crusade into Africa. The Fifth Lateran Council may have swayed his mind, for it ended on 16 March 1517 with a call from Pope Leo X (1513-1521) for a crusade against the Turk.[18] Manuel's pious intention was never fulfilled, for thoughts of a dynastic alliance turned his mind to another Spanish marriage. However, even while secret negotiations had been entered into in order to secure the hand of Manuel's third wife, the 'official line' maintained until the end of February of 1518 was that the king would go on Crusade against the infidel.[19] The play would then have been printed at some point between the summer of 1517 and March 1518. Furthermore, the attack on the Dominicans was in line with royal policy: Manuel had long striven to reform all orders of friars. Between 1501 and 1505, he had negotiated with the pope for the reform of the Poor Clares, the Enclosed Franciscans, the Dominicans, the Carmelites and the Trinitarians. Frei Hurtado de Mendoza came to Portugal in 1513 in order to reform the Dominican provice, but his mission was a failure.[20] Vicente, dependent upon a network of patronage for his social position, was accustomed, both as a goldsmith and as a dramatist, to receive commissions and to please his patrons. The *Auto de Santo Martinho*, for example, is a short piece written expressly to order. It is therefore likely that the *Moralidade* subscribed, at least in part, to the political agenda of his masters.

A specific instance of the reflection in the play of the contemporary blend of religion and politics appears also in the problematic figure of the Jew. When he appears at judgement, the Jew is presented as blind to the reality of condemnation and salvation. He offers to pay the devil to take him to Hell. He insists on being accompanied by the goat he carries upon his back. He is accused by the fool, in one of the more scatalogical passages of the play, of urinating upon graves in a church. Almost all of the common mediæval anti-Jewish stereotypes are gathered together. Yet the play was written at a time when, officially, no Jews were present in

---

18 *The Oxford Dictionary of Popes*, ed. J. N. D. Kelly (Oxford: O. U. P., 1986), 258A.

19 Braamcamp Freire, 125-131.

20 See the excellent article by Claude-Henri Frèches, 'L'économie du salut dans la trilogie des "Barques"', in *Mélanges à la mémoire d'André Joucla-Ruau* (2 vols.; Aix-en-Provence: Éditions de l'Université de Provence, 1977), II, 723-736, at 727.

Portugal, since they had all been forced to convert nearly twenty years earlier.[21]

Although their conversion had been obtained, the Jewish community had not been forced to adopt any Christian practices. The *cristãos novos* were free from any inquisition into their beliefs or behaviour during the reign of Manuel I. The spiritual blindness of the Jew in the *Moralidade* would seem to be an intellectual justification of this split policy of having Jews baptised without enforcing Christian observances. The *Judeu* is simply incapable of recognising the truth, even after death, underpinning the pointlessness of attempting any real conversion, since Jews were predestined to damnation. Vicente expressed an identical view in a rhymed sermon in Spanish preached before Queen Lianor in 1506. The question of whether the Jews should have been forcibly baptised was prudently avoided, but, as to the rest,[22]

Es por demás pedir al Judio	*It is too much to ask the Jew*
que sea Christiano en su coraçon:	*to be a Christian in his heart;*
es por demás buscar perfección	*it is too much to seek perfection*
adonde el amor de dios está frio,	*where the love of God runs cold;*
también está llano	*it is also plain,*
que es por demás al que es mal Christiano	*for it is too much for the bad Christian*
doctrina de Christo por fuerça ni ruego,	*the doctrine of Christ by force or entreaty,*
es por demás la candela al ciego,	*it is too much for the blindman a candle*
y consejo al loco, y don al villano.	*and advice for the madman, and 'sir' for the villein.*

Neither preaching nor compelling Jews towards Christian observance could have any result, any more than providing a blind man with a candle.

Whilst the figure of the Jew may owe a certain amount to popular stereotypes, the figure of the fool has, as Paul Teyssier rightly suspected,[23] been taken from popular drama, since although his name is given in the stage-direction, it is never mentioned in dialogue on stage. *Joane o Parvo* was evidently some kind of folk hero, originating in that mediæval symbiosis of popular and ecclesiastial theatre whose growth had become rank, if one judges from the strictures set out for the liturgical celebration of Christmas by the Bishop of Oporto in 1475:[24]

---

21   See John Edwards, 'Expulsion or indoctrination? The fate of Portugal's Jews in and after 1497', in *Portuguese, Brazilian and African Studies: studies presented to Clive Willis on his Retirement*, ed. T. F. Earle and Nigel Griffin (Warminster, England: Aris & Phillips, 1995), 87-96.

22   *Copilaçam*, f. 253v A.

23   Paul Teyssier, *La langue de Gil Vicente* (Paris: Librairie C. Klincksieck, 1959), 78, 172.

24   Luiz Francisco Rebello, *O Primitivo Teatro Português* (Lisbon: Biblioteca Breve, 1977),

Não cantem chanceletas nem outras cantigas algumas, nem façam jogos no coro
da igreja, salvo se for alguma boa e devota representação como é a do Presépio
ou dos reis magos, ou outras semelhantes a elas, as quais façam com toda a
honestidade e devoção e sem riso nem outra turvação.
Neither ditties nor other songs of any kind may be sung, nor may there be any plays
performed in the choir of the church, unless it be some good and devout representation such
as that of the Crib or of the Three Kings, or others of their kind, which should be performed
with all honesty and devotion, and without any laughter or any other type of distractions.

It is to express the popular origin of the character that I have translated
his name as 'Simple Simon' in my Englishing of the text.

In profiting from the popular appeal of the character, Gil Vicente is able
to exploit the contrast of the fool who is saved with the ship of fools (the
navicula stultorum of Geiler) who are damned. However, it is only through
his idiocy that Joane is saved; those who are less imbecile have to be
concerned more with their own *malitia*, or evil inclinations.

The fool plays an important dramatic rôle, according to Reckert, by
breaking the monotony of the processional form of the drama by his
interjections.[25] His scatological speech has often been characterized as
'carnavelesque' by critics, in the manner identical to that used by Bahktin
to describe Rabelais' characters. Such an equation needs a certain nuance.
The fool, as a character from that mediæval, popular theatre which left no
written trace in Portugal, was probably a carnavelesque figure, providing
a topsy-turvying influence, a critique of arrogance and ill-use of authority.
In the *Auto de Moralidade*, however, the fool's blend of the gross and the
vulgar, his concentration on the excremental and the sexual, is directed
either at the devil or at characters who are clearly damned. The
scatalogical and phallic imagery which, on this side of the grave, may be
said to possess powers of regeneration,[26] is, in the *Auto de Moralidade*,
hurled at those who cannot hope to be regenerated, who are bound for the
place of despair. The fool's humiliating insults are a verbal expression or
prefiguration of the characters' damnation and torture in Hell. Far from
being the voice of unorthodoxy, the fool can speak for the angel, and hand
out God's judgement upon both Jew and friar, who are allowed no
communication with the angelic boatmen. The equation of the friar with

35, quoted by José I. Suárez, *Vicentine Comedy within the Serio-Comic Mode*
(Mississagua, Ontario: Associated University Presses, 1993), 40-41.

25   Reckert, 75-6.

26   Maria José Palla, 'O parvo e o mundo às avessas em Gil Vicente — algumas
reflexões', in *Temas Vicentinos. Actas do colóquio em torno da obra de Gil Vicente; Teatro da
Cornucópia, 1988* (Lisboa: Ministério da Educação, Instituto de Cultura e Língua
Portuguesa, 1992), 87-99, at 91.

the Jew would seem to be another means by which Vicente sought to do down the Order of Preachers. In any case, both Hebrew and Dominican are shown to be furthest away from salvation, for even the usurer could share a joke with the angel. The 'subversive' popular character of the fool is exploited in the *Moralidade* to support the political aims of the hierarchy.

The *Auto de Moralidade* is presented in the chap-book as a play which was seen by the king. This is expressly stated in its introduction and implied by the numerous preterite tenses found throught the text in the stage directions. The presence in the plot of characters known to the court is of a piece with the aura of court drama surrounding the *Moralidade*, and must have been part of the play's appeal, even to an wider audience. The first character to appear on stage, Dom Anrique, was identified by Diogo do Couto in his fifth *Década* as an important nobleman:[27]

> Dom Anrrique de Meneses, irmão do marques de Villa Real — aquelle do Auto da Barca de Gil Vicente que dizia 'o poderoso dom Anrrique que he Vossa Senhoria', porque hera hu[m] fidalgo muy vão e mandava aos criados que lhe falassem por 'Senhoria'; p[e]lo que se conta del Rey Dom João aquella galantaria que, estando falando com o marques, lhe perguntava: 'Como está a Senhoria de vosso irmão?'
> *Lord Henry of Meneses, brother of the Marquis of Vila Real, he of the Auto da Barca of Gil Vicente that said, 'oh powerful Lord Henry, what is your lordship doing here?' because he was a very vain nobleman and ordered servants to call him 'your Lordship', because of which the witticism of King João is told: while speaking to the Marquis, the king asked him, 'How is the Lordship, your brother?'*

The king is question was presumably João II (†1495). Dom Anrique, in spite of his illustrious brother, was obviously something of a whipping-boy. The 'misquotation' of two lines of the play by Diogo do Couto ('o poderoso dom Anrrique/que he vossa Senhoria', now lines 23 and 241 respectively) may well represent an earlier performance of the play which was subsequently reworked into the form that we have it in the *Auto de Moralidade*.

The scene of the Hanged Man was a puzzle to all critics of the play until Américo da Costa Ramalho provided the means to explain the references made to Garcia Moniz.[28] The Hanged Man enters the stage, and the devil immediately asks him, 'What does Garcia Moniz say there?' Garcia Moniz was Gil Vicente's superior whilst the latter was employed in the treasury. Moniz was also, however, a member of the confraternity *da*

---

27 Quoted by Révah, *Recherches*, 106. 'Senhoria' was a title only applied to the Marquis himself.
28 Américo da Costa Ramalho, 'A "feia acção" de Gil Vicente', *Estudos sobre a época do Renascimento* (Coimbra: Instituto de Alta Cultura, 1969), 124-129.

Misericórdia. One of the obligations which this organisation laid upon its members was that of accompanying condemned criminals to their execution.[29] The Hanged Man reproduces a burlesque version of the 'consolations' preached to him by Garcia Moniz. The confraternity had been established by Vicente's patron, Queen Lianor, in 1498. It is likely that this scene is again designed for the consumption of Vicente's patrons and protectors, 'in jokes' for his own faction in court. The only other reference to Garcia Moniz in Vicente's plays comes from the *Velho da Horta* of 1512, produced shortly before Vicente was appointed to the treasury on 4 February, 1513:[30]

Ò sam Gracia	*Oh, saint Garcia*
Moniz, tu que oje em dia	*Moniz, you who nowadays*
fazes milagres dobrados,	*perform redoubled miracles,*
dá-lhe esforço e alegria	*give him strength and joy*
pois que es da companhia	*since you're of the company*
dos penados.	*of the suffering.*

The verses honour him ironically. Yet his pious accompaniment of the condemned is recognized in his being patron saint of the 'penados', both those punished by the law and those who pain with love. The devil's admonishment to the Hanged Man in the *Moralidade*, 'If you'd believed what he said/it's certain that you'd be saved' (ll. 819-20), show that there was no harsh criticism of Moniz intended. Vicente saw fit to sell his position of *mestre da balança* on 3 August 1517, less than a month and a half after Moniz had been replaced as head of the Treasury by Rui Leite on 22 June 1517.[31]

We might summarize the *Moralidade* by saying that it is an instrument of propaganda for a royal policy that sought soldiers for expansion into Africa. The *Moralidade*'s cheap, small, chap-book format destined it for easy distribution among the literate classes, and thence, by reading to small groups of listeners, to the population at large. The *Auto da Barca do Inferno* was next brought to light as part of the collected works of the playwright in 1562. I shall make some general considerations about this collection before turning to the specific text of the *Auto* which is printed therein.

---

29   See Pimenta Ferro Tavares, 103-4.
30   Costa Ramalho, 'A "feia acção"', 124.
31   *Ibid.*, 125, note 2, at 174.

The *Copilaçam de todalas obras de Gil Vicente*

Before his death, Gil Vicente would seem to have attempted a collection of his works on the orders of João III (r. 1521-1557). As early as 1530, Vicente may have set about collecting together those works which had been published as chap-books and begun copying unpublished plays in a manuscript form ready to be sent to the printers.[32] He had reached an advanced stage in this work for he managed to write a prologue dedicated to João III, and according to Luis, his son, 'as it was his [i.e., Gil Vicente's] intention that his works should be printed, he wrote out and brought together a large part of them in a big book, and would have brought all together had not death consumed him.'[33]

Vicente's plays had to wait for many years before they were brought to light as a *corpus*, when Paula and Luis Vicente published the *Copilaçam* in 1562, to take advantage of the favour which the plays had found with the young king, Sebastião (†1578), then only eight years old and in his minority. Paula Vicente gained the usual licence to print from the Regent Queen in 1561.

The ordering of the *Copilaçam* into its five books of devotional works, comedies, tragicomedies, farces and minor works may well have originated with Gil Vicente himself. The playwright, in the letter of dedication to João III that prefaced the *Auto de Dom Duardos* wrote,[34]

Como quiera, excellente Principe y Rey muy poderoso, que las Comedias, farças y moralidades que he compuesto en seruicio dela Reyna vuestra tia, quanto en caso de amores, fueron figuras baxas, en las quales no auia co[n]ueniente rethorica, que pudiesse satisfazer al delicado spiritu de V[uestra] A[lteza].
Although, excellent Prince and very powerful King, the Comedies, farces and moralities that I composed in the service of the Queen, your aunt, as regards the depiction of love, contained only low characters, in whom there was no fitting speech which might satisfy Your Highness's delicate spirit.

This enumeration of genres led Révah to claim that Vicente only ever wrote comedies, farces and moralities. The subsequent five-fold division was, according to the same critic, a later accretion.[35] However, in the

---

32 For the date of 1530, see the introduction to the *Exortação da Guerra* in this volume.

33 From Luis' prologue to the *Copilaçam*, f. 3v: 'porque sua tençam era que se empremissem suas obras, escreveo per sua mão & ajuntou em hum livro muyto grande parte dellas, & ajuntara todas se a morte o nam cõsumira.' Vicente's own prologue to João III is on f. 4r.

34 Braamcamp Freire, 535. This letter was omitted from the *Copilaçam* of 1562 but included in its second edition of 1585, at folio 105v.

35 Révah, *Recherches*, 16-18. Gil Vicente, in his prologue to João III included in the

passage cited, Vicente was attempting to stress that he was writing something quite different for João III. The *Auto de Dom Duardos* is termed a Tragicomedy, a title in vogue since the second edition of the *Celestina*, properly called the *Tragicomedia de Calixto y Melibea*. A Spanish translation of the *Auto de Moralidade* appeared in Burgos in 1532 under the title, *Tragicomedia del paraíso y del infierno*. Of the ten *tragicomédias* included in the relevant book of the *Copilação*, only two were composed before João's reign (the *Exortação da Guerra* and the *Côrtes de Júpiter*), and in both of these, Lianor is not mentioned, ceding her place as patron of the play to Dom Manuel.

In a similar vein, the stitching together of the three *Autos das Barcas* may well be the intitiative of a Gil Vicente seeking to make his *moralidades* appear more 'classical' to his new patron, João III, by presenting the three works as three scenes of the same play. That the *Comédia de Rubena* is divided into three scenes indicates that the concept was not foreign to Vicente. Indeed, the 'vendaval cósmico' which Reckert attributes to Vicente's later years[36] may have less to do with internal spiritual renewal and rather more connection to the end of his favour due to the death of the rather dour Manuel I, who had little interest in Italian humanism. Vicente was then obliged to jockey for position under João III, around whom the refreshing zephyrs of the Renaissance had nemorously begun to breathe.

Whilst Gil Vicente's shadow was clearly cast over the composition of the *Copilaçam*, and filial involvement is indubitable, the interference of another body has been hotly debated: the Portuguese Inquisition.

The rôle of the Inquisition in the edition of the *Copilaçam*

The Portuguese Inquisition had been created by the pope at the request of João III in 1531.[37] Although its first concern was the welfare of the *cristãos novos*, those Jews or their descendants who had been forcibly baptised by Manuel I in the early years of his reign, its activity soon spread to all areas of national life.

Although the Inquisition's first *Index*, or list of prohibited books, published in 1547, did not mention Gil Vicente's works, the Index of 1551,

---

Copilaçam, makes reference to 'obras de devaçam', which may be taken as implying that the first book of *his* collected works was then called by the same name as it was in his children's edition of 1562.

36 Reckert, 36
37 Moura, *Teatro*, 16.

four years later, had noticed him, and instructed seven works to be banned:[38]

O auto de dom Duardos que nom tiver ce[n]sura como foy emendado.	*The Auto de Dom Duardos which has not been censored as it was emended*
O auto de Lusitania com os diabos, sem elles poderse ha emprimir.	*The Auto de Lusitânia with the devils; it may be printed without them.*
O auto de pedreanes, por causa das matinas.	*The Auto de Pedreanes, because of the mattins.*
O auto do Jubileu damores.	*The Auto, Jubiléu d'Amores*
O auto da aderencia do paço.	*The Auto, Aderência do Paço.*
O auto da vida do paço.	*The Auto, Vida do Paço.*
O auto dos phisicos.	*The Auto dos Físicos.*

The subsequent *Index* published in Portugal, in 1561, when the *Copilaçam* was already projected if not already in press, made the following proviso concerning the playwright's works:[39]

Gil Vicente — suas obras correrão da maneira que neste anno de 1561 se Imprimem & nas Impressas ate este anno, guardarse a ho regimento do rol passado.
Gil Vicente: his works will circulate in the manner in which they are printed this year, 1561; and for those printed before this year, the ruling of the previous Index is to be followed.

Révah, in his edition of the *Auto da Barca do Inferno*, inferred from this statement that[40]

au mois de mars, 1561, l'Inquisition maintient ses sept prohibitions et n'a pas perdu l'espoir de faire appliquer ces interdictions dans la *Copilaçam* qui est déjà à l'impression. En effet, il est impossible d'admettre que l'Inquisition ait édicté des règles différentes selon que les *autos* étaient reproduits en *Copilaçam* ou en feuilles volantes.

However, as was later pointed out by Reckert, the comments in the 1561 *Index* need not be taken in quite the way that Révah understood them. The Inquisitors intended that some chap-books be either 'emended' or banned, whilst establishing that the text of the *Copilaçam* was to be the 'official'

---

38   Révah, *Recherches*, 5; Reckert, 238-39. The Spanish Index of 1559 reproduced these condemnations and added the *Auto de Amadís de Gaula* (Révah, *Recherches*, 8).

39   Révah, *Recherches*, 7; Reckert, 240.

40   Révah, *Recherces*, 7. It is not necessarily true that the *Copilaçam* was in press when the Inquisition published its *Index*: publication need only have been planned, since, in the phrase, 'que neste anno se imprimem', the verb may be understood as referring to a future printing rather than a contemporaneous one.

text, to which they gave their seal of approval: 'foy visto pelos deputados da sancta Inquisiçam' (*seen by the representatives of the Holy Inquisition*) was printed on the title page of the *Copilaçam* when it was eventually published a year and a half later.[41]

Révah insisted that the regent Queen, Caterina, had forced the Inquisitors to abandon their attempt to censure Gil Vicente's works;[42] yet such a hypothesis would seem to ignore her favouring of the Jesuits and her insistence that the Inquisition be established in Goa, which came about in 1560, only a year before the 'privilegio' was granted to Paula Vicente to publish the *Copilaçam*. One might also observe that, since the published edition was expressly addressed to the young Sebastião (and as his tutors were all Jesuits at the insistence of the same Caterina), it is most unlikely that the publication would not attract the concerned regard of at least some members of the ecclesiastical and educational establishment.[43]

The rather fantastic explanation of Catarina's 'coup de force' against the Inquisition was motivated by Révah's desire to exculpate its officers for any initial bowlderization of Vicente's work and his wish to show how the destruction worked upon the plays was 'due à l'incurie, à la stupidité et au mauvais goût' of Luis Vicente.[44] This is not the case, as an analysis of the changes made to the two texts of the *Auto da Barca do Inferno* will show below.

The second version of the *Auto da Barca do Inferno*: the *Copilaçam*

The *Copilaçam*, which was published posthumously by the playwright's children, is a de luxe production, designed for a much more sophisticated and aristocratic readership. Much has been changed in the text, alterations that were clearly carried out by various hands, which I propose to identify below as those of Gil Vicente, Luis Vicente, and the Inquisitors. Révah, in his edition of the *Auto da Barca do Inferno*, showed that the source of the *Copilaçam*'s text was the chap-book *Auto de Moralidade*.[45] It is on this basis that a comparison will be made.

---

41   Reckert, 240.
42   Révah, *Recherches*, 9.
43   For Caterina's preference of the Jesuits, see the GEPB, 28, 13A.
44   Révah, *Recherches*, 9, 10.
45   On the basis of line 270; see Révah, *Recherches*, 121.

Changes carried out by Gil Vicente.

It is certainly possible to divide the changes that can be attributed to
Vicente into two phases: a relatively early one, where his alterations would
seem to have been motivated by another performance (perhaps with the
Auto da Barca do Purgatório) in the reign of Manuel I; and a later phase,
most probably to be attributed to the period when Vicente, at the behest of
João III, was compiling the collection of his own works which he never
completed.

In the stage direction which announces the arrival of the knights in the
Copilaçam there is an altered description of the 'quatro cavaleros' of the
Moralidade; they have become 'quatro fidalgos cavaleyros' from a
Portuguese military order, whose emblem was the cross of the crusader.
This was not due, I think, to Luis Vicente's social snobbery, as Révah
would have it, the son forgetful of the plebeian origins of his father.[46] The
characterization of the knights as members of the Order of Christ would
seem to imply that the change may have come at the instigation of Vicente
himself, perhaps annotating his copy of the chap-book with a view to a
later production of the piece, or perhaps to return the text to his original
conception before *raisons d'état* determined that a wider significance be
given to the warriors for the faith. Gil Vicente had been named, as noted
earlier, as overseer of all works carried out in gold and silver at the
mother-house of the Order of Christ, Tomar, in 1509.[47] That the knights
belonged to this order would seem to be an attempt to improve their
public relations, to advertise them at court. The change could only have
been made during Manuel's reign, for one of the early acts of João III's
reign was to reduce the military order to a monastic one, forcing the
warrior monks who fought on horseback to be enclosed within their
monastery walls.[48] This change, then, is indubitably from the early period
of Vicente's life.

Two other changes may also come from the need to bring the play up
to date for a subsequent performance. In the scene of the Hanged Man,
lines 797-99, the *Moralidade* depicts the convict enumerating various
'consolations' proffered him by Garcia Moniz: 'He told me that I'd eat
bread and honey with Saint Michael as soon as I'd been hanged.' In the
Copilaçam, however, a change is made which allows the Hanged Man to
reproduce Moniz's speech directly: 'He said, "You'll go eat bread and
honey with Saint Michael since you've been hanged."' Such a change,

46 Révah, *Recherches*, 27, 82-3.
47 Braamcamp Freire, 76-77.
48 *Ibid.*, 180.

involving the mimicry or impersonation of Garcia Moniz, produces an effect explicable as an attempt to increase the comedy of the scene when played before an audience who were familiar with the mannerisms of the individual concerned.

The following addition to the text is more doubtfully attributable to this earlier period, but the balance of probability lies towards it being an inclusion for the sake of performance. In the *Moralidade*, the devil sings a short ditty, 'You'll come by my hand, by my hand you'll come' (ll. 110-11), to which the *Copilaçam* has added, 'and you'll see/fish in the nets'. The success of the addition leads one to think that its author was Vicente himself: the fish stand for souls caught in the devil's toils, an image which provides an inversion of a story from the Gospel of John. Jesus, after his resurrection, appeared to the disciples on the side of the Lake of Galilee and instructed them where they should cast their nets. The fish that they brought into the boat were symbolic of the whole of humanity that would be brought into the Church. The significance of the devil's boat then serves to contrast it with that given to the boat to Paradise in the *Auto da Barca do Purgatório*. The effectiveness of the addition is not limited to its religious significance. The image of fish caught in nets would seem to have had a proverbial force, used to express how the beauty of a woman would 'catch' men,[49] an image particularly suitable to the noble whose life had been based upon the pursuit of sensual pleasure.

The insults hurled at the Jew are softened. He is still damned, but no longer is he accused of urinating upon graves. This may reflect a revision by the author to his play in the light of his later Jewish sympathies, represented, for example, by his depiction of the Jewish family as loyal supporters of the crown at the beginning of the *Auto de Lusitânia*, first performed in 1532.

The 'powerful Lord Henry' of the *Moralidade* becomes 'precious Lord Henry' (l. 23). Another figure from the court was given the 'precious' epithet in the *Velho da Horta*, Dom Henrique de Noronha, grand-master of the Order of Santiago.[50] Vicente's loyalties may well have shifted, necessitating the alteration. Lord Henry's sins are also ameliorated: no longer accused of being a tyrant, he is condemned for his desire to be tyrannous.

---

49   Cp. 'A pescar salió la niña/tendiendo redes/y en lugar de peces/las almas prende', Tirso de Molina, *Don Juan Tenorio o El burlador de Sevilla*, Jornada Primera. ll. 981-984. [The girl went to fish,/hanging out nets/and in place of fish/she catches souls], in Antonio Prieto, ed., *Tirso de Molina: Marta la piedosa — El burlador de Sevilla* (Madrid: Editorial Magisterio Español, 1974), at 226.

50   Révah, *Recherches*, 107.

The characterization of the fool would seem to have been altered by Gil Vicente himself. In the *Moralidade*, the fool, when asked by the angel who he is, replies, "Appen, someone' (l. 298). In the *Copilaçam*'s version, the reply has become, 'I be nobody', a shift which allows a character originally from popular theatre to be transformed into an allegorical figure. In the *Auto da Lusitânia*, an allegorical figure is indeed called 'Ninguém', Nobody.[51] This new-found religious significance given to the fool may well explain why his insults are toned down in a rather haphazard way.

The devil's final words to the hanged man are radically altered. Rather than informing the thief that, had he believed what Moniz had said, he would have been saved, the *Copilaçam*'s devil orders him not to wait for his father but to board. The latter concurs, and the devil expresses his pleasure. The dramatic force of the alteration again makes it likely that Gil Vicente was the author of the change. The mention of the Hanged Man's father points back to the first character on stage, the noble, who is told that his father had preceded him to Hell. In the *Moralidade*, the thief had been the only character to express no acceptance of the need to go on board; in the *Copilaçam* he agrees to embark on the boat to Hell. Reckert has claimed that the characters' recognition of their damnation gives the drama the shape of a classical tragedy, with its characteristic moment of *máthema*.[52] Indeed, the version of the *Copilaçam*, where this feature is made complete, probably corresponded to that period when Gil Vicente was consciously striving to be more 'classical'.

Alterations carried out by Luis Vicente.

The same impulse towards making the text conform more to classical paradigms led Luis Vicente to make other changes to the *Auto da Barca do Inferno*, as he himself admits in his prologue to the *Copilaçam*, comparing himself to the early editor of Homer's text who 'cleaned and purified' it.

In general terms, the spellings and vocabulary of the *Moralidade* are modernized in the *Copilaçam*, although occasionally more modern forms in the former are turned back into archaic forms in the latter. The earlier text, clearly designed for performance, is transformed into a text for reading by the judicious addition of 'ca', 'cá', 'lá', 'que' and '&', conjunctions which make the connections between lines or statements

---

51 See João Nuno Alçada, 'Para um novo significado da presença de Todo o Mundo e Ninguém no *Auto da Lusitânia'*, *Arquivos do Centro Cultural Português*, 21 (1985), 199-271, and José I. Suárez, *Vicentine Comdy within the Serio-Comic Mode* (Mississauga, Ontario: Associated University Presses, 1993), 111.

52 Reckert, 70.

more logical, or which conceptually express place, more usually done by gesture and tone in speech.

Whilst the numerous hispanisms due to the printer of the *Moralidade* are corrected, so too is the macaronic speech of Magistrate and Advocate, whose garbled Latin is made slightly (but only slightly) more correct. Thus 'nom som pecatus meus', distinguishable from the Portuguese by only one letter ('t'), becomes 'non sunt peccatus meus'. Generally, however, the Latin is so 'corrupt' that it is impossible to translate it. In my translation therefore, the Latin is not rendered into English (unless a 'Latin' word is really a Portuguese word 'in disguise'),[53] and an explanation is attempted in the notes.

As we have seen, Gil Vicente altered one stage direction. It is likely that his son continued this process, suppressing or shortening stage directions, and including any information they contained in the dialogue. For example, when the magistrate arrives at the devil's boat, the *Moralidade* has the stage-direction, 'A magistrate enters loaded with judicial processes and, arriving at the boat of Hell with his rod in his hand, says…'. Four lines later, the devil exclaims 'you bring a noble load!' (l. 609); the *Copilaçam*'s devil is less ironic but much more explicit, 'how many processes you've brought!', for the *Copilaçam* had substituted the earlier text's descriptive stage directions with the terse, 'A magistrate enters, and says, reaching the boat of Hell, …'. This type of change seems to be an attempt to make the play fit more easily into the canons of the classical literature which was then so much in vogue. Luis Vicente's changes are, however, in the same trajectory as that which his father had already embarked upon.

The *Copilaçam* states that the setting for the first performance of the *Auto da Barca do Inferno* was before 'Queen Dona Maria, while she was sick with the illness from which she died, the year of our Lord, 1517'. I am in complete accord with Révah, who thought that Luis Vicente, having learnt that the *Auto de Moralidade* was printed in 1517, linked the date, thanks to the otherworldly subject matter, with the death of Maria that had occurred that same year.[54]

53' 'At a time when the use of Latin had certainly achieved an air of snobbery, … "Portuguesifying"Latin in the mouths of popular characters probably had a comic air for those who knew its correct use, and these were then numerous enough': Américo da Costa Ramalho, 'Uma bucólica grega em Gil Vicente', in *Estudos sobre a época do Renascimento* (Coimbra: Instituto de Alta Cultura, 1969), 130-149, at 130-31 [my translation; to assist non-Portuguese speakers, critics writing in Portuguese will henceforward be rendered into English in my own translation].

54 Révah, *Recherches*, 74-6.

Changes wrought by the Inquisition.

The two editions of the *Copilaçam* in the sixteenth century bear witness to a difference in Inquisitorial method. The first *Copilaçam*, that of 1562, displays a care over theological statements, whereas the second edition is just as concerned with what we might term 'taste and decency'. In the second edition, the scenes of the friar and the Hanged Man are wholly excised, and significant changes made to Brísida Vaz's enumeration of her brothel-madam's wares. In the first edition, the changes are much more subtle and are clearly the product of a keen intelligence.

The Dominican friar in the *Copilaçam*'s version of the *Auto da Barca do Inferno* is no longer presented as the representative of a completely corrupt religious order, as in the *Moralidade*. The transformation worked on the scene makes it likely that the inquisitor was a Dominican, since mention of the friar's maintaining his mistress with monastery funds is omitted. Furthermore, the revelation that 'they all do the same thing' (l. 383) with their mistresses is subtly changed. Instead of this line from the *Moralidade*, the *Copilaçam* has something quite different. The friar, when asked about the reaction of his confrères in the priory, replies, 'I was well whipped'. The image presented is no longer that of an order which fails to live by any of its ideals. It is of an order which punished 'black sheep', which was in no need of reform and which functioned as a religious organization should, despite the weakness of some of its members.

Other changes made to the friar's scene display a stricter moralistic intention. The devil's approbation of the friar's actions because of Florença's beauty (l. 380) is omitted by the *Copilaçam*, which stresses that the punishment of Hell is to be meted out to the friar's concubine as well by the devil's instruction, 'that lady is to board here' (l. 375).

Towards the end of the play, the friar is not identified as Frey Babriel (a combination of Gabriel, the name of a Dominican, and Babel, an ironic comment on the friar's vocation of preaching) and told to help push the boat out; rather, that honour is given to the noble and the magistrate.

As we have seen above, the stage direction which announces the arrival of the knights killed in Africa is adopted from the *Moralidade*, but, together with changes worked by Vicente himself, the *Copilaçam* text also omits the theologically suspect proclamation of the knights' being free from all guilt and punishment. The changes wrought are indicative of a change of attitude, a care in theological statements. Ernst Kantorowicz expressed the following view concerning the spiritual status of crusaders in the thirteenth century:[55]

> A crusader who battled against the infidels for the Christian faith and died for the cause of the Holy Land in the service of Christ the King was entitled, according to common belief, to expect immediate entry into the celestial Paradise and, as a reward for his self-sacrifice, the crown of martyrdom hereafter. ... Whether this confidence in other-worldly reward was dogmatically sound or rather a misunderstanding of papal decrees (which granted crusaders no remission of sins, but remission of such punishments as the discipline of the church might have imposed) made little difference then.

By the mid-sixteenth century, however, there was a difference: in the *Copilaçam*, the knights are 'saints', not 'martyrs', surely saved, but not at the highest level of honour.

The same theological care is witnessed in the noble's scene. In the *Moralidade*, the devil informs the illustrious 'senhoria' that, 'before you died, you gave me a sign' that he would embark upon the devil's boat. The *Copilaçam* adjusts the line to a hypermetric one, '*when* you died ...', being precise that the moment that the soul is damned or saved is at the moment of death, not before.

Conclusion.

It would be too laborious to consider each of the minor changes to the text in turn. They will be dealt with in the notes to the relevant lines. The changes to the text of the *Auto* in the *Copilaçam* betray several interests. On a first level of alteration, Gil Vicente's own hand has adjusted certain aspects of the play relatively soon after the printing of the *Auto de Moralidade*. On a second level, alterations were again carried out by Vicente to allow for a change in his interests and his patrons, to make a more devotional reading of the play possible through the allegorical figure of the fool who is 'Nobody', and to present the material in a more classical form to suit the tastes of João III. On a third level, this conformity to classical paradigms was continued by Luis Vicente, and, on the fourth, the Inquisition provided changes that witness to theological constraints being

---

55 Ernst H. Kantorowicz, *The King's Two Bodies: a study in mediæval political theology* (Princeton, 1987), 238-9. Bonaventure, in the thirteenth century, 'was concerned lest the crusade indulgence be taken as a flat guarantee of eternal salvation ... crusaders who failed to live righteously would risk eternal damnation', James A. Brundage, *Medieval Canon Law and the Crusader* (Madison: University of Wisconsin Press, 1969), 151.

placed upon the text of the play. These 'levels' of composition reflect various moments in the history of the play: an initial adaptation of the work for a performance during the life of Manuel I; a second adaptation by Vicente as he sought to prepare a collection of his own works; and a third series of adaptations, by Luis Vicente and the Inquisition to provide an 'official text' of which the Inquisition approved and which could be printed in the *Copilaçam*. These four types of changes came together in that text, published in 1562.

In view of the different hands at work in the re-elaboration of the *Auto* for the *Copilaçam*, an edition of a definitive text appears impossible. Whilst the *Moralidade* can claim to be the authentic production of the playwright, elements of the text in the *Copilaçam* would also seem to come from Gil Vicente's quill. Yet these alterations change the focus of the play and leave us with two clearly distinct versions of the same work. It is for these reasons that I have chosen the *Moralidade* as my base text, yet also provide, when variants warrant it, the reading of the *Copilaçam*'s text in parallel. The reader may then see clearly the major differences between the versions of the play. This edition does not seek to reconstruct an archetype of the text, the perfect creation of the artist's mind; rather, it aims to present the history of the text within the evidence that we possess.

Note to the Critical Edition

I have used a combination of sigilla and style of letters to indicate the sources of the critical edition.

M indicates the *Auto de Moralidade*, represented by normal text.
C indicates the text of the *Auto da Barca do Inferno* found in the *Copilaçam*, which is represented by italic script.
My own interventions are signalled by bold script.

Censorship by the Inquisition in subsequent editions of the text or in a later *Index* is identified in the notes. Two later printed versions of the play have been consulted according to their editions in Paolo Quintela, ed., *Gil Vicente: Auto de Moralidade da Embarcação do Inferno, textos das duas primeiras 'edições avulsas' e das 'Copilações' ... com um apêndice que contém a 'Tragicomedia Alegorica del Parayso y del Infierno'* (Coimbra: Atlântida, 1946):

μ: a chap-book reprinting of the *Auto de Moralidade*, censored by the Inquisition.
D: the second edition of the *Copilaçam*, published in 1586.

Original spellings have been maintained, although 'v' and 'u' have been differentiated. In *M* and *C*, 'v' and 'u' are used to signify both sounds, 'v' being used for the beginning of words (e.g., 'vxore', 'vt') and 'u' being used within a word (e.g., 'louuores'). The forms of the definite article occasionally found in both texts, 'ho', 'ha' have been modernized to 'o', 'a'; these 'modern' forms are, however, occasionally found in the text. The initial 'h' is merely a typographical convention to signal the beginning of a new word. The forms 'hũ', 'hũa' have also been rendered ũ, although the more archaic 'huũ' has been retained when it occurs. The form 'he', when it signifies 'he/she/it is' has been modernized to 'é'. The original forms are always given in the *apparatus criticus*. Letters supplied to expand marks of abbreviation are underlined.

Double letters, 'oo', 'aa', etc., have been represented by an accent: 'ò', 'ó', 'à', 'á', etc. Whilst the gothic script of both *M* and *C* bears no accents, the Humanist type that *C* uses for stage directions occasionally contains 'á' where one might expect 'aa'.

The presentation of the text may be surprising to those readers accustomed to editions which wholeheartedly modernize following the eminently logical system of Paul Teyssier.[56] As there are several excellent

---

56   Paul Teyssier, 'Normes pour une édition critique des œuvres de Gil Vicente', *Critique*

modernized texts of the plays that I present in this volume,[57] I have felt free to strike a balance between the demands of modern readers for clarity, regularity and accessibility with the desire to retain as much of the original text as possible. Spellings have therefore been retained largely unchanged. I hope that this halfway house will serve as an introduction and encouragement for students to approach unmodernized editions of mediæval texts. The edition thus seeks to be another contribution to the 'bibliographical spectrum' of editions of Gil Vicente, attempting to fill an area which is not covered by the range of modernized editions.[58]

The words of a text are not just the sum of their phonetic integrity; they have a beauty and a charm in their presentation on the page, in the way in which they are spelt. If the archaic forms in the play give pleasure to the reader in and of themselves (as they do to this reader), this is one thing; if they serve to remind the reader that the text was written 'long ago and [therefore] far away', that the play represents a world different to any text written in modern Portuguese orthography, then that is a far greater success. This edition is, then, an unhappy and probably illogical compromise between authenticity and modernization. It is inauthentic because modern readers cannot be expected to read the gothic type of the originals. Yet that inability is also their misfortune. And so, this edition attempts to preserve as much as the editor thought it possible to preserve, so that the experience of reading might thereby be enriched. In any case, the luxury of a facing translation can often allow the reader the opportunity to clarify unfamiliar forms and phrases by comparing the original with its translation.

---

textuelle portugaise: actes du colloque, Paris, 20-24 octobre 1981 (Paris: Fondation Calouste Gulbenkian, 1986), 123-130.

57 Not least of which are those provided in the modernized edition of the *Copilaçam de todalas obras de Gil Vicente* by Maria Leonor Carvalhão Buescu (2 vols.; Lisboa: Imprensa Nacional-Casa da Moeda, 1984).

58 On the 'bibliographical spectrum' or 'campo bibliographico' of editions, see Ivo de Castro and Maria Ana Ramos, 'Estrategia e táctica da transcrição', *Critique textuelle portugaise: actes du colloque, Paris, 20-24 octobre 1981* (Paris: Fondation Calouste Gulbenkian, 1986), 99-122, esp. 114. Révah produced transcriptions of both versions of the *Barca do Inferno* in his edition; a simple reproduction of one or other of the texts was therefore not necessary.

Auto de Moralidade

Morality Play of the Boats

Autos das Barcas: escena primeira

The Boat Plays: Act One.

Auto de moralidade composto per Gil Vicente. Por contemplaçam da serenissima & muyto catholica reynha dona Lianor nossa señora, & representada per seu mandado ao poderoso principe & muy alto rey dom Manuel, primeyro de Portugal deste nome. Começa a declaraçam & argumento da obra:

¶Primeyramente no presente auto se segura que no ponto que acabamos d'espirar chegamos supitamente a huũ ryo, o qual per força avemos de passar em huũ de dous batés que naquelle porto estam, scilicet, huũ delles passa pera o parayso, & o outro pera o inferno, os quaes batés tem cada huũ seu arraez na proa, o do parayso huũ anjo, & o do inferno huũ arraez infernal & huũ companheyro. O primeyro entrelocutor é huũ fidalgo que chegua com huũ page que lhe leva huũ rabo muy comprido & huũa cadeyra d'espaldas. E começa o arraez do inferno desta maneyra ante que o fidalguo venha.

Representa-se na obra seguinte ũa prefiguração, sobre a regurosa acusaçam que os immigos fazem a todas as almas humanas, no ponto que per morte de seus terrestes corpos se partem. E por tratar desta materia, põe o autor por figura que no dito momento ellas chegão a um profundo braço de mar, onde estam dous bateis: ũ delles passa pera a gloria, o outro pera o purgatorio. É repartida em tres partes, scilicet, de cada embarcaçam ũa cena. Esta primeyra é da viagem do inferno: trata-se pollas figuras seguintes.

Primeyramente, a barca do inferno: arraiz & barqueyro della, diabos. Barca do parayso: arraiz & barqueyros della, anjos.

¶Passageyros: ¶Fidalgo, Onzeneyro, Joanne, Çapateyro, Frade, Florença, Alcouviteyra, Judeo, Corregedor, Procurador, Enforcado, quatro cavaleyros.

¶Esta præfiguração se escreve neste primeyro livro, nas obras de devação: porque a segunda & terceyra parte forão representadas na capella, mas esta primeyra foy representada de camara, pera consolação da muyta catholica & sancta Raynha dona Maria, estando enferma do mal de que faleceo, na era do Senhor, de 1517.

---

o · ho (throughout) é · he *um profundo* · *hum profundo* ũ · hũ é · he **Onzeneyro** · *Honzeneyro* **Joanne** · *Ioanne*

Morality Play written by Gil Vicente, for the most serene and Catholic queen, Dona Lianor, our lady, and performed, on her order to the powerful prince and very exalted king, Dom Manuel, the first of this name in Portugal. The description and plot of the work follows:

Firstly, in the present work it is posited that, at the moment when we have breathed our last, we suddenly come to a river, which we, by force, have to cross in one of two boats that are in that port, that is, one goes across to Paradise and the other to Hell. These boats each have their bosun on the prow: the boat of Paradise having an angel; the boat of Hell, an infernal pilot and a companion. The first speaker is a noble who arrives with a page who is carrying his extremely long train and a high-backed chair. And the pilot of hell begins in this way before the noble arrives,

Represented in the following work is a prefiguration concerning the rigorous accusation [over their sins] which the enemies, [the devils], make of all human souls at the moment in which they depart [this life] due to the death of their earthly bodies. And, in order to deal with this subject, the author figuratively sets out that, at the said moment, the souls arrive at a deep inlet of the sea, where there are two boats: one of which passes to glory, the other to purgatory. It is divided into three parts, namely, a scene is given to each embarcation. This first scene is of the voyage to Hell, and it is dealt with by the following figures:

First, the boat of Hell: her bosun and boatman, devils. Boat of Paradise: her pilot and boatman, angels.

Passengers: Noble, Usurer, John, Shoemaker, Friar, Florence, Bawd, Jew, Magistrate, Advocate, Hanged Man, Four Knights.

This prefiguration appears in this, the first book, in the works of devotion, because the second and third part were performed in the chapel, but this first part was represented in her chamber, for the consolation of the very Catholic and holy queen, dona Maria, who was ill with the sickness from which she died, in the year of our Lord, 1517.

DIABO:	¶À barca, à barca, oulá,	[*M f.* 1v A; *C f.* 43v A]
	que *temoſ* gentil maré!	
	Ora venha o caro a ré.	
COMPANH.:	Feyto, feyto!	
DIABO:	Bem est*á*!	
5	Vay tu, muytieramá:	
	atesa aquelle palanco,	
	& despeja aquelle banco	
	pera a gente que vinrá.	

	¶À barca, à barca, h*ú*	[*C f.* 43v B]
10	asinha que se quer ir!	
	Ó que tempo de partir,	
	louvores a Berzebú!	
	Ora sus, que fazes tu?	
	Despeja todo esse leyto.	
15	COMP.:	Em boa ora, feyto, feyto!	
	DIABO:	Abaxa, 'ma-ora, esse cú.	

	¶Faze aquella poja lesta	[*C f.* 44r A]
	& alija aquella driça.	
COMPANH.:	Ó caça! Ó yça, yça!	
20	DIABO:	Ó que caravella esta,	
		põe bandeiras que é festa,	
		verga alta, ancora a pique!	
		Ó poderoso dom Anrrique,	*Ó precioſo dom Anrique*
		c*á* vindes v<u>os</u>, <u>que</u> cousa é esta?	

¶Vee<u>m</u> o fidalgo & chega<u>n</u>do ao batel infernal	[om *C*]
diz:	

25	Esta barca, onde vay ora,
	que assy est*á* apercebida?

---

1 di.¶Aa barca aa barca · *Arraiz ∂o inferno.* / *Haa barca, ha barca,* 2 tenemos · *temoſ*
3 ho caro aree · *a caro a ree.* 4 cõ. feyto feyto. dia. bem esta · *feyto, feyto, bem eſtaa.*
5 vaytu · *Vay alíj* 6 atesa · *e͂ʒ̃ ateſa* 8 vinraa. · *viraa.* 9 ¶Aa barca aa barca huũ ·
¶*Haa barca, ha barca, huu* 10 hir · *yr,* 11 o que · *oo que* 15 em boa ora feyto feyto ·
Em bonora, logo he feyto.

30

DEVIL: Board the boat, board the boat, ho!,
we have a favourable tide.
Now draw astern the mizzen.
MATE: It's done, it's done!
DEVIL: That's good.
5   Hellfire and damnation — go
tighten that rope
and clear that bench
for those who are to come.

Board the boat, board the boat, hey!
10   Quickly, we must be gone.
Oh, what a time to sail
to Beelzebub be praise!
Now, come on, what are you doing?
Clear all that berth.
15 MATE: With luck, it's done, it's done.
DEVIL: Lower the damned block and tackle!

Bring that clew in to the wind
and throw out that halyard!
MATE: Oh, catch it! Oh, raise it, raise it!
20 DEVIL: Oh what a caravel this is:
put out flags, it's a holiday!
Raise the yard-arm, weigh anchor.
Oh, powerful Lord Henry,
you've come; well, what'd you say?

A nobleman enters, and, reaching
the infernal boat, says:

25   Where's this boat now bound
that it is decked out so well?

---

16 abaxa maora · *abayxa aramaa* cuu · *cu* 19 o o caça: o o yça yça · *Hoo caça, hoo
ciça.* 20 oo · *Ho* carauella · *carauela* 21 bandeiras · *bandeyras* é · he *he* 23 o · *hoo*
24 ca · *ca* é · he *he* **stage direction underlined in** *M* **by later hand;** o · ho 26 assy
esta apercebida · assi estaa percebida.

	DIABO:	Vay pera a ylha perdida
		& *há* de partir logo e essora.
	FIDALGO:	*Pera* lá vay a senhora?
30	DIABO:	Senhor, a vosso serviço.
	FIDALGO:	Parece-me ysso cortiço. [*M f.* 1v B]
	DIABO:	Porque a vedes lá de fora.

	FIDALGO:	¶Pore<u>m</u>, a qu<u>e</u> terra passaes?
	DIABO:	Pera o inferno senhor.
35	FID.:	Terra é bem sim sabor.
	DIABO:	Qué? E tambem cá zo<u>m</u>bais?
	FIDALGO:	E passageiros acha<u>e</u>s
		pera tal habitaçam?
	DIABO:	Vejo vos eu em feiçam
40		pera ir ao nosso caes.

	FIDALGO:	¶Parece-te a ty assy?
	DIABO:	Em qu<u>e</u> esperas ter guarida?
	FIDALGO:	Que leyxo na outra vida
		quem reze sempre por mi.
45	DIABO:	Quem reze sempre por ti? —
		hi hi hi hi hi hi hi hi! —
		& tu viveste a teu prazer
		cuydando cá guarecer
		porque rezem lá por ty?

50		¶Embarcae, ó embarcae,
		que aveis d'ir à derradeira:
		mandae meter a cadeira
		que assi passou vosso pay.
	FIDALGO:	Que, que, que? Assy lhe vay?
55	DIABO:	Vay ou ve<u>m</u>, embarcae p<u>re</u>stes:
		segundo lá escolhestes [*C f.* 44r B]
		assi cá vos contentae.

---

28 & a departir logo eessora · *e³ ha de partir logo essora* **29** por la · *Pera la* **31** ysso
· *isso* **32** la · *la* **33** passaes · *passais* **34** ho · *o* **35** sim · *sem* **36** quee: & · *Quee, e³* ca
zõbaes · *ca zombais* **37** & passageiros achaees · *E passageyros achais* **39** feiçam ·
feyçam **40** hir ao nosso caes · *yr ao nosso cais* **41** aty assy · *a ti assi* **43** leyxo · *deyxo*
46 hi hi hi hi hi hi hihi· *hi hi hi hi hi hi,* **48** la · *la*

	DEVIL:	It's going to the Lost Isle,
		and must depart right now.
	NOBLE:	That's where this lady's to head?
30	DEVIL:	My lord, if you please ...
	NOBLE:	She looks a wreck to me.
	DEVIL:	Because you see her from the outside.

	NOBLE:	But to what land will you cross?
	DEVIL:	To Hell, my lord.
35	NOBLE:	A land with no good in store!
	DEVIL:	What? Even here will you scoff?
	NOBLE:	And do you find passengers
		for such an abode?
	DEVIL:	I see you well-disposed
40		to travel to our harbour.

	NOBLE:	Does it seem like that to you?
	DEVIL:	In what do you hope to find a haven?
	NOBLE:	In that I've left, in the other life,
		those who'll always pray for me.
45	DEVIL:	Who'll always pray for you?
		He, he, he, he, he, he, he!
		And you lived as you pleased
		thinking here you'd be saved
		since there they'll always pray for you!

50		Get on board, oh, get on board,
		for you'll have to go, in the end:
		order your chair to be brought on
		for your father went the same way.
	NOBLE:	What, what, what? So that's his fate?
55	DEVIL:	Come or go, get on board soon.
		Here you must content yourself
		according to what you chose there.

---

49 la · *la* ty · *ti* 50 ¶Embarcae ou embarcae · *¶Embarca, ou embarcay* 51 dir aa derradeira · *ðir aa ðerraðeyra* 52 mandae · *manðay* cadeira · *caðeira* 54 que. que.que.assy lhe vay. *Que que que, & assi lhe vay.* 55 embarcae · *embarcay* 56 la · *la* 57 ca · *ca* contentaee · *contentay*

¶Pois que ja a morte passastes
avés de passar o ryo.
60 FID.: Nam há aqui outro navio?
DIABO: Nam senhor, que este fretastes,
[*M f.* 2r A] & primeiro que espirastes   *& ja quando espirastes*
me destes logo sinal.   *me tinheis dado sinal.*
FID.: Que sinal fuy este tal?
65 DIABO: Do que vos vos contentastes.

FIDALGO: ¶A estoutra barca me vou.
*H*ou da barca! Para onde iis?
Ah, barqueiros, nam me ouvis?
Respondey-me, *h*oulá, *h*ou.
70 Par deos, aviado estou:
quant'a ysto é ja peor
que giricocins, salvanor;
cuydam que sam eu grou?

ANJO: ¶Que querés?   *Que mandais?*
FIDALGO: Que me digaes,
75 poys parti tam sem aviso,
se a barca do parayso
é esta em que navigaes?
ANJO: Esta é; que demandaes?   *Esta é; que lhe buscais?*
FIDALGO: Que me leixaes embarcar:
80 soo fidalgo de solar,
é bem que me recolhaes.

ANJO: ¶Nam se embarca tirania
neste batel divinall.
FIDALGO: Nam sey porque aveis por mal
85 que entr'a minha senhoria.
ANJO: Pera vossa fantesia
muy estreyta é esta barca.   *muy pequena é esta barca*

---

58 Pois · *¶Pois* 59 auees de passar ho ryo · *aueis de passar o rio.* 60 nam ha · *Não ha*
61 nam · *Não* 64 sinal: fuy · *sinal foy* 67 ou · *Hou hijs · ys,* 68 aa barqueir⁹ nam
me ouuis · *ah barqueyros, não mouuis,* 69 respondeme oula ou · *respondeyme, houla,*
hou. 71 quanta ysto he · *canta isto he* 71 é · he *he*

As you've already passed through death
you have to pass over the river.
60 NOBLE: Is there no other galley here?
DEVIL: No, my lord; this is what you've chartered,
and before you breathed your last
you gave me straightaway a sign.
NOBLE: And what sign was that?
65 DEVIL: The things that made you satisfied.

NOBLE: I'll go to this other boat.
Ho there, boat! Where do you go?
Ah, boatmen, can't you hear me?
Answer me, hello, ho!
70 By God, I'm well served!
As for this, it's already worse
than asses (excuse the word).
Do you think I'm here to wait?

ANGEL: What do you want?   *What do you demand?*
NOBLE: For you to say,
75 since I left with no warning,
if the boat of Paradise
is this one that you sail?
ANGEL: It is; what do you ask for?   *It is: what do you seek?*
NOBLE: That you allow me to embark.
80 I am of ancient and noble blood:
it would be good to welcome me on board.

ANGEL: You cannot bring tyranny
upon this godly gig.
NOBLE: I don't know why you take so badly
85 that my noble self should board.
ANGEL: This boat is too narrow   *This boat is too small*
for your arrogance.

---

72 giricocius · *gericocins* 73 cuydam que sam · *cuydam ca que sou* 74 qu̲e digaes ·
¶*Que digais* 75 poys · *pois* 76 ha · *a* 77 é · he *he* nauigaes · *nauegais* 78 é · he *he,*
79 leixaes · leyxeis 80 soo · *sou* solar · *sollar* 81 é · he *he* recolhaes. · *recolhais.* 82
Nā · *Não* 83 diuinall · *diuinal* 84 nam se embarca · *Não sembarca* 85 entra · *entre*
87 é · he *he*

FIDALGO: Pera senhor de tal marca
nom há aqui mais cortesia?

90   ¶Venha prancha & atavio:
levae-me desta ribeyra!
ANJO: Na_m_ vindes vos de maneira
pera ir neste navio: *pera entrar neste navio*
esſoutro vay mais vazio   **[M f. 2r B; C f. 44v A]**
95   a cadeira entrar*á*,
& o rabo caber*á*,
& todo vosso senhorio.

¶Vos yrés mais espaçoso
com fumosa senhoria,   *vos e³ vossa senhoria,*
100   cuydando na tirania   *contando da tirania*
do pobre povo queyxoso;   *de que ereis tam curioso,*
& porque de generoso
desprezastes os pequenos
achar-vos-és tanto menos
105   quanto mais fostes fumoso.

DIABO: ¶À barca, à barca, senhores!
Ó que maré tam de prata,
huũ ventezinho que mata
e valentes remadores!

Diz cantando: **[C in margin:** *Cantando.***]**

110   Vos me venirés a la mano   *Vos me veniredes a la mano*
a la mano me veniredes   *a la mano me veniredes*
                        e³ vos veredes
        [om. *M*]   *peyxes nas redes.*

FID.: ¶Ao inforno toda via,
inferno há hy pera my?

---

89 nom ha aqui · *não haqui* **90** ¶Venha prancha & atauio · *Venha a prancha e³ o atauio* **91** leuaeme · *leuayme* **92** nã · *Não* maneira · *maneyra* **93** pera hir · *pera entrar* **94** esoutro · *essoutro* **95** entrara · *entraraa* **96** ho · *o* cabera · *caberaa*

NOBLE: Is there no more respect here
for a lord of such degree?

90 Set down the plank, put out the flags,
take me from this river bank!
ANGEL: You've not come the proper way
to travel in this barque;
that other one sails emptier,
95 your chair will go on,
and your train fit in,
and all of your lordliness.

You'll go more at your ease
with your vain 'noble self',
100 thinking on your tyranny
over the complaining poor;
and because, being nobly born,
you despised the humble,
you shall find yourself all the less
105 for however vain you were.

DEVIL: Board the boat, board the boat, my lords,
oh what a silvery tide,
and a little breeze that could kill,
and strong men at the oars.

He sings:

110 You'll come holding my hand,
holding my hand you'll come.
*and you will see
fish from the sea.*

NOBLE: Am I bound for Hell, still?
Is it to be Hell for me?

---

98 Vos yres · *Ireis la* 104 acharuos es · *acharuos eis* 106 Aa barca aa barca señores ·
¶Ha barca, ha barca senhores 107 *oo* · ho 108 huũ · *hum* 109 e · *he e²* 110 **venirés** ·
venires 112 inforno · *inferno* 113 ha hy pera my · *ha hi pera mi*

Ó triste! Em quanto vivi

115   nam cuydey que o hi havia: *nunca cri que o hi havia,*
tive que era fantasia.
Folgava ser adorado,
confiey em meu estado
& no<u>m</u> vi que me perdia.

120   ¶Venha essa pra<u>n</u>cha; veremos
esta barca de tristura.

DIABO: Embarca vossa duçura
que cá nos entenderemos:
tomarés ũ par d<u>e</u> remos,

125   veremos como rema<u>e</u>s,   [*M f.* 2v A]
& chegando ao nosso caes
todos bem vos serviremos.   *nos vos desembarcaremos.*

FIDALGO: ¶Esperar-me-és vos aqui:
tornarey à outra vida,

130   veer minha dama querida   [*C f.* 44v B]
que se quer matar por mi.

DIABO: Que se qu<u>er</u> matar por ty?

FIDALGO: Ysto bem certo o sey eu.

DIABO: Ó namorado sandeu,

135   o mayor que nunca vy!

FIDALGO: ¶Como podrá ysso ser,   *¶Era tanto seu querer*
que m'escrevia mil dias?   *que m'escrevia mil dias.*

DIABO: Quantas mentiras que lias,
e tu, morto de prazer!

140 FID.: Pera que é escarnecer,
que no<u>m</u> avia mais *no* bem.

DIABO: Assi vivas tu, amem,
como te tinha querer.

---

114 o triste em · *oo triste que em* 115 o · ho auia · *auia* 116 ¶Tiue · *tiue* fantasia · *fantasia* 119 nõ · não 120 venha · *¶Venha* veremos · *e³ veremos* 122 Embarca · *Embarque* duçura · *doçura* 124 Tomares hũ · *tomareis hum* 125 remarees · *remais* 126 caes · cais

| | | Oh, alas! Whilst I lived | |
| 115 | | I never thought it existed! | *I didn't believe it existed* |

Oh, alas! Whilst I lived
115 I never thought it existed!   *I didn't believe it existed*
I held it was a vain invention:
I enjoyed being adored,
I trusted in my postion
and didn't see I was damning myself.

120 Set down that plank — we'll see
this boat of sadness.
DEVIL: Come on board, your sweetness,
for we'll understand each other here:
you'll take a pair of oars,
125 we shall see how you row,
and when we come to our harbour,
we'll all serve you well indeed.   *we will disembark you.*

NOBLE: You will wait for me here:
I'll go back to the other life
130 to see my beloved lady,
who wants to kill herself for me.
DEVIL: Who wants to kill herself for you?
NOBLE: I am quite sure of that.
DEVIL: Oh foolish lover!
135 The most foolish that I've ever seen!
                                      She loved me so much / that
NOBLE: How could that be?   *she wrote a thousand*
For she wrote to me each day for years!   *days to me*
DEVIL: And how many lies you'd read,
and you — dying with pleasure.
140 NOBLE: Why should you sneer?
I loved no other thing better.
DEVIL: May you ever live thus, amen,
just as you were loved.

---

128 esperarmees vos · *¶Mas esperayme* 129 aa · *ha* 130 veer · *ver* 132 ¶Que · *Que* ty · *ti* 133 ysto · *Isto* ho · *o* 134 oo · *Ho* 135 ho major · *o mayor* vy · *vi.* 136 ¶ om. *M* podrá · *podra* 139 e · he *es* 140 ¶Pera · *Pera* é · he *he* 141 nõ · *nam* nom bem · *no bem.*

FIDALGO: ¶Ysto quanto ao que eu conheço —
145 DIABO: Poys estando tu espirando,
se estava ella requebrando
com outro de menos preço.
FIDALGO: Dá-me licença, te peço,
que vá ver minha molher.
150 DIABO: E ella por nam te ver
despenhar-s'-á dũ cabeço.

¶Quanto ella oje rezou
antre seus gritos & gritas
foy dar graças infinitas   *foy dar glorias infinitas*
155 a quem a desasombrou.   *a quem na desabafou.*
FIDALGO: Quanto ella bem chorou!   *Quant'a ella, bem chorou.*
DIABO: Nom há hy choro d'alegria?   **[M f. 2v B]**
FIDALGO: E as lastimas que dezia?
DIABO: Sua may lhas ensinou.

160   ¶Entrae, entrae, entrae: *¶Entray, meu senhor, entray,*
ey-la prancha, ponde o pé.   *venha a prancha, ponde o pé*
FIDALGO: Entremos pois que assi é.
DIABO: Ora senhor descansae,   *Ora agora descansay,*
passeae & sospirae,
165 em tanto vinrá mais gente.
FIDALGO: Ó barca como es ardente:
maldito quem em ty vay!

¶Diz o diabo ao moço da cadeyra:

[C f. 45r A]   Nom entras cá; vay-te d'hy,   *¶Tu seu moço vay-te d'hi,*
a cadeyra é cá sobeja:
170 cousa qu' esteve na ygreja
nom se há d'embarcar aqui,
ca lha daram de marfym

---

144 Ysto · *¶Isto* ao · *o* 145 poys · *Pois* 147 outro · *outra* 148 ¶Dame · *Dame* 149
vaa · *va* 150 & ella por nam · *E ella por não* 151 dhũ · *dum* 152 quanto · *¶Quanto*
154 graças · *glorias* 155 quem a · quem ha 156 ¶Quanto · *Canta* 157 Nom ha hy
· *E não ha hi*

NOBLE: This, as far as I know —
145 DEVIL: Well, while you were dying
she was making eyes
at someone of lower rank.
NOBLE: Give me leave, I pray you,
to go and see my wife.
150 DEVIL: And she, in order not to see you,
will throw herself from a cliff.

Today, whatever she prayed,
among her shouts and screams,
was to give untold praise
155 to the one who gave her such good cheer.
NOBLE: She cried so very much.
DEVIL: There, are there no tears of joy?
NOBLE: And the laments she voiced?
DEVIL: Her mother taught them to her.

160 Come on board, come on board, come on board:
here's the plank, step up on it.
NOBLE: We'll board, since it's like this.
DEVIL: Now my lord, be at your ease,
walk about, and breathe:
165 in the meantime, more people will come.
NOBLE: Oh boat, how you burn:
Cursed be those you take to sea!

The devil says to the boy carrying the chair,

You don't board here, get away from there,
here the chair isn't needed:
170 a thing which used to be in church
may not be stowed in here,
for they'll give him one of ivory

---

158 & · *E* 159 may · *mãy* 160 ¶ om. *M* 161 ho · *o* 162 é · he *he* 164 ¶Passeae ·
paʃʃeay sospirae · *ʃoʃpiray* 165 vinra · *viraa* 166 Oo · *o* 167 ty · *ti* **stage direction**
ho · *o* 168 ca · *ca* 169 a · *que a* é cá · he ca *he ca* 170 consa · *couʃa* 171 nom se ha ·
nam ʃaa 172 ¶Ca · *ca* daram · *ʃarão* marfim · *marfi*

marchetada de dolores
com taes modos de lavores
175   que estará fora de sy.

¶À barca, à barca, boõa gente,
que queremos dar a vella:
chegar a ella, chegar a ella   **[*C* in marg.,** *Chega*
muytos, & de boa mente.   *ũ onzeneiro, & diz,*]
180   Ó que barca tam vallente!

¶Vem ũ onzeneyro & pregunta ao arraez do inferno dizendo,

Pera onde caminhaes?
DIABO: Ó que má ora venhaes,
onzeneyro meu parente!

Como tardastes vos tanto!   [*M f.* 3r A]
185 ONZ.: Mays quisera eu lá tardar
na çaffra do apanhar;
me deu Saturno quebranto.
DIABO: Ora muy muyto m'espanto
nom vos livrar o dinheyro.
190 ONZ.: Solamente pera o barqueiro   *Nem tam sois pera o*
nom me leixarom, nem tanto.   [*barqueyro*

DIABO: ¶Ora entrae, entrae aqui.
ONZ.: Nam **h**ey eu hy d'embarcar.
DIABO: Ó que gentil recear
195   & que cousas pera mi!
ONZ.: Aynda agora faleci,
leixa-me buscar batel.
Pesar de Sam Pimentel,   *DIABO: Pesar de Jam Pimentel,*
nunca tanta pressa vy!   *porque nam yrás aqui?*

---

174 taes · *tais* **175** estara · *estaraa* sy · *si* **176** a barca a · ¶*Ha barca ha* boõa · *boa*
177 a · *aa* **178** · *chegar ella, chegar ella* **stage direction (C)** ũ · *hũ* **180** ¶Ó · ¶O
¶*Ho* vallête · *valente* **stage direction (M)** ũ · hũ **181** caminhaes · *caminhais.*
182 o que maa ora venhaes· *Ho que maora venhais*

inlaid with such travails
and with such a type of work
175   that he will be beside himself.

Board the boat, board the boat, good people,
for we want to set sail.   [*C* in marg.:
Come up to her, come up to her,   *A usurer*
many of you, and well.   *enters and says,*]
180   Oh, what a splendid caravel!

    A usurer enters, and questions the boatman of hell,
                  saying,

              Where are you going?
     DEVIL: Oh what a bad time to turn up,
             usurer, my cousin!

              What a long time you took!
185   USUR.: I'd have liked to stay there more
             in the harvest of my profits;
             I felt Saturn's evil influence.
     DEVIL: Now I'm very much surprised
             that money didn't free you from it.
190   USUR.: They didn't leave me enough
             for the boatman, not even so much.

     DEVIL: Now come on board, come on board here.
  USURER: I won't be boarding there.
     DEVIL: Oh what a promising fear,
195   and what things for me!
     USUR.: I've only just died —
             let me look for a ferry.
             Saint Pimentel's grief!
             I've never seen such a hurry.

---

183 onzeneyro · *honzeneyro*   184 di. Como · *¶Como* tardaste · *tardastes* 185 mays ·
Mais la · *la* 186 çaffra · *çafra* 189 nom · *nam* 191 nom · *nam* leixarom · *deyxaram*
192 ora entrae entrae · *¶Ora entray entray* 193 ey · *ey* hy · *hi* 195 Aynda agora ·
Indagora 196 leixame · *deyxayme* 199 **irás** · *iras*

200   ¶Pera onde é a viagem?

DIABO: Pera onde tu *h*ás d'ir —

ONZ.: Avemos logo de partir?   [*DIABO:*] *Estamos pera partir.*

DIABO: Na<u>m</u> cures de mais lingoage<u>m</u>.

ONZ.: Pera onde é a passage<u>m</u>?

205 DIABO: Pera a infernal comarca.

ONZ.: Dix! No<u>m</u> vou eu em tal barca,   *Dixe, na<u>m</u> m'e<u>m</u>barco*

[*C f.* 45r B] estoutra tem avantagem.   *[eu nessa barca,*

[om. *M*]   ¶*Vay-se à barca do anjo, & diz,*

¶*H*ou da barca, houl*à*, *h*ou,

avés logo de partir?

210 ANJO: E onde queres tu yr?

ONZ.: Eu pera o parayso vou.

ANJO: Pois quan<u>t</u>'eu muy fora estou

de te levar para l*á*;

essa barca que l*á* está   *essoutra te leverá,*

215 vay pera que<u>m</u> te enganou.

ONZ.: ¶Porqu<u>e</u>?

ANJO: Porqu<u>e</u> esse bolsam   [*M f.* 3r B]

tomara todo o navio.

ONZ.: Juro a d<u>eos</u> que vay vazio.

ANJO: Nam ja no teu coraçam.

220 ONZ.: Lá me fica de rodam   *Lá me ficam de rondam*

minha fazenda & alhea.   *vinte & seis milhões nũa arca,*

ANJO: Ó o<u>n</u>zena como es fea   *pois que onzena tanto abarca*

& filha de maldiçam!   *nam lhe dais embarcaçam*

¶Torna o onzeneyro **à** barca do inferno & diz,   ¶*Torna ao*
                                                          diabo, & diz.

¶*H*oulá, *h*ou, demo barqueyro:

225 sabes vos no que me fundo?

Quero lá tornar ao mundo,

---

200 pera · ¶*E pera* é · *he he* **201** dyr · *dir* **204** ¶Pera · *Mas pera* é · *he he* **208** ou
da barca oula ou · ¶*Hou da barca, oulaa, hou,* **209** auees · *aueis* **210** & · *E* hyr · *yr.*
211 ho · *o* **212** quanteu muy · *canteu bem* **213** para la · *pera laa*

200   Where's the journey to?

DEVIL: To where you are to go.

USURER: Are we to leave straightaway?   *DEV.: We're about to*

DEVIL: Don't say another word.   *[leave.*

USURER: Where does the fare go to?

205   DEVIL: To the infernal domain.

USURER: Phew! I'll not go in such a boat —
the other cuts a better figure.

He goes to the Angel's boat and says

Ho there, boat, hello, ho!
Are you to leave soon?

210   ANGEL: And where do you want to go?

USURER: I'm off to Paradise.

ANGEL: As for me, I'm much disinclined
to take you there;
over there, that boat

215   goes to the one who deceived you.

USURER: Why is that?

ANGEL: Because that pouch
will take up all the galley.

USURER: I swear to God that it's empty.

ANGEL: But in your heart it's not.

220   USUR.: There I've left in a mound
mine and other's property   *twenty-six million in a chest:*

ANGEL: Usury: oh, how ugly,   *since usury makes such profit*
and daughter of   *you won't take it on board.*
          damnation!

The usurer returns to the   *He returns to the*
boat of Hell and says   *devil & says*

Ho, hullo, demon boatman!

225   You know what I've decided?
I want to return to the earth

---

214 **lá está** · la esta **215** te enganou · *tenganou.* **216** tomara todo o nauio · *tomaraa todo nauio* **220-223 spoken by onzeneiro in C stage direction (M)** à · a **224** Oula ou · ¶*Oula, hou* **225** sabes · *sabeis* me · *meu* **226** la · *la* ao · *oo*

       & trarey o meu dinheyro.
       Aquel outro marinheiro
       porque me vee vir sem nada
230   dá-me tanta borregada
       como araes lá do Barreyro.

DIABO: ¶Entra, entra, remarás:
       nom percamos mais maré.
ONZ.: Toda via?
DIABO: Per forç'é;
235   que te pes, cá entrarás,
       yrás servir Satanas
       porque sempre te ajudou.
ONZ.: *Ó* triste! Quem me çegou?
DIABO: Cal-te, que cá chorarás

¶Entrando o onzeneyro no batel
que achou o fidalgo embarcado, diz tirando o
       barrete,

                                    ¶Entrando no batel
                                      diz ao fidalgo,

240   ¶Sancta Joana de Valdés,
       cá é vossa senhoria?
FIDALGO: Dá *ó* demo a cortesia!
DIABO: Ouvis? Falae vos cortés!   [*M f.* 3v A]
       Vos, fidalgo, cuydarés   [*C f.* 45v A]
245   que estays na vossa pousada?
       Dar-vos-ey tanta pancada
       com o remo, que renegues.

¶Vem Joane o Parvo & diz ao araes do   *¶Vem hum parvo, & diz ao*
       inferno: *arraiz do inferno.*

       ¶Hou daquesta!   *¶Hou daquella!*
DIABO: Quem é?

---

227 trarey o · *trazelo*   228 ¶Aquel outro marinheiro · *que aquelloutro marinheyro*
229 vee · *ve* 230 da · *da* 231 araes la · *arraiz la* 232 entra remaras · *entra & remaras*
233 nom · *nam* 234 per forçe · *por força he* 235 ca entraras · *ca entraras* 236 ¶Yras ·
yraas 237 porque · *pois que* te ajudou · *tajudou* 238 o · *Oo* çegou · *cegou* 239 ca
chorarás · *ca choraraas.* **stage direction** o · ho achou · acho

and I'll bring back my money.
That sailor over there,
since he sees me without a penny,
230   treats me with derision,
like a Barreiro pilot.

DEVIL: Board, board the boat: you'll pull an oar.
Let's lose no more of the tide.
USURER: Already?
DEVIL: Of necessity;
235   no matter what, it's here you'll board:
you'll go to serve Satan
since he ever came to your aid.
USURER: O alas! Who made me blind?
DEVIL: Shut up; here's where you'll cry.

When the usurer boards the boat,   *Boarding the boat,*
he finds the nobleman embarked,   *he says to the*
and says, taking off his cap,   *nobleman,*

240   Saint Joanna de Valdes!
It's not your lordship!
NOBLE: Give your manners to the devil.
DEVIL: You hear? Mind what you say!
You, *fidalgo*, do you consider
245   your noble self at home?
I'll give you so many blows
with the oar, you'll swear and curse.

Simple Simon enters and   *A fool enters, and says to*
says to the pilot of Hell,   *the pilot of Hell,*

Ho, thingummyjig!
DEVIL: Who is it?

---

240 ¶Sancta joana de valdes · ¶Santa Joanna de valdees 241 ca he · *ca he* 242
daa ho demo · *Da ho demo* 243 falae vos cortes · *falay vos cortees*, 244 ¶Vos · *vos*
cuydarees ·*cuydareis* 245 estays na · *estais em* 246 dar vos ey · *daruos ey* 247 cõ
hõ remo · *cum remo* renegues · *arregueis* **stage direction** o · ho 248 Ou da
questa. di. quẽ he. io eu so · ¶*Ou daquella / di / quẽ he / pa / eu soo*

JOANE: Eu so!
                É esta *naviarra* nossa?

250   DIABO: De que<u>m</u>?
       JOANE: Dos tol<u>os</u>.
       DIABO: Vossa:
       entra!
       JOANE: De pullo ou de voo?
       Ó pesar de meu avoo,
       soma vim adoecer
       & fuy má ora a morrer

255   & nell*a* pera my soo.

       DIABO: ¶De que morreste?
       JOANE: De que?
       Samicas de caganeyra!
       DIABO: De que?
       JOANE: De caga merdeira,
       má ravugem que te d*é*!

260   DIABO: Entra, põe aqui o pé.
       JOANE: Houl*á*, no<u>m</u> tombe o zambuco!
       DIABO: Entra tolazo enuco,
       que se nos vay a maré.

       JOANE: ¶Aguarda**e**, aguardae, houl*á*!

265   & onde avemos nos d'ir ter?
       DIABO: Ao porto de Lucifer.
       JOANE: Ha-a-a.   *PARVO: Como?*
       DIABO: *Ó* inferno, e<u>n</u>tra c*á*!
       JOANE: *Ó* inferno, era má?
       Hiu, hiu! Barca do cornudo!

270   P<u>er</u>o Vinagre beiçudo,
       rachador d'alverca, hu ha!

---

249 É · he *he* arauiara nossa · *nauiarra voſſa.* 251 entra · *entray* pullo · *pulo,* 252 Ou · *ho* 253 adoecer · *hadoecer* 254 a morrer · *morrer* 255 nello pera my · *nella pera mi* 256 de que · ¶*De que* 257 samicas · *ſamica*

SIMON: It be me!
Be this hulkin' tub ours?
250 DEVIL: Whose?
SIMON: The fools'.
DEVIL: It's yours:
come on board.
SIMON: Should I jump or should I fly?
Oh, ma grand-daddy's grief,
at th' end I fell right sick,
an' I died damn quick,
255   it were ma' number that come up.

DEVIL: What did you die of?
SIMON: O' what?
'Appen, o' t' trots.
DEVIL: Of what?
SIMON: O' t' pooey shits,
tha' mangy git!
260 DEVIL: Come on board, put your foot down there.
SIMON: Oh, oh, tha' sampan's tippin' over!
DEVIL: Board, you great ball-less fool,
for the tide's slipping away.

SIMON: Wait a mo', wait a mo', oh!
265   And where are we goin' ta go?
DEVIL: To the port of Lucifer.
SIMON: Ah, ha, ha!   *FOOL: What?*
DEVIL: Oh, Hell, get on board!
SIMON: Hell, hellfire and damnation!
Phew, phew, cuckold's carrack,
270   thick-lipped Peter Pickle,
water-butt breaker, hoo ha!

---

258 merdeira · *merdeyra* 259 rauugem · *raugem* de · *dee.* 261 oula nõ · *Oula, não* ho
· *o* 262 enuco · *euuco* 263 aguardaee aguardaee oula · *Aguarday aguarday, oulaa*
267 ho · *oo* ca · *ca* 268 O inferno era maa · *Oo inferno yeramaa* 269 hiu hiu: · *hio
hio,* 270 po vinagre beiçudo beiçudo · *beyçudo beyçudo,*

49

¶Çapateiro da Candosa,
antrecosto de carrapato,   [*M f.* 3v B]
hiu, **hiu**! Caga no çapato!
275   Filho da grande aleyvosa,
tua molher é tinhosa
& **há** de parir ũ çapo
chentado no guardenapo,
neto de cagarinhosa.

280   ¶Furta cebola, hiu, hiu!
Escomungado nas erguejas,   [*C f.* 45v B]
burrella, cornudo sejas,
toma o pam que te cayo;
a molher que te fogio
285   per'a ylha de Madeyra.
Cornudo atá mangueyra,   *ratinho da Siesteyra*
toma o pam que te cayo   *o demo que te pario.*

¶Hiu, hiu! Lanço-te ũa pulha:
dede pica na … aquella!
290   Hump! Hump! Caga na vela!
Hio, cabeça de grulha!
perna de cigarra velha,
caganita de coelha,   *pelourinho da pampulha,*
pelourinho de Pampulha,   *rabo de forno de telha.*
295   mija n'agulha, mija n'agulha!   *[om.]*

¶Chega o parvo ao batel do anjo, & diz,   *¶Chegando à barca da*
                                                    gloria diz.

JOANE: ¶*H*ou do barco!
ANJO: Que me queres?   *Tu que queres?*
JOANE: Queres-me passar alem?
ANJO: Quem es tu?
JOANE: Samica, alguem!   *Nam sou ninguem.*
ANJO: Tu passarás se quiseres.

---

272 capateiro · ¶*Capateyro* 274 hiu: caga no çapato · *çapato çapato,* 276 ¶Tua · *tua*
é · he *he* 277 **há** · ha *ha* **um** · hũ *hum* 278 guardenapo · *guardanapo* 279
cagarinhosa · *cagarrinhosa* 280 furta cebola: hiu: hiu · ¶*Furta cebolas, hio hio* 281
erguejas · *ygrejas* 282 burrella · *burrela* 283 ho pam · *o pão* 284 ¶A · *a*

Candosa cobbler,
beef-rib from a tick,
phew, phew: poo on tha shoe!
275 Son of the great whore,
tha's got a mangy wife
who'll give birth to a toad
stuffed into an 'ankerchief,
a fœtus from t' fæces!

280 Onion-pincher, phew, phew!
Excommunicate in ev'ry church,
may tha be an 'orned ass:
take up t' bread tha dropped;
tha wife who ran off
285 to t' island of Madeira
left tha cuckoled up to tha spout: *Siesteyra hick,*
take up t' bread tha dropped.   *the devil bore you.*

Phew, phew, I'll trade insults wi' you:
take a pinch o' that!
290 Hump, hump: poo on t' sail!
Phew, tha tongue never fails,
leg of a cricket that's past it,
dirty droppin' from a rabbit,   *Pampulha whippin-post*
whippin' post o' Pampulha,   *brick-kiln tail.*
295 pee on t' compass, pee on t' compass!   *[om.]*

The fool goes to the Angel's boat and says,

SIMON: Ho, galley there!
ANGEL: What do you want me to do?
SIMON: Will tha take me over there?
ANGEL: Who are you?
SIMON: 'Appen, someone.   *I be nobody.*
ANGEL: You shall cross if you wish.

285 pera ylha de · *pera a ilha da* 287 (*M*) o · ho 288 hiu: hiu: · *¶Hio hio,* ũa · hũa
hũa 289 dede · *de* 290 hũp: hũp: · *hio hio,* 291 hio cabeça · *cabeça* 292 ¶Perna ·
perna **stage direction** o · ho 296 ou do barco · *¶Hou da barca* 297 queresme ·
Queresme alem · *aalem* 299 passaras · *passaras*

300 Porque em todos teus fazeres
per malicia nom erraste;
tua simpreza t'abaste
para gozar dos prazeres. [*M f.* 4r A]

¶Espera em tanto per hy
305 veremos se vem alguem
merecedor de tal bem,
que deva de entrar aqui.

¶Vem ũ çapateiro com seu avantal, &
carreguado de formas, & chegua ao batel
infernal. Diz,

*¶Vem um çapateyro
carregado de formas, &
diz na barca do inferno,*

*H*ou da barca!
DIABO: Quem vem hy?
Sancto çapateyro honrrado,
310 como veens tam carregado!
ÇAPATEIRO: Mandaram-*me* vyr assy;

¶& pera onde é a viagem?
DIABO: Pera o lago dos danados. *Pera a terra dos danados.*
ÇAPATEIRO: Os que morrem confessados —
315 onde tem sua passagem?
DIABO: Nom cures de mais linguajem:
esta é tua barca, esta.
ÇAPATEIRO: Arrenegaria eu da festa,
[*C f.* 46r A] & da puta da barcagem! *& da barca, & da barcagem.*

320 ¶Como poderá ysso ser,
confessado & comungado?
DIABO: E tu morreste escomungado,
nom o quiseste dizer:
esperavas de viver;
325 calaste dous mil enganos:
tu roubaste bem trint' annos

---

301 nom · *nam* **303** para · *pera* **304** espera · *¶Espera* hy · *hi* **307** de entrar · *dentrar*
stage direction ũ · *hũ um · hum* **308** Ou · *Hou* hy · *hi* **309** sancto · *santo* **310** vês · *vês*
311 mandaram vyr assy · *Mandarãme vir assi.*

52

300   Because, in all of your deeds,
               you did not sin through malice,
               your simplicity will suffice
               for you to share in heavenly joys.

               Wait in the meantime around there,
305   we shall see if anyone comes
               deserving such a good
               that they should be taken in here.

A cobbler enters wearing his apron and   *A cobbler enters loaded*
loaded with lasts and comes up to the   *with lasts and says into*
hellish boat. He says,   *the boat to Hell,*

               Ho, the boat!
DEVIL: Who goes there?
               Oh, Saint Cobbler the honourable,
310   how you've come so laden.
COBBLER: I was ordered to come like this.

               And to where's the journey?
DEVIL: To the lake of the damned.   *To the land of the damned*
COBBLER: Those who've confessed before they died,
315   where do they have their passage?
DEVIL: Don't say another word:
               this, this one is your galley.
COBBLER: Oh, I renounce this holiday,
               and the sodding ferry-fare   *& the boat, & the fare.*

320   How could this come to be,
               if I confessed and took communion?
DEVIL: You died an excommunicate,
               and you didn't say:
               you were hoping you'd live on;
               you hushed up two thousand tricks,
               you've been robbing quite thirty years

---

312 & · ¶*Mas* é · he *he* 314 os · *E os* 316 Nõ · *Não* linguajẽ · *lingoagem*   317 esta
he · *que esta he* 318 arrenegaria · *Renegaria* 320 como podera ysso · ¶*Como poderaa
isso* 322 & · *E* 323 nom o · *& nam no* 324 ¶Esperauas · *esperauas* 325 dous · dez
326 robaste · *roubaste* trintannos · *trinta anos*

        o povoo com teu mester.

        ¶Embarca era má pera ty,
        que *h*a ja muyto que t'espero.

330   ÇAP.: Pois digo-te que nom quero.   *Digo-te que re-nam quero.*
    DIABO: Que te pes, **hás** d'ir: sy, sy.   *Digo-te que ſi, re-ſi.*
   ÇAPATEIRO: Qua*n*tas missas eu o*u*vy!   **[*M f.* 4r B]**
        Nom me ham ellas <u>de</u> prestar?
    DIABO: Ouvir missa, entam roubar
335   é caminho per'aqui.

   ÇAPATEIRO: ¶E as offertas que daram,
        & as horas dos finados?
    DIABO: E os dinheiros mal levados,
        que foy da satiſfaçam?
340   ÇAP.: Ah! no<u>m</u> praza **ao** cordova<u>m</u>
        ne<u>m</u> à puta da badana
        se é esta boa traquitana
        em que se vee Joanatam.

        ¶Ora juro a d<u>eo</u>s que he graça.   [*C* **in margin:**

       Vay-se à barca do anjo & diz,   *Vay à*
                         barca do
345   *H*ou da sancta caravella: *parayſo*]
        poder**és** levar-m*e* n*e*lla?
    ANJO: A carrega t'embaraça.
   ÇAPATEIRO: Nom **há** mercé <u>que</u> me d<u>eo</u>s faça —
        ysto uxiquer ir*á*.
350   ANJO: Essa barca que *lá* est*á*
        leva quem ro*u*ba de praça

        ¶*a*s almas embaraçadas.   ¶*Ó almas embaraçadaſ!*
   ÇAPATEIRO: Ora eu me maravilho
        averdes por gram pegilho
355   quatro forminhas cagadas

---

327 povoo · *povo* mester · *miſter* **328** embarca · ¶*Embarca* ty · ti **329** aja · *ha ja*
tespero · *te eſpero* **331** **hás** · *as* **332** ¶Quautas · *Quantaſ* ouy · *ouuy* **333** nom me
ham · *não mão* **335** é · *he* peraqui · *pera aqui* **336** & · ¶*E* daram · *darão* **338** & ·
E dinheiros · *dinheyroſ* **339** satiffaçam · *ſatiſfaçam*

54

the people with your craftmanship.

Get on board, damn you,
I've been waiting for you a long time.
330 COB.: Well, I tell I don't want to.
DEVIL: Like it or not, you have to, oh yes.
COBBLER: I heard so many masses —
won't they be of any use?
DEVIL: If you hear mass, and then you thieve,
335 that's the way you get to here.

COBBLER: And the offerings they'll give,
and their prayers for the dead?
DEVIL: And as regards the money stolen,
what reparations have been made?
340 COB: Ah, curse the cordovan leather,
and the sodding sheep's skin,
if this is not that fine old rattletrap
in which you might see Jonathon.

Now God knows, I'm in a state of grace.

He goes to the angel's boat and says,

345 Ho there, holy caravel,
might you take me in her?
ANGEL: Your load stands in the way.
COBBLER: Can God give me no mercy —
this load can be stowed anywhere.
350 ANJO: That boat that's over there
takes those who openly steal

from souls laden with sin.
COBBLER: Now I'm much taken aback
that you consider great obstacles
355 four little bloody lasts

---

340 ¶Aa nõ · *Ho nam* ho cordouã · *ho cordouão* 341 aa · *ha* 342 é · e *he* traquitana ·
tranquitana 343 joanatam · *Janantam* 345 ou · *Hou* 346 poderes leuarmo neella ·
poderei̇́ leuarme nella 348 nom ha mercee · *Não ha merce* 349 ysto vxiquer hira · *ịsto*
hu ̇xiquer yraa. 350 que esta · *que la e̬staa* 351 roba · *rouba* praça · *praça.* 352 as ·
¶*Oo*

55

que podem bem ir hy chantadas
nuũ quantinho desse leyto.   [C f. 46r B]
ANJO: Se tu viveres dereyto
ellas forem cá escusadas.

360   ÇAP.:   ¶Assy que determinaes   [M f. 4v A]
que vá coser ò inferno.
ANJO: Escripto estás no caderno
das emmentas infernaes.

¶Torna-se à barca dos danados & diz,   [om. C]

Hou barqueiros que aguardais?   Pois diabos, que
365   Vamos, venha a prancha logo   [aguardais?
& levae-me àquelle fogo.
Nam nos detenhamos mais.   Pera que é a guardar mais?

¶Vem ũ frade com ũa moça pela mão & ũ   ¶Entra um frade
bruquel & huũa espada na otra, & ũ casco   com ũa moça pola
debaixo do capello: & elle mesmo fazendo a   mão, & vem
baixa, começou de dançar, dizendo: dançando fazendo a
Tay ray ray ra rã! Ta-ry-ry-rã!   bayxa
Ta-ray ray ray-rã! Táy-ri-ri-rã!   com a boca,
Tã tã! Ta-ri rim rim rã hu há!   & acabando
                                                   diz o
370   diabo,
DIABO: ¶Que é ysso padre? Que vay lá?
FRADE: Deo gracias, som cortesaão!
DIABO: Sabes tambem o tordiam?
FRADE: Porque nam? Como ora sey!   He mal que m'esquecerá.
375   DIABO: Pois entrae: eu tangerey   Essa dama há d'entrar cá
& faremos huũ seraão!   [FRA.: Nam sey onde embarcarey
DIA.: Ella é vossa?
Essa dama: é ella vossa?   [FRA.:   Eu nam sey:
FRADE: Por minha a tenho eu,   por minha a trago eu cá.
e sempre a tive de meu.   [om.]
380   DIABO: Fezestes bem, que é fermosa.   [om.]

_____

356 hir hy chãtadas · yr chentadas 357 nuũ quantinho · no cantinho 358 viueres ·
viueras 359 forem ca · foram ca 360 assy · ¶Assi 361 vaa · va ò · hoo ao 362
escripto estas · Escrito estaas 366 leuaeme· leuayme 367 é·he stage direction

that could well be stuffed
in a corner of that berth.

ANGEL: If you had lived a-right,
here they would be put aside.

360   COB.: And so you've got it fixed
that my soul must go to Hell.

ANGEL: For you there can be no repair
from the infernal caravel.

He returns to the boat of the damned, and says,

Ho, boatmen, what are you waiting for?
365   Come on, set the plank down quick,
and take me to that fire.
Let's waste no more time.   *Why should I wait any more?*

A friar enters holding a girl by the hand,   *A friar enters*
having a shield and a sword in the other, and   *holding a girl by the*
a helmet beneath his hood, and he himself   *hand, dancing &*
singing the bassedanse, begins to dance,   *singing*
saying   *a bassedanse,*
   and when he
Tay-ray-ray, ra ram! Ta-ri-ri-ram!   *finishes, the*
Ta-ray, ray, ray-ram! Ta-ay ri-ri-ram!   *devil*
370   Tam, tam! Ta-ri, rim, rim, ram, hoo ha!   *says,*

DEVIL: What's this, father? What's going on there?
FRIAR: Thanks be to God, I'm a courtly fellow!
DEVIL: Do you know the tordion?
FRIAR: Why not? I know it indeed!   *It'd be bad to forget it!*
375   DEVIL: Well, board: I'll play   *That lady boards here.*
and we'll make a fine do!   *F: Don't know where to board.*
   D: Is she yours?
This lady: is she yours?   *F:*   *I don't know:*
FRIAR: I consider her my own   *I bring her here as my own.*
and so I've always kept her.   **[om. C]**
380   DEVIL: You did well, for she's beautiful.   **[om. C]**

ũ · hũ **ũa** · hũa ũ · hũ (twice) *um* · *hum* **ũa** · *hũa* **368-70 om.** *C*   **371** é · he *he* la · *laa.* **372** sõ cortesão · *sam cortesam* **373** sabes · *Sabeis* tordiam · *tordião* **375** bá · *ha* **cá** · *ca* **377** é · he *he* **378** a · la **cá** · *ca* **380** é · he

DIABO: E na<u>m</u> vos punh**am lá** grosa
no vosso co<u>n</u>vento sancto?   *nesse convento sagrado?*

FRADE: E elles fazem outro tanto!   *Assi fuy bem açoutado.*

DIABO: Que cousa tam preciosa!   **[*M f.* 4v B]**

385   ¶Entrae, padre reverendo.

FRADE: Para onde levaes gente?

DIABO: Pera aquelle fogo ardente
que no<u>m</u> temestes vivendo.

FRADE: Juro a d<u>eo</u>s <u>que</u> no<u>m</u> t'e<u>n</u>tendo:

390   & est' abito no<u>m</u> me val?

DIABO: Gentil padre mundanal,
a Berzabu vos encomendo!

FRADE: ¶Ah, corpo de d<u>eo</u>s co<u>n</u>sagrado!
Pella f<u>é</u> de Jesu Christo,

395   <u>que</u> eu nom posso ente<u>n</u>der isto!
Eu **h**ey de ser condenado?
Huũ padre ta<u>m</u> namorado   **[*C f.* 46v A]**
& tanto dado a virtude?
Assi deos me d<u>é</u> saude,

400   que esto<u>u</u> maravilhado!

DIABO: ¶Nom cures de mais detença: *Nam façamos mais*
embarcae & partiremos.   *[detença,*
Tomarés u<u>m</u> par de remos.

FRADE: Nom ficou ysso n'avença.

405   DIABO: Pois dada est<u>á</u> ja a se<u>n</u>tença

FRADE: Pardeos essa seri'ella:
nam vay em tal caravella
minha senhora Florença.

          ¶Como por ser namorado

410   & folgar com ũa molher,

---

381 E · ¶E ¶*E* punha la · *punhão la* **383** E · & **385** ¶ **om.** *M* and *C* entrae ·
Entray **386** para · *Pera* leuaes · *leuais* **388** no temestes · *nam temeste* **389** ¶Juro ·
¶*Juro* no · *nam* **390** estabito no · *este habito nam* **393** ¶ **om.** *M* and *C* Aa corpo ·
Corpo **394** pella fe · *polla fee* **395** nom · *nam* **396** **h**ey · ey *ey*

DEVIL: And didn't they make a big fuss
in your holy monastery?   *in that sacred convent?*
FRIAR: But they all do the same!   *So I was well whipped.*
DEVIL: What marvellous news!

385   Come on board, reverend Father.
FRIAR: Where do you take people to?
DEVIL: To that burning fire
that you didn't fear alive.
FRIAR: I swear to God, I don't understand you:
390   won't this habit protect me?
DEVIL: Oh Father, pagan and worldly,
to Beelzebub I commend you!

FRIAR: Ah! By the holy eucharist,
by the faith of Jesus Christ,
395   I can't make head or tail of this!
Am I to be condemned,
a priest so enamoured
and so given to virtue?
So may God give me health,
400   for I'm struck with wonder!

DEVIL: Don't think of delaying any more,   *Let's make no more*
get on board and we'll depart.   *[delay*
You'll take up a pair of oars.
FRIAR: That didn't feature in the contract.
405 DEVIL: The judgement's already been given.
FRIAR: By God, that would be just it:
my lady Florence
will not go in such a caravel.

Just for being a lover
410   and frolicking with a woman

---

397 ¶Huũ · *¶Hum* 399 de · *dee* 400 estoy · *estou* 401 ¶ om. *M* and *C* 402
embarcae · *embarcay* 403 tomarees hũ · *tomareis hum* 404 Nom · *Nam* ysso
nauença · *isso na auença* 405 ¶Pois · *¶Pois* esta · *estaa* 406 seriella · *seria ella* 407
nam · *nam, nam* 409 ¶ om *M* and *C* 410 ũa · hũa *hũa*

se há ũ frade de perder
com tanto psalmo rezado?

DIABO: Ora estás bem aviado.

FRADE: Mais estás bem corregido.

415 DIABO: Devoto padre-marido,
avés de ser cá pinguado. [*M f.* 5r A]

¶Descobrio o frade a cabeça tirando o capello & [om. *C*]
apareceo o casco, & diz o frade.

¶Mantenha deos esta coroa!

DIABO: *Ó* padre, Frey Capaçete,
cuydey que tinheis barrete?

420 FRADE: Sabe que foy da pessoa.
Esta espada é roloa
& este broquel rolam!

DIABO: *Dé* vossa reverença liçam
d'esgrima, que é cousa boa.

Começou o frade a dar liçam desgrima com a espada
& broquel que eram d'esgrimir & diz desta maneira [om. *C*]

425 FRADE: ¶Deo gracias, demos caçada!   *Que me praz, demos caçada.*
Pera sempre contra sus,   *Entam logo um contra sus,*
huũ fendente: ora sus!   **[*C* in marg.: *Esgrime*]**
Esta é a primeira levada
Alto levantay a espada,

metey o diabo na cruz
[om. *M*]   *como o eu agora pus,*
sahi coa espada rasgada
& que fique anteparada,

430   talho, largo, & ũ reves!
& logo colher os pés,
que todo o al nom é nada. [*C f.* 46v B]

---

411 ha hũ · *ha hum* 412 psalmo · *salmo* 413 ¶Ora estas · *¶Ora estas* 414 mais
estas · *Mas estas* 415 padre marido · *padre, & marido* 416 auees · *aueis* ca pinguado ·
ca pingado **stage direction om.** *C* o · ho (three times) 417 ¶ om. *M* & *C* 418 Oo ·
ho 420 sabe que foy · *Sabey que fuy* 421 ¶Esta · *¶Esta* é · he *he*

60

a friar has to be damned
when he's prayed so many psalms?
DEVIL: Now everything's in order.
FRIAR: Yes, indeed, you're smart.
415 DEVIL: Devout father — and devoted husband —
here you shall be scourged.

The friar, removing his hood, uncovers his head and
the helmet can be seen, and the friar says,

May God preserve this tonsured crown!
DEVIL: Oh Father, fray Bascinet,
did you think you had a biretta?
420 FRIAR: Know that I'm always well turned-out.
This sword's like Roland's
and this shield's like Roland's, too.
DEVIL: Reverend Father, give a lesson
in fencing, for it's such a good thing.

The friar begins to give a fencing lesson with the
sword and the shield, which were for fencing, and
says in the following manner,

425 FRIAR: Thanks be to God, let's begin to fence!
Always to be facing upwards,
parry one blow — now, courage,
this is the first guard:
raise the sword up high,

put the devil on the cross
just like I have done,
step out dragging the sword,
so that it remains in front,

430 cut right to left, step back, cut left to right,
then pull back your feet,
nothing else is worth your while.

---

422 broquel rolam · *bruquel rolão* 423 de · *Dee* reuerença liçam · *reuerencia lição* 424
desgrima · *disgrima* é · he *he* **stage direction** a · ha 426 *um* · *hum* 427 huũ · *hum*
428 é · he *he* primeira · *primeyra* 429 ¶Alto leuantay · *¶Aleuantay* 430 largo & hũ ·
largo, hum 431 pees · *pes* 432 ho al no he · *o al nam he*

¶Qua_n_do o recolher se tarda,
o ferir no_m_ é prudente:

435 ora sus muy largamente,
cortae na segunda guarda.
Guarde-me d_eo_s d'espi_n_garda,
mais de homem denodado;   *ou de barão denodado*
aqui estou tambe_m_ guardado

440 como a palha n'albarda.

¶Sayo com mea espada,   [*M f*. 5r B]
houlá guardae as queixadas!
DIABO: **Ó** que valentes levadas!
FRADE: Ainda *i*sto nom é nada.

445 Demos o_u_tra vez caçada:
contra sus, & ũ fendente,
& cortando largamente
ex aqui *a* seysta feytada.

¶Daqui sayo com ũa guya

450 & ũ reves da primeira.
Esta é quinta verdadeira.
Ó quantos daqui feria!
Padre que tal aprendia
no inferno *há* d'aver pingos?

455 **Ah**, no_m_ praz a Sam Domi_n_gos
co_m_ tanta descortesia.

                                           ¶Prosigamos nossa historia
¶Tornou a tomar a moça pella   *nam façamos mais detença:*
        mão dizendo,   *day cá mão, senhora*
                                                        Florença,
    Vamos *à* barca da gloria   *vamos à barca da gloria*

¶Começou o frade a fazer o tordia_m_ & fora_m_
dan_ç_ando até o batel do a_n_jo desta maneira: [om. *C*]

---

432 quãdo · *¶Quando* 433 ho · *o* 434 ho · *o* no he · *nam he* 435 ora · *eya* 436
cortae · *cortay* 437 despigarda · *despingarda* 439 · *mas aqui estou guardado* 441 sayo ·
¶Sayo 442 oula · *oula* guardae · *guardar* queixadas · *queyxadas.* 443 Ó · *o Ho* 444
ainda esto nom he · *Inda isto nam he*

When you're slow in stepping back,
striking out would not be wise;
435 now, upwards, in an arc,
cut down from the second guard.
May God protect me from the gun,
above all from intrepid men,
but here I am quite safe,
440 like straw stuffed in a pillion.

I step out with half a blade,
watch it! Mind your face!
DEVIL: Oh, what marvellous plays!
FRIAR: You haven't seen anything yet!
445 Let's begin to fence again.
Upwards, and then to parry,
and then to cut, in an arc,
here is the sixth pose;

from here I step out, throw a feint,
450 and cut left to right, from the first;
This guard is, in faith, the fifth.
Oh, how many did I strike from here!
Will the priest who's learnt such things
be scourged in Hell with whips?
455 Oh, spite on Saint Dominic
for such discourtesy!

He again takes the girl by the
  hand, saying,

Lets continue our story;
let's waste no more time:
give me a hand, my lady Florence,

Let's go to the boat of glory

The friar begins to dance the tordion and they both
dance to the angel's boat in the following way:

---

445 ontra · *outra* 446 & hũ · *ora hum* 448 ex aqui seysta feytada · *eis aqui a seista* *guarda.* 449 sayo com hũa guya · *se sae com hũa guia* 450 ũ · hũ *hum* primeira · *primeyra* 451 é · he *he* verdadeira · *verdadeyra* 452 Ó · o *ho* 453 ¶Padre · *padre* 454 há · a *ha* 455 ha nõ · *ha nam* 456 con · *com* 456'-456''' om. *M* 456''' cá · *ca* 457 a · *aa* **stage direction** o · ho (three times)

FRIAR:	Ta-ra-ra-ray-rã! Ta-ri-ri-ri-ri-ram!	[*C* in marg.:
	tay-ray-rã-ta-ri-ri-ram! Ta-ri-ri-rã!	*Chega à barca*
460	Hu ha!	*da gloria e3 diz,*
	¶Deo gracias! Há lugar cá	*Deo gracias, há cá lugar*
	pera minha reverença,	
	& a senhora Frorença	
	pollo meu entrará lá?	*pollo meu há lá d'entrar.*
465 JOANE:	Andar muytieramá,	
	furtaste o trincham frade?	
FRADE:	Senhora dá-m' à vontade,	
	que este feito mal está.	[*M f.* 5v A]
	¶Vamos onde avemos d'ir:	
470	nam praz a deos com a ribeira;	[*C f.* 47r A]
	eu nam vejo aqui maneyra	
	senam em fim concrudir.	
DIABO:	Aveys, padre, de viir.	*Padre, aveys logo de vir.*
FRADE:	Agasalhae-me lá Frorença,	*Si, tomay-me lá Florença*
475	& compra-se esta sentença,	*e3 cumpramos esta*
	& ordenemos de partir!	[*sentença*

¶Ta<u>n</u>to qu<u>e</u> o frade foy <u>e</u>mbarcado veo ¶*Vem ũa alcouviteyra*
ũa alcouveteira <u>per</u> nome Brísida Vaz a *per nome Brísida Vaz,*
qu<u>al</u>, chegan<u>do</u> à barca infernal, diz *e3, chegando à barca*
desta maneyra, *do inferno, diz.*

	¶*H*oulá da barca, *houlá*	
DIABO:	Que<u>m</u> chama?	
BRÍS.:	Brísida Vaz!	
DIABO:	E aguarda-me, rapaz,	
480	como nom vem ella ja?	
COMP.:	Diz que nom há de viir cá	
	sem Joana de Valdés.	

458-460 om. *C* 463 frorença · *Florença* 461 Há · ha cá · ca *Há cá* · *ha ca* 464
entrará lá · entrara la *há lá* · *ha la* 465 andar · ¶*Andar* 466 ho trincham · *esse*
trinchão 467 *FRADE* om. *M* da maa vontade · *dame ha vontade* 468 feito mal esta. ·
feyto mal estaa 469 ¶Vamos · *vamos* 470 praz a d's com a · *praza a Deos coa* 472
concrudir · *comcrudir* 474 lá · la *lá* · *la*

	FRIAR:	Ta-ra-ra-ray ram! Ta-ri-ri-ri ram!
		Tay-ray ram, ta-ri-ri-ri ram! *[C in marg.: He reaches*
460		Ta-ri-ri ram, hoo ha! *the boat of glory & says,]*
		Thanks be to God! Is there a place
		for my reverend self,
		and will the lady Florence
		enter on my account?
465	SIMON:	Get away, Hellfire an' damnation!
		Friar, 'as tha stole yon' crumpet?
	FRIAR:	Lady, it seems to me,
		that we're in a bad situation.
		Let's go where we must;
470		this riverbank is God-forsaken,
		and I see no other way
		except by agreeing in the end.
	DEVIL:	Father, you have to come.
	FRIAR:	Take charge there of Florence,
475		and so fulfil this sentence,
		and let's order that we leave.

As soon as the friar is embarked, a   *A bawd called Brísida Vaz*
bawd by the name of Brísida Vaz   *enters and,*
enters, who, reaching the infernal boat,   *reaching the boat*
          says in this manner,   *of Hell, says,*

		Yoo-hoo there, boat, hullo!
	DEVIL:	Who is it?
	BRÍSIDA:	Brísida Vaz!
	DEVIL:	Well, boy is she waiting for me —
480		she hasn't come yet, how's that?
	MATE:	She says she won't come here
		without Joanna de Valdés.

---

476 & ordenemos · *ordenemos* **stage direction (M)** ũa · huma **alcouviteteira** ·
alcouitera **Brísida Vaz** · brisida vaz *(C)* **Vem** · Vã ũa · *hũa* **Brísida Vaz** · *Brísida
vaz* 477 ¶Oula da barca oula · *¶Hou da barca, hou laa* 478 brisida · *Brísida* 479 E ·
& *Ea* 480 como nom · *porque nam* 481 **COMP.:** ·BRISIDA. *BRISIDA* nom ha ·
nam ha vijr ca · *vir ca* 482 valdes · *valdeis*

      DIABO: Entrae-vos & remarés.
      BRÍSIDA: Nom quero eu entrar lá.

485 DIABO: ¶Que sabroso arrecear!
      BRÍSIDA: Nom é essa barca que eu cato.
      DIABO: E trazes vos muyto fato?
      BRÍSIDA: O que me convem levar.
      DIABO: Que é o qu'avés d'embarcar?
490   BRÍS.: Seys centos virgos postiços,
          & tres arcas de feytiços
          que nom podem mays levar.

          ¶Tres almareos de mentir,
          & cinco cofres de enlheos,
495   & alguns furtos alheos,
          assy em joyas de vestir,   **[*M f.* 5v B]**
          guarda roupa d'encobrir:
          em fim, casa movediça,
          ũ estrado de cortiça
500   com dous coxyns d'encubrir.   *com dez coxins d'embayr.*

          ¶A mor carrega que é,
          essas moças que vendia;
          daquesta mercaderia
          trago eu muyta, bó fé!
505 DIABO: Ora, ponde aqui o pé.
      BRÍSIDA: Huuy! & eu vou pera o parayso.   **[*C f.* 47r B]**
      DIABO: E quem te dixe a ty ysso?
      BRÍSIDA: Lá hey d'ir desta maré.

          ¶Eu soo ũa martella tal,
510   açoutes tenho levados
          & tormentos soportados
          que ninguem me foy ygual.

---

483 entrae · *entray* remarees · *remareis* **484** nom · *nam* la · *laa*. **485** Que sabroso ·
¶*Que saboroso* **486** No esa barca que eu · *Nam he essa barca a queu* **487** & trazes · *E
trazeis* **488** ho · *O* **489** é · he *he* quaues · *que aueis* **490** seys · *Seis* **492** nom · *nam*
mays · *mais* **494** de enlheos · *denleos* **496** assy · *assi*

66

DEVIL: Get on board, you shall row.
BRÍSIDA: I don't intend to board there.

485 DEVIL: What a pleasant sign of dread.
BRÍSIDA: This isn't the boat I'm looking for.
DEVIL: Have you brought much freight?
BRÍSIDA: What was fitting for me to bring.
DEVIL: What do you have to put on board?
490 BRÍS.: Six hundred false maidenheads
and three chests of spells,
'cause I couldn't bring any more.

Three wardrobes of lies,
and five coffers of plots and plans,
495 ill-gotten gains from others' thefts
(such as jewels one might wear),
a wardrobe full of ruses;
in sum, household furniture
a table made of cork
500 with two cushions for cover.   *with ten cushions to*
                                                      deceive.

The greatest load that I've got,
these girls I used to sell —
of that type of merchandise
my word, I've brought a lot.
505 DEVIL: Now, set your foot down here.
BRÍSIDA: Humph! But I'm off to Paradise.
DEVIL: And who could have told you that?
BRÍSIDA: I shall go there with this tide.

I am a martyress, and some:
510 whippings have I borne,
and torments have I endured,
such as none could equal.

---

499 ũ · hum *hum* 500 coxyñs · *coxins* 501 é · he *he* 504 muyto boo fe · *muyta, ha boofee* 506 huuy · *Huy* voy · *vou* 507 & · *E* ty ysso · *ti isso* 508 Lá hey · la ey *la ey* 509 soo hũa martella · *som hũa martele* 510 açotes tenho leuados · *acoutes tenho eu leuados*

Se fosse ò fogo infernal
lá yria todo o mundo.
515   A est'outra barca cá fundo
me vou, que é mays real.

      [om. *M*]   *¶E chegando à barca da gloria, diz ao*
                                            [anjo,
¶Barqueiro, mano, meus olhos:
prancha a Brisida Vaz!
ANJO: Eu nam sey quem te cá traz.
520 BRÍS.: Peço-vollo de giolhos,
cuydaes que trago peolhos?
Anjo de Deos, minha rosa,
eu so aquella preciosa   *eu sou Brisida preciosa*
que dava as moças a molhos.   *que dava as moças os*
                            [molhos

525   ¶A que criava as meninas
pera os conegos da sé.
Passae-me por vossa fé,
meu amor, minhas boninas,   **[*M f.* 6r A]**
olhos de perlinhas finas!
530   E eu som apostolada,
engelada & martallada,
& fiz cousas muy divinas.   *& fiz obras muy divinas.*

    ¶Santa Ursula nom converteo
tantas cachopas como eu:
535   todas salvas pollo meu
que nenhũa se perdeo;
& prouve aquelle do céo
que todas acharam dono.
Cuydaes que dormia sono?
540   Nem punto se me perdeo.   *nem ponta, & nam se perdeo.*

ANJO: ¶Ora vay lá embarcar:
nam estés emportunando.

---

513 se fosse ho · *se eu fosse ao* 514 lá · la *la* 515 ca fundo · *ca em fundo* 516 vou que
he mays · *vou eu, que he mais* *stage direction* om. *M* 517 ¶ om. *M* 519 cá · ca *ca*
520 peço vollo · *Peçouolo* 521 cuydaes · *cuydais* peolhos · *piolhos* 524 a molhos · *bos*
molhos 527 passaeme · *passayme* 529 olho · *olhos* perlinhas · *peerlinhas*

If I went to the fire of Hell,
so would everybody else.
515   I'll go to that boat down there,
since it is much more royal.

And arriving at the boat of glory, she says to the
[angel,

Boatman, dear, my darling,
put down the plank for Brísida Vaz!
ANGEL: I don't know who brought you here.
520   BRÍS.: I beseech you on bended knee,
do you think I've got lice?
Angel of God, my rose,
I'm that precious thing   *I'm precious Brísida*
that gave away the girls in loads.   *that gave girls broth.*

525   I'm she who brought up little girls
for the canons of the Cathedral.
Take me across, by your faith,
my love, my sweetheart,   [*M f.* 6r A]
my little teeny-weeny pearl.
530   I have been apostolicked,
angelized and martyressed,
and I did things that were really divine.

Saint Ursula did not convert
as many girls as me:
535   all saved on my account,
so that not one of them was lost.
And may it please Him up there
for all of them to find masters.
D' you think I was half asleep?
540   I never missed a stitch!

ANGEL: Now go and board over there,
cease your importunate entreaties.

---

530 E · & *&* som apostolada · *sou hapostollada* 531 engelada · *angellada*
martallada · *martellada,* 533 nõ · *nã* 534 como eu · *comeu* 537 proue aquelle ·
prouue haquelle ceeo · *ceo* 538 acharam · *acharão* 539 cuidaees · *cudais* dormia sono
· *dormia eu sono,* 541 la · *la* 542 estes · *estes*

[C v A] BRÍS.: Pois estou-vos eu contando   *Pois estou-vos alegando*
                 o porque me avés de levar.
545   ANJO: Nam cures de emportunar,
                 que nom podes ir aqui.
       BRÍSIDA: E que má ora eu servi
                 pois nam m'há d'aproveitar

       ¶Torna se Brísida Vaz à barca do inferno dizendo,   [om. *C*]

              ¶Hou barqueiros da má ora!
550   Que é da prancha, que ex me vou,
              & há ja muyto que aqui estou,   *& tal fada me fadou*
              & pareço mal cá de fora.   *que pareço mal cá fora.*
       DIABO: Ora entrae, minha senhora,
              & serés bem recebida;
555   se vivestes sancta vida
              vos o sentirés agora.

       ¶Tanto que Brisida Vaz se em/barcou veo   [*M f.* 6r B]
              ũ judeu com ũ bode às costas; &   ¶*Vem um Iudeu com um*
              chegando ao batel dos danados, diz: *bode às costas, & diz ao*
                                                        diabo,

       JUDEU: ¶Que vay cá? Hou marinheiro!
       DIABO: Ó que má ora vieste!
       JUDEU: Cuj'é esta barca que preste?
560   DIABO: Esta barca, é do barqueyro.
       JUDEU: Passai-me, por meu dinheyro.
       DIABO: E o bode, há cá de vir?
       JUDEU: Poys tambem o bode há d'ir.
       DIABO: Que escusado passageyro!   *Ó que honrrado passageyro.*

565   JUDEU: ¶Sem bode como yrey lá?
       DIABO: Nem eu nom passo cabrões.
       JUDEU: Ex aqui quatro testoões,

---

544 ho · *o* me auees · *mauei* 545 de emportunar · *demportunar* 546 nom · *nam* hir ·
yr 547 & · *E* maa ora · *maora* 548 ma daproueitar · *maa daproueytar*   549
Ou barqueir⁹ · ¶*Hou barqueyros* maa ora · *maora* 550 que he da · *pôde a* ex · *eis*
551 há · ha *ha* 552 cá · ca *cá* · *ca* 553 entrae · *entray* 554 serees · *sereis*

BRÍS.: Well, I'm trying to tell you
why you have to take me. [C f. 47v A]

545 ANGEL: Don't think of entreating any more,
since you cannot cross here.

BRÍS.: What a damned time I served
for it'll provide me with no profit.

Brísida Vaz returns to the boat of Hell,
saying,

Ho there, boatmen of damnation!
550 Where's the plank, here I come!
I've already been here a while,
and I look bad from outside.

DEVIL: Now embark my lady,
and you'll be well received:
555 if you've lived a holy life,
you're going to feel it now.

Whilst Brísida Vaz embarks, a Jew   *A Jew comes carrying a*
enters carrying a goat on his back, and   *goat on his back and*
reaching the boat of the damned, says,   *says to the Devil,*

JEW: What's going on here, sailor?
DEVIL: Oh what a bad time to come!
JEW: Whose is this pretty boat?
560 DEVIL: This boat belongs to the boatman.
JEW: Take me across, for my money.
DEVIL: And the goat, it has to come?
JEW: Well, the goat has to come too.
DEVIL: What an unwanted passenger!

565 JEW: How can I get there without a goat?
DEVIL: I don't take any goats across.
JEW: Here are four florins:

---

556 sentires · *sentireis* **stage direction (M)** ũ · hũ (twice) às · as (C) um · *hum*
(twice) 557 Que · ¶*Que* ca: ou marinheiro · *la ou marinheyro.* 558 oo · *Ho* maa ora
· *maora* 559 cuje · *Cuja* he 560 é · he *he* 561 passaime · *passayme* 562 & ho · *E esse*
há · ha *ha* 563 poys tambê ho bode ha · *O bode, tambem ha* 565 la · *laa.* 566 nem eu
nom · *Pois eu nam* 567 ex · *Eis* testoões · *tostões*

	& mais se *v*os pagar*á*
	(por vida do Semifar*á*!)
570	que me passeys o cabram.
	Queres mais outro tostam?
DIABO:	Nenhũ bode **há** de vir c**á**.

Nem tu nam bás de vir cá.

JUDEU:	¶Porque no<u>m</u> yr*á* o judeu
	*o*nde vay Brisida Vaz?
575	Ao senhor meirinho apraz,
	senhor meyrinho, yrey eu.
DIABO:	E o fidalgo, que<u>m</u> lhe deu —
JUDEU:	O mando, dizes, do batel?
	Corregidor, coronel,
580	castigae este sandeu!

[*C*, in margin: *Fala ao*
fidalgo

[*DIABO*: *o mando deste batel?*
[*JUDEU*: *Corregedor, Coronel,*

	¶Hazar*á*! Pedra meuda!
	Lodo! Chanto! Fogo! Lenha!
	Caganeira que te venha,
	má corrença que te acuda!
585	Para'l deu qui te sacuda,
	co*m a* beca nos focinhos,
	fazes burla dos meirinhos:
	dize, filho da cornuda!

[*C f.* 57v B]

[*M f.* 6v A]

JOANE:	¶Furtaste a chiba cabra<u>m</u>?
590	Parece-me vos a mim
	guafanhoto d'Almerim
	chacinado em ũ seiram
DIABO:	Judeu, lá te passaram
	porque vã mais despejados.
595 JOANE:	E elle mijou nos finados
	n'ergueja de sam Gião!

carrapato d'Alcoutim
enxertado em camarão.
Judeu, lá te levarão
porque hã d'ir descarregados.
E s'elle mijou nos finados
no adro de sam Gião?

---

568 os pagara · *vos pagaraa* 569 do semifara · *de se ma faraa* 570 passeys ho cabram · *passeis o cabrao* 571 queres · *quereis* tostam · *tostão.* 572 **há** · a cá · ca **bás** · *bas* **cá** · *ca* 573 nõ yra ho · *nam yraa o* 574 honde · *onde* 575 meirinho · *meyrinho* 576 hyrey · *yrey* 577 & ho · *& ao* 578 ho · *ho* 580 castigae · *castigay*

and you'll be given more,
(by the life of Semifarah!),
570   for you to take the goat across.
Do you want another florin?
DEVIL: No goat will come here.   *Nor are you to come here.*

JEW: Why can't the Jew go to
where Brísida Vaz goes?
575   If you please, sheriff, sir,   **[C, in margin:** *He speaks*
sheriff, sir, I shall go!   *to the noble*
DEVIL: And the noble, who gave him —
JEW: You mean, the command of the boat?
Magistrate, colonel,
580   punish this lunatic!

Hazarah! Small stone of grief!
Mud! Mourning! Fire! Wood!
May the trots come upon you:
may the runs catch up with you!
585   By the God who shakes you,
with your robe stuffed up your snout,
you make fun of the sheriffs,
say, son of the horned one!

SIMON: Goat, did tha' steal yon' kid?
590   Tha' seems, tha' does, ta me
a locust from Almerim,   *a tick from Alcoutim*
chopped up in a basket.   *stuck on a prawn.*
DEVIL: Jew, they'll take you across   *Jew, they'll bear you there*
so they can travel emptier.   *as they have to go*
595 SIMON: And 'e pee'd on t' dead   *[unburdened.*
in t' church o' Saint Julian?   *And if 'e pee'd on t' dead*
                                                  In Saint Julian's church-
                                                     yard?

581 ¶Hazara · *¶Azaraa* 583 caganeira · *caganeyra* 584 te acuda · *tacuda:* 585 paral deu qui · *por el deu que* 586 coa · *com a* 587 meirinhos · *meyrinhos* 589 cabrã · *cabrão,* 590 parece me · *pareceísme* 591 dalmerim · *Dalcoutim* 592 ũ · hũ 593 lá · la *lá · la* 595 E · & 596 n'ergueja · neegueja

¶E comia a carne da panella
no dia de nosso Senhor,
& aperta o salvanor

& mais elle — salvanor —

600 & mija na caravella.

cada vez mija naaquella.

DIABO: Sus! Sus! Demos a vella!
Vos, judeu, yres à toa
que soys muy roym pessoa;
levae o cabram na trella!

Vem ũ corregedor carregado de feit<u>os</u>, & chegan<u>do</u> à barca do inferno co<u>m</u> sua vara na mão, diz,

¶Vem um Corregedor, & diz chegando à barca do inferno,

605 ¶Hou da barca!

DIABO: Que querés?

COR.: Est*á* aqui o senhor juyz.

DIABO: Ó amador de perdiz,
gentil carregua trazés!

quantos feytos que trazeis!

COR.: No meu ar co<u>n</u>hecereys

610 que nom é ella do meu geyto.

qu'elles nam vem de meu [*geyto*

DIABO: Como vay l*á* o direyto?

COR.: Nestes feytos o verés.

DIABO: ¶Ora, pois, entrae, veremos
que diz hy nesse papel.

615 COR.: E onde vay o batell?

DIABO: No inferno vos poeremos.

[*M f.* 6v B]

COR.: Como? À terra dos demos
h*á* d'ir ũ corregedor?

[*C f.* 48r A]

DIABO: Sancto descorregedor,

620 embarcae & remaremos.

¶Ora entrae, pois que viestes.

COR.: Nom é de regule juris, na<u>m</u>,

Non est de regule juris, não.

DIABO: Ita, ita, day c*á* a mão:

---

597 E · ¶E da · *na* 601 sus sus · *Ora sus* a · *aa* 602 hyres · *yreis* 603 soys · *sois* roym · *roim* 604 leuae ho · *leuay o* **stage direction** ũ · *hũ* um · *hum* 605 Ou · ¶*Ou* querees · *quereis* 606 esta · *estaa* ho · *o* 609 ar cõhecereys · *aar conhecereis* 610 é om. *M* 611 la o · *la ho* 612 ho verees· *o vereis* 613 Ora · ¶*Ora*

74

And 'e ate meat from t' kettle
on t' day o' our Lord.
And 'e'll open 'is arse   *and 'e even – 'scuse me! –*
600   and pee on t' caravel.   *always pees on that thing…*
   DEVIL: Come, come, let's set sail,
       Jew, you'll be dragged behind,
       for you are a bad person indeed;
       take the goat on its leash.

A magistrate enters loaded with legal   *A magistrate enters*
processes and, reaching the boat of Hell with   *and says reaching*
his rod in his hand, says,   *the boat of Hell,*

605   Ho there, boat!
   DEVIL: What do you want?
   MAG.: Be upstanding for the judge!
   DEVIL: Oh, you lover of partridges,
       you've brought a promising load!
   MAG.: From my air you'll recognise
610   that it isn't really in my style.
   DEVIL: How's the law down there?
   MAG.: You can see it in these processes.

   DEVIL: Now then, come on board, let's see
       what's written on that paper.
615   MAG.: And where is the boat bound?
   DEVIL: We'll set you down in Hell.
   MAG.: What? Is my honourable self
       to go to the land of devils?
   DEVIL: Your holy dishonour,
620   come on board and we'll row.

Now come on board, since you've come.
   MAG.: It's not de regule juris, not at all.
   DEVIL: Ita, ita, give me here your hand,

---

(613) entrae · *entray* **614** hy · *hi* **615** & honde · *E onde* batell · *batel.* **616** poeremos · *poremos* **617** aa · *ha* **618** ha· *ha* hũ · *hum* **620** embarcae · *embarcay* **621** Ora entrae · *¶Ora entray*

		remaremos u<u>m</u> remo destes,
625		fazé conta que nacestes
		pera nosso companheyro.
		Que fazes tu, barzoneyro?
		Faze-lhe essa prancha prestes.

	COR.:	¶Ó, renego da viagem,
630		& de quem m'**h**á de levar!
		H**á** 'qui meirinho do mar?
	DIABO:	Nam **h**á **cá** tal custumagem.
	COR.:	No<u>m</u> entendo esta barcagem,
		nem hoc non potest esse.
635	DIABO:	Se ora vos parecesse
		que no<u>m</u> sey mais q<u>ue</u> linguaje<u>m</u>...

		¶Entrae, entrae, corregedor!
	COR.:	Ó, videtis qui petatis?
		Super iure magestatis
640		tem vosso mando vigor?
	DIABO:	Quando ereys ouvidor,
		no<u>n</u>ne accepistis rapina?
		Pois yres pella bolina
		onde nossa merce for.

645		¶*Ó* que ysca esse papel
		pera ũ fogo que eu sey.
	COR.:	Domine, memento mei!
	DIABO:	Nom es tempus bacharell,
		imbarquemini in batel
650		quia iudicastis malicia.
	COR.:	Semper ego *in* iusticia
		fecit e² bem per nivel.

	DIABO:	¶E as peitas dos judeus
		que vossa molher levava?

[*M f. 7r* A]

---

624 remaremos hũ · *remareis hum* **625** fazee · *fazey* **629** ¶O · *¶Ho* **630** ma · *maa*
631 há · ha *ha* meirinho · *meyrinho* **632** ha ca · *ha ca* custumagem · *custumagem.*
633 nõ · *Nã* barcagem · *barcajem* **636** nõ · *nam* linguajẽ · *lingoagẽ* **637** ¶Entrae
entrae · *¶Entray, entray* **638** ou · *Hou* **639** iure · *jure*

625   we'll row one of these oars:
you'd better realise you were born
to be our very own.
What are you doing, lazybones?
Get that plank ready for him.

MAG.:   Oh, I curse the voyage,
630   and the one who is to take me!
Is there no officer on duty?
DEVIL: Such is not our custom.
MAG.:   I do not comprehend this journey,
nor hoc non potest esse.
635   DEVIL: If, by chance, you might think
that I don't know more than Portuguese:

come on board, come on board, magistrate.
MAG.:   Oh, videtis qui petatis?
Super iure magestatis,
640   does your authority stretch?
DEVIL: When you were a justice
nonne accepistis rapina?
So you'll have to sail
wherever is our pleasure.

645   Oh, that paper'll make fine kindling
for a fire I've got in mind!
MAG.:   Domine, memento me.
DEVIL: It non is tempus, your honour.
Imbarquemini in caravel,
650   quia iudicastis malitia.
MAG.:   Semper ego in iustitia
fecit, and all on the level.

DEVIL: And the bribes the Jews gave
that your wife accepted?

---

641 ereys · *ereis* 643 hyres pella · *yreis polla* 645 ¶O · *¶Oo* ysca · *isca* 646 ũ · hũ
hum 648 nom · *Non* bacharell · *bacharel* 650 iudicastis · *judicastis* 651 ego iusticia ·
ego in iusticia 652 & fecit · *fecit, e³* per · *por* 653 peitas · *peytas* linguajẽ · *lingoagẽ* 637
¶Entrae entrae · *¶Entray, entray* 638 ou · *Hou*

655   COR.: Ysso eu nam o tom*a*va.
          Eram l*á* percalços seus,   **[C** *f.* **48r B]**
          nom som pecatus meus,   *non ʃunt peccatuʃ meuʃ,*
          pecavit uxore mea.
    DIABO: *Et* vobis quoqu̲e̲ cum ea,
660   nam temuisitis deus.   *nemo tĩmuiʃtiʃ ∂euʃ.*

         ¶A largo modo adquiristis
         sanguinis laboratorum,
         ignorantes pecatorum
         ut quid eos nom audistis.
665   COR.: Vos, arraez, non̲ne legistis
         que o dar qu̲e̲bra os pined̲o̲s̲;
         os dereytos estam quedos
         sed aliquid tradidistis.   *ʃi aliqui∂ tra∂i∂iʃtiʃ.*

         ¶Ora e̲ntrae nos negros fados:
670   irés ao lago dos caães,
         & verés os escrivaães
         coma estam tam prosperados.
    COR: E na terra dos danados
         estam os evangelistas?
675   DIABO: Os mest*r*es das burlas vist*a*s
         l*á* estam bem freguados.

      ¶Estando o corregedor nesta pratica co̲m̲ o   *¶Vem um*
[M   arraez infernal, chegou huũ procurador   *procura∂or, e³ ∂iz o*
f. 7r   carre/gado de livros, & diz o corregedor ao   *correga∂or quan∂o o*
B]   procurador: *vee,*

         ¶*Ó* senhor procurador!
    PRO.: Bejo-v*o*-*l*as maãos juyz.
         Que diz esse arraes, que diz?
680   DIABO: Que serés boõ remador.
         Entrae, bacharel, doutor,

---

655 ysso · *Iʃʃo* nam ho tomova · *nam no tomava* 656 la · *laa* 658 pecauit · *peccauit*
659 & · *Et* 661 adquiristis · *a∂queriʃtiʃ* 663 pecatorum · *peccatorum* 664 nom · *non*
665 arraez · *arraiz* 666 ho · *o* pined⁹ · penedos 669 Ora · ¶*Ora* ẽtrae · *ẽtray* 670
hires · *yreiʃ* caães · *cãeʃ* 671 verees · *vereiʃ* escriuaães ·

655 MAG.: Those I didn't have any part in,
that was her own business.
They are not peccatus meus,
peccavit uxore mea.

DEVIL: Et vobis quoque cum ea.
660 You didn't temere deus.

Wholesale you adquiristis
sanguinis laboratorum,
ignorantes peccatorum,
ut quid eos non audistis.

665 MAG.: Boatman, nonne legistis
that giving you will receive:
rights can be silenced
if aliquid tradidistis.

DEVIL: Now board upon your unhappy doom.
670 You'll go to the lake of hounds
where you will see the scribes
and how prosperous they've become.

MAG.: And are the evangelists found
in the land of the damned?

675 DEVIL: There the masters of public fraud
are properly doctored.

¶Whilst the magistrate is saying these
things to the infernal boatman, an advocate
arrives, burdened with books, and the
magistrate says to the advocate,

An advocate enters,
and the magistrate
says as soon as he
sees him,

Oh, it's you, advocate.
ADVOCATE: I kiss your hands, your honour.
This pilot — what does he say?

680 DEVIL: That you'll be handy with an oar.
Board, bachelor, doctor of the law,

escriuães **672** coma · como **673** & · *E* **675** mesters · *mestres* burlas vistes · *bulras vistas* **676** lá · la *la* freguados · *fragoados* **stage direction** o corr. · ho … **livros** · libros **um** · *hum* **677** ¶O · *¶Oo* **678** bejo vos las maãos · *Beyjouolas mãos* **679** esse arraes · *este arraiz* **680** serees boõ · *sereis bom* **681** entrae · *entray*

79

        & yrés dando na bomba.
PRO.: E este barqueiro zomba?
       Jogatays de zombador?

685   ¶Essa ge<u>n</u>te que a<u>h</u>y está
       pera onde a levays?
DIABO: Pera as penas infernaes.
PRO.: Dix! Nom vou eu pera *lá*:
       outro navio está *cá*
690   muyto milhor assombrado.
DIABO: Ora estás bem aviado:
       entra, muytieramá.

COR.: ¶Co<u>n</u>fessastes-vos, doutor?   [*C f.* 48v A]
PRO.: Bacharel som, do*u-me* o demo.
695   Na<u>m</u> cuydey que era estremo
       nem de morte minha door;
       & vos senhor corregedor?
COR.: Eu muy bem me confessey,
       mays tudo quanto roubey
700   encubry ao confessor.

PRO.: ¶Porq<u>ue</u>, se o nom tornays   [*C* om. PRO.]
       nam vos querem absolver,
       & é muy mao de volver
       depoys que o apanhaes.
705 DIABO: Pois porq<u>ue</u> no<u>m</u> embarcays?
PRO.: Quia speramus in deo.   *COR.: Quia esperamus in Deo.*
DIABO: Inbarquimini in barco meo!   [*M f.* 7v A]
       Pera que esperatis mais?

  ¶Va<u>m</u>-se ambos ao batel da gloria, &   *¶Vam-se à barca da gloria,*
  chegando diz o corregedor ao anjo,   *e³ diz o Corregedor,*

     ¶*Hou*, ara<u>e</u>z dos gloriosos,

---

682 hyrees · *yreis* na bomba · *aa bonba* **683** & · *E* barqueiro · *barqueyro* **684**
jogatays · *jogatais* **685** ha hy esta · *hi estaa* **686** leuays · *leuais* **687** infernaes ·
infernais. **688** dix nom · *Dixe, nam* la · *laa* **689** esta ca · *estaa caa*

and you will have a bale.
ADVOCATE: Is this boatman joking?
Are you playing at the jester?

685   Over there, those people,
where are you taking them?
DEVIL: To infernal punishment.
ADVOCATE: Phew! I won't be going there.
Here there's another ship
690   with a much better shape.
DEVIL: Now you're quite ready:
board, hellfire and damnation!

MAG.: Have you confessed, Doctor?
ADVOCATE: I'm only a Bachelor of law, damn it.
695   I didn't think it would be final
nor the pain I felt be fatal;
and what about yourself, magistrate?
MAG.: I made a very good confession,
but all that I had stolen
700   I kept hidden from the priest.

ADVOCATE: Since, if you don't return it
they won't give you absolution,
and returning something's really bad
once you've got your hands on it.
705 DEVIL: Well, why don't you embark?
ADVOCATE: Quia speramus in Deo.
DEVIL: Imbarquimini in barco meo!
Why wait any more?

¶Both go to the boat of glory and, once they have
arrived, the magistrate says,

Ho there, pilot of the blessed!

691 hora estas · *Ora estais* 692 entra · *Entray* 694 som domo o · *sou doume o* 699
mays · *mas* 700 encubri · *encobri* 701 nom tornays · *nam tornaes* 703 é · he *he* 704
depoys · *depois* ho · *o* 705 nõ embarcays · *nã embarcaes* 707 inbarquimini ·
Imbarquemini **stage direction o** · ho 709 O araeez · ¶*Hou arraiz*

AUTO DA BARCA DO INFERNO

710   passae-nos neste batel!
    ANJO: Ó pragas pera papel,
           pera as almas odiosos,
           como vindes preciosos
           sendo filhos da ciencia!
715   COR.: Ó, abeatis clemencia,
           & passae-nos como vossos!

  JOANE: ¶Ó homens dos briviayros,
           rapinastis coelhorum,
           & pernis perdiguytorum
720   & mijaes nos campaneyros!
    COR.: Ó nam nos sejaes contrairos,   *Anjos, nam sejaes*
           pois nom temos outra ponte.   *[contrayros,*
  JOANE: Beleguynis, ubi sunt?
           Ego latinus macayros!

725   ANJO: ¶A justiça divinal
           vos manda vir carregados
           porque vades embarcados
           nesse batel infernal.
    COR.: Ó nom praza a sant Malçal   *[C f. 48v B]*
730   com a ribeyra nem com o ryo!
           Cuydam lá que é desvario
           aver cá tamanho mal.

    PRO.: ¶Que ribeira é esta tal?   **[om. C to l. 737]**
  JOANE: Pareces-me vos a my
735   como cagado nebry,
           mandado no sardoall.   *[M f. 7v B]*
           Embarquetis in zambuquis!

    COR.: ¶Venha a negra prancha cá,
           vamos ver este segredo.
740   PRO.: Diz ũ texto do degredo —   *Dix um teisto do decreto,*

---

710 passaenos neste · *passaynos nesse* 711 oo · *Ho* 714 ciencia · *sciencia.* 715 o abeatis · *Ho habeatis* 716 pasaenos · *passaynos* 717 Ou · ¶*Hou* briuiayros · *breuiayros* 719 perdiguytorum · *perdigatorum* 720 campaneyros · *campanayros*

82

710		Take us over in this ferry.
	ANGEL:	Oh, you plagues on paper,
		hateful to all souls.
		How preciously you come
		as sons of knowledge.
715	MAG.:	Oh, abeatis clemency,
		and take us over as your own.

	SIMON:	Ah, men of breviaries and books,
		rapinastis rabbitorum
		et pernis perdiguitorum,
		an' peed on t' bell-towers.
720	MAG.:	Oh, do not be against us,
		for we've no other bridge across.
	SIMON:	Sherifforum, ubi sunt?
		Ego latinus macairos!

725	ANGEL:	The justice of Heaven
		orders you to come burdened
		because you will travel
		on that infernal ferry.
	MAG.:	Oh, Saint Martial cannot be pleased
730		with the shore, nor with the river!
		There they think it's folly
		to have such evil here.

	ADVOCATE:	What sort of riverbank is this?
	SIMON:	Tha' seems ta me, tha' does,
735		like a soddin' falcon
		sent into t' trees.
		Embarquetis in t' sampanis!

	MAG.:	Set down here the damned plank,
		let's go and see this secret.
740	ADV.:	A text says in the Decretals —

---

721 Ó · o 722 nom · *nam* 723 beleguynis · *Beleguinis* sunt · *sunte* 728 neste · *nesse*
729 o nom · *Ho nam* sant malçal · *sam Marçal* 730 com a · *coa* cõ o ryo · *co rio*
731 lá · la *la* é · he *he* 733 é · he cá · ca *ca* 738 venha · ¶*Venha* cá · aca*ca* 740 ũ ·
hũ *um* · *hum*

Entrae, que cá se dirá.

¶E tanto que foram dentro no batel
dos condenados, disse o corregedor a
Brisida Vaz porque a conhecia:

¶Entram no batel dos
danados, & diz o
Corregedor a Brisida Vaz.

Ó, estés, muytieramá
senhora Brisida Vaz.

BRÍSIDA: Ja siquer estou em paz

745   que nam me leixaveys lá.

¶Cada ora sentenciada:
"Justiça que manda fazer...".

¶Cada ora encoroçada:

COR.: E vos — tornar a tecer
& urdir outra meada.

750   BRÍS.: Dizede, juyz d'alçada,
vem lá Pero de Lixbõa?
Leva-llo-emos à toa,
& irá nesta barcada.

¶Vem ũ homem que morreo enforcado &
chegando ao batel dos malaventurados, disse
o araez tanto que chegou,

¶Vem ũ enforcado,
& diz o diabo,

¶Venhaes embora, enforcado,

755   que diz lá Garcia Moniz?

ENF.: Eu te direy que elle diz:
que fuy bem aventurado,
em morrer dependurado
como o tordo na buyz,

[*M f.* 8r A] & diz que os feitos que eu fiz
me fazem calonizado.

que pollos furtos que eu fiz
sou sancto canonizado
pois morri dependurado
como o tordo na buiz.

762   DIABO: ¶Entra cá, governarás
atá as portas do inferno.

¶Entra cá & remarás

ENF.: Nom é essa a nao que eu governo

---

741 entrae · *Entray* **cá** · ca *ca* dira · *dira* **stage direction disse** · dise a · ha 742
¶O estees muytiera má · *¶Esteis muyto arama* 743 brisida · *Brisida* 745 leiyaueys ·
leixaueis 746 cada hora · *¶Cada ora* 748 & · E 749 hurdir · *vrdir* 751 lá · la *ja*
lixbõa · *Lisboa* 752 leualloemos · *leualoemos* 753 hira nesta · *yraa*

Come on board, here it can be said.

¶And when they are on board the boat
of the damned, the magistrate says to
Brísida Vaz because he knew her:

*They board the boat of
the damned, and the
magistrate says to
Brísida Vaz.*

Oh, you're here, by the fires of Hell,
Senhora Brísida Vaz.

BRÍSIDA: At least I'm in peace now,
745   which you wouldn't allow me there.

Sentenced at every moment,
"By the power vested in me…".

MAG.: And you … you'd begin to weave
and spin some other intrigue.

750 BRÍS.: Tell me, circuit judge,
will Peter of Lisbon come?
We'll drag him along behind us
and he'll go in this ferry-load.

A man who has been hanged enters, and
arriving at the boat of the ill-fated, the pilot
of that boat says,

*A hanged man
enters and the devil
says,*

Come along, hanged man,
755   what did Garcia Moniz say?

THEIF: I'll tell you what he says,
that I was fortunate
to die upon the gallows,
like a thrush in a springe,
and he says that my deeds
make me a canonized saint.

*that by the thefts I did,
I'm a canonized saint,
since I died by hanging
like the thrush in a springe.*

762 DEVIL: Come on board: you'll steer
up to the gates of Hell.

THEIF: That's not the ship I'll pilot.

Board, and you shall row.

---

desta **stage direction** ũ · hũ **disse** · dise *ũ* · *hũ* **754** Venhaes · ¶*Venhais* **755** la
garcia · *la Gracia* **756** te · *vos* **759** o · ho **762** ¶ *om.* M cá governerás · ca
gouernaras · *cá* · ca **remarás** ·*remaras* **763** ataa · *atee* **764** nõ e · *Nã he*

765 DIABO: Mando teu, que aqui irás.   *Entra que inda caberás.*
       ENF.: Ó, nom praza a Barabás!   *Pesar de sam Barrabás!*
             Se Guarcia Moniz diz
             que os que morrem como fiz
             sam livres de Satanás.

770   ¶E disse-me que a deos prouvera   [*Cf.* 49r A]
             que fora elle o enforcado,
             & que fosse deos louvado,
             que em bo' ora eu cá nacera:
             & que o senhor m'escolhera,
775   & por meu bem vy beleguyns,
             & com ysto mil latins,
             muy lindos feitos de cera.   *como seu latim soubera.*

           ¶E no passo derradeyro
             me disse nos meus ouvidos
780   que o lugar dos escolhidos
             era a forca & o Limoeyro;
             nem guardiam de moesteyro
             nam tinha tam sancta gente
             como Affonso Valente
785   que é agora carcereyro.

      DIABO: ¶Dava-te consolaçam
             isso, ou alguũ esforço?
       ENF.: Com o baraço no pescoço
             muy mal presta a pregaçam.
790   E elle leva a devaçam
             que há de tornar a gentar;
             mas quem há d'estar no ar   [*Mf.* 8r B]
             avorrece-lh' o sermam.

      DIABO: ¶Entra, entra no batel,

---

765 irás · hiras. **caberás** · *caberas* **766** barabas · *Barrabas* **767** guarcia · *Garcia* **768** como fiz · *como eu fiz* **769** liuras · *liures* satanas · *Satanas.* **770** & disseme que · ¶*E disse que* **771** ho · *o* **773** ca · *ca* **774** ¶E · *c̃* **775** vy beleguyns · *vi beleguins* **776** ysto · *isto* **778** & · ¶*E* **781** ho · *o*

86

765 DEVIL: As you wish, but cross you will.   *Board, you'll still fit.*
    THIEF: Oh, spite upon Barabbas!   *Spite on St Barabbas!*
    So says Garcia Moniz,
    that those who died like me
    are freed from Satan.

770   And he told me that would to God
    it were he who was hanged;
    and that God was to be praised
    for I was born in a lucky hour;
    and that I'd been chosen by the Lord
775   and that for my good I saw the constables,
    and with that a thousand relics   *and many Latin words*
    very pretty things of wax.   *as he knew his Latin.*

    And, as I was being hanged,
    he whispered in my ear
780   that the place of the chosen
    was the gallows and the prison;
    not even a monastery's keeper
    would have such holy men
    as has Afonso Valente
785   he that's now the gaoler.

    DEVIL: Did that bring you consolation
    or did it give you any strength?
    THIEF: With the noose around your neck
    preaching doesn't go down well.
790   And you can stand devotion
    if you're going back to dine,
    but if you're about to swing
    you just can't bear a sermon.

    DEVIL: Come on board, board the ferry,

---

782 Nã · *nem* moesteyro · *mosteyro* **783** tam · *mais* **785** que he agora · *o que agora he* **786** daua · *¶Daua* **787** ou ysso · *isso, ou* alguũ · *algum* **788** cõ ho · *Co* **789** pregaçam · *preegaçam* **790** ¶E elle · *elle* **791, 792 há** · ha *ha* **793** auorecelho sermam · *auorecelhe o sermão* **794** entra · *¶Entra*

795   que ao inferno *h*ás d'ir
  ENF.:   O Moniz há de mentir?
            Disse-me que com sam Miguel   *Dixeme, 'com sam Miguel*
            gentaria pam & mel   *yrás comer pão & mel*
            tanto que fosse enforcado.   *como fores enforcado.'*
800   Ora ja passey meu fado
            & ja feito é o burel.

            ¶Agora nam sey que é ysso:
            nam me falou em ribeyra,
            ne<u>m</u> ba*r*queiro ne<u>m</u> barqueyra
805   senam logo o parayso
            (ysto muyto em seu syso),
            & era sancto o meu baraço.
            Eu nam sey que aqui faço:
[C *f.* 49r B]   <u>que</u> é desta gloria emproviso?   *ou se era mentira isto.*

810 DIABO: ¶Falou-te no purgatorio?
     ENF.:   Diz que foy o Limoeyro
             & ora por elle, o salteyro,
             & o pregam vitatorio,
             & que era muy notoryo
815   que aquelles deciprinados
             eram oras dos finados
             & missas de sam Gregorio.

     DIABO: ¶Quero-te desenganar   *¶Ora entra, pois hás d'entrar*
             se o que disse tomaras,   *nam esperes por teu pay.*
820   certo é que te salvaras: *[ENF: Entremos pois que assi vay.*
             nam o quiseste tomar.   *[DIA: Este foy bom embarcar:*
             Alto todos a tirar   *eya todos apear*
             que está em seco o batel!
[*M f.* 8v A]   Sahi vos, fray Babriel,   *vos, doutor, bota batel,*
825   ajuday ally a botar.   *fidalgo saltay ò mar.*

---

795 ao inferno as · *pera o inferno has* 796 ho moniz ha · *E Moniz ha* 797 **disse-me** · diseme que 801 feito he · *feyto he* 802 agora · ¶*Agora* he ysso · *he isso* 804 baqueiro · *barqueyro* 805 ho · *oo* 806 ¶Ysto · *& isto* 807 & era · *& que era*

795   for you are to go to Hell.
   THIEF Old Moniz was lying?
          He told me that I'd eat   *He said "You'll go eat*
          bread and honey with Saint Michael
          as soon as I'd been hanged.   *since you've been*
800   Now I've passed through my fate   *[hanged."*
          and the time for sackcloth's over.

          Now I don't know what this is:
          he didn't tell me of a riverbank,
          neither boatman nor woman,
805   except straightaway — Paradise
          (and that very much in his wits),
          and that my noose was holy.
          I don't know what I'm doing here:
          what's immediate about this glory?   *or was that a lie?*

810 DEVIL: Did he tell you about Purgatory?
   THEIF: He said that it was the prison,
          and now, for him, the praying of psalms
          and his final sermon,
          and that it was well-known
815   that being flogged with whips
          were prayers for the dead
          and masses for the Holy Souls.

   DEVIL: I'd like to undeceive you:
          if you accepted what he said
820   it's sure you'd have saved yourself,
          but you didn't manage to accept.
          Get up, all of you and pull
          for the ferry's stranded!
          Get out, fray Babriel,
825   and help to push over there.

---

808 eu nam · *porem nam* 809 é · he 810 faloute · *¶Faloute* 812 ho · *o* 813 ho pregam · *o pregão* 814 ¶E · *&* muy notorio · *muyto notorio* 817 missas · *missa* 818 ¶ om. *M hás · has* 819 o · ho 820 é · he 821 (*M*) o · ho 822 (*M*) Alto · ¶Alto 823 esta · *estaa* ho · *o*

¶Vem quatro cavaleyros cantando os quaes
trazem cada ũ a cruz de Christo pello qual señor
& acrecentamento de sua sancta **fé** catolica
morreram em poder dos mouros. Absoltos a
culpa & pena per privilegio que os que assi
morrem teem dos misterios da paixam da quelle
por quem padecem, outorgados per todos os
presidentes summos pontifices da madre sancta
ygreja, & a cantiga que assi cantavan (quanto **à**
palavra della) é a seguinte:

¶Vem quatro
fidalgos
cavaleyros da
ordem de
Christo, que
morreram nas
partes
d'Africa, &
vem cantando
a quatro vozes
a letra que se
segue:

¶À barca, à barca segura,
barca bem guarnecida:
à barca, à barca da vida.

guardar da barca perdida

830 ¶Senhores que trabalhaes
polla vida transitoria,
memoria, por deos, memoria,
deste temeroso caes.
À barca, à barca, mortaes,
barca bem guarnecida
835 à barca, à barca da vida.

porem na vida perdida
se perde a barca da vida.

¶Vigiae-vos, pecadores,
que despois da sepultura
neste rio está a ventura
de prazeres ou dolores.
840 À barca, à barca, senhores,
barca muy nobrecida,
à barca, à barca da vida.

[om. *C* to line 842]

[*M f.* 8v B]

¶E pasando per diante da proa do batel dos danados **[om. *C*]**
assy cantando com suas espadas & escudos, disse o
araez da perdiçam desta maneira:

DIABO: ¶Cavalleyros, vos passeaes
& nom preguntays onde is

Cavaleyros, vos passaes
& nam me dizeis pera onde is

---

stage direction cavaleyros · caualeros **ũ** · hũ **per** · por **é** · he **à** · a ***d'Africa*** ·
Dafrica **829 ¶Señores** · *¶Senhores* **trabalhaes** · *trabalhais* **832 caes** · *cais*

Four knights enter singing, each of whom bears *Four noble*
the cross of Christ, the Lord for whom and for the *knights of*
increase of whose holy Catholic faith they died in *the Order of*
Christ who
the power of the Moors. Absolved from all guilt *had died in*
and punishment through the privilege that those *Africa*
who thus die recieve from the mysteries of the *enter,*
passion of the one for whom they suffer, *singing in*
authorized by all the popes of Holy Mother *four voices*
the words
Church and the song they sing as they enter (as to *which follow*
the words) is the following:

Board the boat, the secure boat,
the well-provisioned boat. *keep from the lost boat*
Board the boat, the boat of life!

Men, you who strive
830   for the life that will not last,
keep in mind, by God, in mind
this fearful riverside.
Board the boat, the boat, oh mortals,
the well-provisioned boat, *but in the lost life*
835   board the boat, the boat of life. *you'll miss the boat of*
[life.

Sinners, watch yourselves,
for after you're in the grave
on this river is your fate
of pleasures or of sorrows.
840   Board the boat, the boat, oh men,
the very noble boat,
board the boat, the boat of life.

And passing before the prow of the boat of the damned
singing in this way with their swords and shields, the pilot of
perdition says to them in this manner:

DEVIL: Knights, you walk about *Knights, you go past*
       and don't ask where you're to go. *& don't say where*
you're going.

---

833 mortaes · *mortais* 838 está · esta stage direction assy · asy 843 ¶Caualleros
· *¶Caualeyros* passeaes · *passaes* 844 nom · no is · his

845 CAV.: Vos, Satanás, presumis?   *E vos Satam presomis,*
             Atentae com quem falaes.
       OUTRO: Vos que nos demandaes,
               siquer conhecey-nos bem:
               morremos das partes d'alem   [*C f.* 49v A]
850   & nam querays saber mays.

       DIABO: ¶Entrae cá, que cousa é essa?   [om. *C* to line 855]
               Eu nom posso entender ysto.
       CAV.: Quem morre por Jesu Christo
               nam vay em tal barca como essa

       ¶Tornam a perseguir cantando seu caminho   [om. *C*]
direito à barca da gloria &, tanto que chegam, diz
                      o anjo:

855   ¶*Ó* cavalleyros de deos,
             a vos estou esperando,
             que morrestes pelejando.
             Por Christo, senhor dos çéos:
             soys livres de todo mal,   [*C f.* 49v B]
             martyres da madre ygreja,   *sanctos por certo sem falha*
860   que quem morre em tal peleja   *que quem morre em tal*
             mereçe paz eternal.   [*batalha*

       ¶E assy embarcam.   *¶Aqui fenece a primeyra cena.*

       ¶Auto das barcas que fez Gil Vicente per seu
mão. Corregido & empremido per seu mandado.   [om. *C*]
Pera o quall & todas suas obras tem privilegio del
Rey nosso senhor. Com as penas & do tehor que
pera o Cancioneyro Gèral Portugues se ouve.

---

845 **Satanás** · satanas **846** atentae · *atentay* falaes · *falais*. **847**
'where *C* has *Outro*' to mark the second speaker, *M* bears a sign.

845 KNIGHT: You, Satan, do you dare?
     Pay heed to whom you speak.
2ND KNIGHT: You who are asking this
     take good note of who we are,
     we died in lands over the sea
850   and do not seek to know more.

  DEVIL: Board here, what's all this about?
     I can't make all this out.
 KNIGHT: He who dies for Christ Jesus
     shall not go in a boat like this.

They again continue singing on their way straight
to the boat of glory, and as soon as they arrive, the
angel says,

855   Oh, God's own knights,
     I have been waiting for you,
     you who have died fighting.
     Through Christ, Lord of the Heavens
     you're free from all evil,
     martyrs of Mother Church,   *saints without any doubt,*
860   for whoever dies in such a struggle *for whoever dies in*
     deserves eternal rest.   *[such a battle*

  And so they embark.   *Here ends the first scene.*

The Play of the boats which Gil Vicente made by his
own hand. Corrected and printed by his own order.
For this and for all of his works he has a privilege
from our lord, the King, with the same conditions
and penalties that were obtained for the Portuguese
Cancioneiro Geral.

---

847 vos · *E vos* demandaes · *demandais* 848 conhecenos · *conheceynos* 849 das · *nas*
850 querays · *queraes* mays · *mais* 851 cá · ca é · he **stage direction** o · ho 855
¶O · *¶Oo* 858 Por xpo · *por Christo* çeeos · *ceos,* 858 soys · *soes* 861 mereçe · *merece*
final note Auto · Autos o · ho **(twice)**

NOTES TO THE *AUTO DA BARCA DO INFERNO*

Introduction: *M*.

por contemplaçam: Morais, I, 456A, 'em respeito, por obséquio, temor'.

mui: a shortened form of *muito*, now obsolete.

comença: the modern form *começa* is also used in the introduction. There was a certain amount of vacillation over nasalized versus un-nasalized vowels during the early sixteenth century. Cp. *page* instead of *pagem* in this introduction.

fegura: the modern form is *figura*.

pera: this form died out from Portuguese at the beginning of the seventeenth century; *C* uses *pera* throughout. On three occasions, *M* prefers *para* before an adverb of place (lines 67, 303, 386: *onde* and *lá*). See Révah, *Recherches*, 162.

gloria: see Paul Teyssier, '*Glória* dans Gil Vicente et Camões', *Ibérica*, 1 (1977), 295-311, for the full range of Vicente's use of the word.

entrelocutor: the modern form is *interlocutor*.

um rabo mui comprido: the train or tail of the noble's coat. J. Cardoso, 1562, f. 90v, glosses *rabo de vestidura* as 'scirma, atis' (Révah, *Recherches*, 163).

ante que: the modern form is *antes que*.

Introduction: *C*.

prefiguração: 'prefiguration' in this passage may have been used with a generic meaning, indicating that we are not meant to take literally what we experience in the play: it is a putting into material shape what is a spiritual event.

terrestres corpos: there would seem to be an implied contrast between 'earthly bodies' which die and 'spiritual bodies', the souls who inhabit these 'earthly bodies'.

escena primeira: the 'first scene' refers to the first play in the trilogy of Boat Plays. The second and third scenes deal with Purgatory (located on the riverbank) and the boat to Heaven. These works are not published in this volume.

purgatorio: editors generally accept that 'inferno', hell, should have been printed. However, I am puzzled how the mistake can have been made, and so have left 'purgatório' in the text rather than supress it.

3   a summary of opinions on this verse is given by Moura, *Teatro*, 163-7; Quirino da Fonseca proved *M*'s reading to be preferable to that of *C* in his 'Comentário ao verso, "Ora venha ho caro a ree" do *Auto de Moralidade* de Gil Vicente, edição de 1516 ou 1517 (*Auto da Barca do Inferno*), in *Gil Vicente: vida e obra. Série de conferências realizadas na Academia das Ciências de Lisboa* ... (Lisboa: Academia das Ciências de Lisboa, 1939), 489-547.

5 *muytieramá*: according to Teyssier, *La Langue de Gil Vicente*, 500, the words *eramá*, *aramá*, and *earamá* have their origin in *em hora má* which, though the denazalization of the first consonant ought to have given *°e ora má*. The popular character of such words in Gil Vicente's Portuguese is without doubt. Even *embora* (from *em boa ora*) and variants of it does not belong to the upper register of speech; the words are found amongst popular characters.

6 *atesar*: a variant of *entesar*, 'to stretch, make taut' (*T* 253A).

   palanco: Morais, II, 213, 'corda que passa por um moutão que está na ponta da vela; serve de a içar'.

14 *leito*: cf. Morais, II, 213, '*leito do barco*: a tilha, ou coberta que traz á popa'.

15 *emboa ora* counted three syllables: cp. line 773. Teyssier comments that *C*'s *bonora* is a manifest printer's error, for this form is unknown in the language of the time (*La Langue de Gil Vicente*, 496, note 1, at 497).

16 *'maora*: a running together of 'em má ora'.
   cu: the lower part of a block and tackle (*A* 505B). A Spanish phrase, cited by Berardinelli, *Antologia*, 138, *abajar el lomo* means 'to work with care', although I doubt whether this could be an underlying meaning here.

17 *poja*: 'clew' (*T* 497A). Révah, *Recherches*, 164-5, followed by Spina, *Obras-primas*, 108, gives *poja* the meaning of a rope that is used to turn the sail on the starboard side.

18 *driça*: a form of *adriça*, 'halyard' (*T* 20B).

22 *a pique*: Quintela, 255 gives the meaning as 'ready, prepared', cf. *Auto da Índia*, l. 26, 'A armada está muyto a pique'; the anchor was said to be 'a pique', when it had been raised to beneath the poop and hung almost vertically (Révah, *Recherches*, 165).

23 *C*: 'Oh, precious Lord Henry'. The *Anrique da âncora* is a rope used to raise the anchor, according to Augusto C. Pires de Lima, *Os autos das Barcas de Gil Vicente* (Porto, 1985?), 49. If a pun were intended, *poderoso*, powerful, would then refer to the strength of the rope as well.

29 *a senhora*: Révah, *Recherches*, 165, considers the noble to be asking about the boat; one should note, however, that at l. 804 the Hanged Man exclaims that he had been told of neither 'barqueiro nem barqueyra'. It may be that the devil's *companheiro* is really a *companheira*.

31 *cortiço*: 'a cilindrical container made of cork and used as a beehive' (*A* 487C; *T* 186A). The noble may well mean that the boat is 'overcrowded', just as a beehive. However, as only the Devil and his mate are on board, it seems an odd statement for the noble to make — unless, in a hypothetical earlier version of the play, the noble's entrance came much later, when several characters had already been embarked.

53 The noble's father and his wife's mother are both implicitly condemned: a dramatic irony, since the noble puts such stress upon his birth.

62-63 *C*: 'and just when you died/you had given me a sign'. An alteration probably imposed by the Inquisition.

63 With Révah, *Recherches*, 166, I see little reason to accept the version of Braga, II, 43, who considered *sinal* to be a 'deposit' for the journey.

64 *foi*: there would seem to be a certain amount of confusion between *foi* and *fui* in the text. I have retained *M*'s reading. Révah corrected this to *fui*.

72 *salvanor*: 'excuse the word'. The modern form of the expression is 'com perdão da má palavra': Cleonice Berardinelli, ed., *Antologia do teatro de Gil Vicente* (Rio de Janeiro: Grifo, 1971), 140. The word is used by countryfolk when mentioning animals lest the person being spoken to think that he or she is being called a pig, donkey, horse, etc.
giricocins: perhaps a cross between *jerico* (ass) and *rocim* (a small, weak horse): see Révah, *Recherches*, 166.
μ substitutes 'bribante' (Quintela, 146).

73 *grou*: Cf. Luis de Camões, *Filodemo*, ed. José Cardoso e Domingos Guimarães de Sá, in *Luís de Camões: Teatro (Anfitriões, El-Rei Seleuco e Filodemo)* (Braga, 1980), 171-262, lines 100-101, at 178, 'Por ventura sou eu grou?/Sempre hei d'estar vigiando?' [perchance am I a crane? Am I always to keep watch?]; Carolina Michaëlis de Vasconcellos, ed., *Poesias de Francisco de Sá de Miranda* (Halle, 1885), 243, note to lines 170-171, 'E des o grou...'. According to mediæval bestiary lore, the crane would stand with one foot on the ground, holding a stone in the other, so that, if it fell asleep, it would drop the stone and wake itself up. The figure of the constantly watching bird had evidently become proverbial. According to a work attributed to Albertus Magnus (†1280), the *Libellus de natura animalium*, 'Natura sive proprietas gruge talis est quod quando dormiunt alie, una ipsarum semper vigilat et custodit...' (ed. Paola Navone, in *Le proprietà degli animali*, Testi della cultura italiana, 5 (Genova: Costa & Nolan, 1983), 196-346, at 216).

74 *C*: 'what do you demand?' An alteration in *C* by which the angel is made to ironise the haughty attitude of the noble, and which is therefore probably by the hand of Gil Vicente.

80 *fidalgo de solar*: a nobleman by birth; Morais, II, 30A, 'o que já descende de outros; o que tem nobreza conhecida pelo Solar'.

83 *batel*: a small boat, used with ships and galleons (cf. *A* 240A).

86 *fantasia*: Morais, II, 84A, 'presumpção'.

87 *estreyta* would seem to be a reference to Matthew 7: 13-14, 'Make your way in by the narrow gate. It is a broad gate and a wide road that leads on to perdition, and those who go in that way are many indeed; but how small is the gate, how narrow the road that leads on to life, and how few there are that find it!' (Ronald Knox, tr., *The Holy Bible: a translation from the Latin Vulgate in the light of the Hebrew and Greek originals* (New York: Sheed and Ward, 1956), 6B).

89 *cortesia*: not only courtesy, but also manners befitting the court.

93 *C*: 'to board this ship'.

99-101 *C*: 'you and your noble self/counting upon the tyranny/for which you had such curiosity'; *curioso* (*C*) would seem to have two meanings, according to Morais, I, 505A: the first, 'curious'; the second, which one might translate as 'amateur', 'se diz de que é *curioso de alguma arte*, o que não deu annos a aprendè-la com mestre, e não a sabe a fundamento' (*he is said to be* curioso *in an art whoever has not spent years learning it with a master, and does not know it in depth*).

100 *tirania*: a line which has suggested that Lucian's *Scaphidium* was a source for the play. A tyrant is forced by Hermes (who acts as psychopomp) to leave his cloak and riches and 'airs' before he is allowed to board the boat across the Styx. See Asensio, 60-64.

102 *generoso*: of noble birth; Morais, II, 84A, 'Que vem de boa casta, ou geração, de pais nobres, e ilustres'.

stage direction *C*: 'Singing'.

111 Cp. l. 456''' (*C*) or the equivalent stage direction in *M*, after line 456.

115 The noble's sin is intensified in *C*, from the ignorance or forgetfulness of the existence of Hell (*M*) to rejection of the Church's teaching on Hell. A change probably carried out by the Inquisition.

125 *M*'s reading of 'remarees' may hide an original reading of 'remaees' (cf. l. 263) which the printer mistakenly read as a future tense ('remarees') due to the other future tenses which surround it.

127 *C*'s version is irreduceably hypermetric. Perhaps the possibility that 'servir', to serve, might have been understood in a way which ignored the irony of its use by the devil was too much of a risk for the Inquisitors to take. According to Morais, II, 695A, 'servir damas' can mean to court women with pleasantries: the devil is thus making an ironic reference to the noble's devotion to courtly love.

128 The noble's wish to return to earth and his wife's behaviour at his death recall Lucian's *Tyrranus*: Megapenthes requests one of the Fates to let him return to the world to warn his wife and his concubine, who had succumbed to the charms of his own servant before his corpse. The concubine, when people arrived, went away weeping and screaming the tyrant's name. See Asensio, 64.

132 *M* records the speaker with the archaic form, 'Diaboo'.

136-7 A change probably carried out by Luis Vicente to improve the grammatical sense of the original.

137 A thousand days are roughly two years and eight months. The figure has a religious resonance, recalling the thousand years of the millenium.

141 This line represents another courtly turn of phrase.

154-56 *C*: 'was to give infinite glories/to he who released her./NOBLE: As for her, she cried a lot'.

160-61 *C*: 'Board, my lord, board, / bring the plank, step on it.'

163 *C*: 'Now, now, rest'. Braga, II, 47, notes that the devil, once he has persuaded the noble to embark, is no longer in such a hurry.

168 *C*: 'You, his boy, go away from here'.

172 The chair made of ivory is reminiscent of numerous mediæval accounts of Hell in which rulers are punished for their sins by being seated upon thrones which torture them.

180 In *M* it is the devil who speaks this line; in *C*, the usurer.

187 *quebranto*: 'exhaustion, weakness, prostration; a spell of depression, illness, etc., inflicted by another's "evil eye", especially upon children and animals' (*T* 526A).
μ has 'mas deume grande quebranto' (Quintela, 152).

188 *livrar*: according to Berardinelli, *Antologia*, 143, one should understand 'free from Hell'.

198 *C*: '*John Pimentel's grief!*' The tendency to euphemize oaths by invoking personalities of the time is perhaps a reflection of contemporary customs, for heavy legal penalties were threatened in law codes for those who swore by God or the saints in vain. See Quintela, 264-5.

207 *avantagem*: the modern form is *vantagem*. Quintela, 266, comments that it is the form used by Gil Vicente and is today preserved above all in Trás-os-Montes.

stage direction: Révah, *Recherches*, 168, thought that a reference to the usurer's *bolsão*, purse, had been omitted by Gil Vicente or the printer in the stage direction, and consequently inserted it. However, it is most probably the case that the readership would have inevitably conceived of the usurer having a bag, for it was thus that the profession was always depicted.

217 *tomara*: See Révah, *Recherches*, 168, who considered the word a pluperfect tense with a conditional value. *C*'s alteration, *tomaraa* (a future indicative), was, he thought, unacceptable.

218 μ has 'Juro a mi...' (Quintela, 153).

220 *de rodam*: the sense of the word seems to be, in the words of Agostinho de Campos, in his edition of the *Auto da Cananeia*, (Lisboa, *s. d.*,) 102): 'Here there is no idea of movement, but rather of accumulation or making round' (cited by Révah, *Récherches*, 168). Ley, 64, also believed that there may have been a cross of the word with *rodar*.

221 This line indicates to the audience or reader that the spiritual significance of the symbols the characters bring with them is to be understood as paramount; here, the usurer is still attached to his money, too attached to be admitted onto the boat to Heaven.

231 *Barreyro*: a town upstream from Lisbon on the Tagus (*GEPB* 4, 265A).

234 *per*, here and lines 301, 304 and 652, and in three stage directions (those before lines 477, 826 and 843), has the meaning, as in Latin, of 'through', 'by', or of spatial or temporal duration. The distinction of *per* and *por* was lost during the sixteenth century, *per* only being retained in set phrases. See Révah, *Recherches*, 162.

248 *aquesta* is a characteristic of dramatized rustic speech, and substitutes a noun which the rustic may not know or wish to say. All the other

characters call the boat a *barca*, and only the parvo refers to it as a generic, 'that'. See Quintela, 270.

249 *naviarra* seems to be an augmentative of *navio*, as with *bocarra* (Quintela, 271). *M* has *araviara*, which may be a misprint, a word the fool has garbled (Révah, *Recherches*, 169), or an older form of the word (Ley, 65). *µ* has 'arauia' (Quintela, 156).

251 Perhaps an allusion to the acrobatics that the character of the fool was expected to perform on stage, or to make the fool better resemble one of the animals (Palla, 91).

252-55 *voo, avoo, soo*: I am unsure quite how these words were pronounced, and so I have made an exception to the norms of transcription I have used thoughout this piece.

255 *nella* (*C*): this refers to *má-ora*, 'evil hour'. It is preferable to *M*'s reading, *nello*, which does not seem to have a referent.

257 *samicas*: the peasant adverb *par excellence*, stressed on the penultimate syllable. This is its first appearance in the *corpus* of Vicente's works. See Teyssier, *La Langue de Gil Vicente*, 84-88; cp. line 298.

261 *zambuco*: The sambook was a small sailing-boat used in the Indian Ocean, sewn together with ropes. The word is from the Arabic *sanbūk*, the initial letter being either sâd or sîn. See *The Portuguese off the South Arabian Coast: Hadramî chronicles with Yemeni and European accounts of Dutch pirates off Mocha in the seventeenth century* (Oxford, Clarendon Press, 1963), 135-36, and, for an illustration, Alan Moore, *Last Days of Mast and Sail*, 128. As the sambook is relatively little known in English, I have preferred another Oriental craft more familiar to English readers, the Chinese sam pan.

262 *tolazo*: this would seem to be an example of hesitation or confusion between endings in –*azo* and -*aço* (Révah, Recherches, 169). It may be an ironic imitation of a more cultured style: Sá de Miranda and António Ferreira use endings in -*az* (beliguinaz, fafianaz, ladravaz).

262 *enuco*: the more normal form was *eunuco*.

272 *Candosa*: a town connected to wine production (Quintela, 272).

273 *antrecosto*: the modern form is *entrecosto* (see *A* 665a).

276 *tinhoso*, while meaning 'mangy, scabby', is, according to *T* 611A, also a colloquial term for the Devil. Such a dual sense of the word would fit well here.

278 *chentar*: chantado, meaning planted out with stakes, occurred as early as 1275. Fr. Joaquim de Santa Rosa de Viterbo, *Elucidário das palavras, termos e frases que em Portugal antigamente se usaram e que hoje regularmente se ignoram*, ed. Mário Fiúza (2 vols.; Porto-Lisboa: Livraria Civilização, 1966; 1ª edição, 1798-1799), II, 93, gives the meaning of *chentar* or *chantar*, as being also 'to unite in affection', and *chantado* as meaning 'united to or rooted in someone's heart'. Teyssier points out that *chentar* is a familiar synonym for *pôr*, to put (*La Langue de Gil Vicente*, 483).

281 *burrella*: although the word in the *Cancioneiro Geral* would seem to indicate a rite of humiliation whereby the offending subject would be forced to ride backwards on a donkey whilst being insulted by onlookers (Révah, *Recherches*, 169; see also I. S. Révah, 'Quelques mots du lexique de Gil Vicente', *Revista Brasileira de Filologia*, 2 (1956), 143-54, at 143-49), here, surely, the insult merely refers to the devil as a 'stupid ass'. The movement from the *burella* to *cornudo sejas* is probably explained by the ass's ears being suggestive of horns.

286 *atá*: again a rustic or popular form of the word in the mouth of the fool, a form which reflects more closely its derivation from the Arabic *hatta* (Teyssier, *La Langue de Gil Vicente*, 137).

mangueira: whilst the word can signify 'mango-tree', it is more likely, in the phallic field of reference used by the fool, to suggest a 'tube' (*A* 1080A).

ratinho: the name given to the rural-urban migrants who flowed into Lisbon from the Beira (Michaëlis, 447).

288 *pulha*: 'contest in which one person wished all sorts of misfortunes, for the most part obscene, upon another, who replied in a similar strain' (J. P. Wickersham Crawford, 'Echarse pullas:—A popular form of *tenzone*', *Romanic Review*, 6 (1915), 150-164, at 157).

287 *pam*: M. Rodrigues Lapa, *Vocabulário galego-português* (Coimbra: Galaxia, 1965), 69A, gives as one of the meanings of *pan* that of a 'small, valueless thing'.

290 *μ* has 'ay damalo caga na vella' (Quintela, 53).

291 *grulha*: 'chatterer' (*T* 327B), loquacious person (*A* 870C), as well as the more explicit 'grouse'.

294 *pelourinho*: the public whipping-post, set in a main square of a town, and beside which punishments were carried out (Berardinelli, *Antologia*, 147).

forno de telha (*C*): it would seem that this image implied, in popular usage, a state of irremediable permanance. In Vicente's *Romagem dos agravados*, 'feito é o forno da telha' occurs at line 406, which Maria de Lourdes Saraiva, in her *Gil Vicente: Sátiras sociais* (Lisboa: Publicações Europa-América, 1975), 230, glosses as a popular aphorism, which seems to signify, 'now there is no remedy'. It is, perhaps, equivalent to the English, 'It's no use crying over spilt milk'. Devils, in Christian belief, were created as angels, but rebelled against God and were thus condemned for all eternity to Hell. Thus the devil's 'brick-kiln tail' is a reference to his fallen state, from which there could be no redemption.

302 *simpreza*: the modern form is *simpleza*; *abastar*: the modern form is *bastar*, *ser bastante*

309 *μ* has 'Hum çapateiro honrado' (Quintela, 160)

311 *viir*: Révah, *Recherches*, 171, thought that this word was pronounced with the first 'i' nasalized, (vĩ-ir).

313 *lago*: the Book of the Apocalypse asserts several times that the wicked will be thrown into a lake of fire: Revelation 19:20, 20:14, 21:8.

333 μ has 'nem me ham daproueitar' (Quintela, 161)

338-39 Satisfaction was 'an act of reparation for an injury committed. In Christian theology it is usually applied to the payment of a penalty due to God on account of sin. … *satisfactio operis* came to be regarded as a necessary means of avoiding punishment in Purgatory after the sin itself had been remitted by sacramental absolution' (*The Oxford Dictionary of the Christian Church*, ed. F. L. Cross (2nd edn.; Oxford: OUP, 1974), 1237B). The 'satisfaction', at least in popular conceptions, need not come from the cobbler himself; it may come from his heirs, who might return the proceeds of theft in order to free him from Purgatory. The omission of Purgatory from the afterlife leaves no option but that the cobbler go to Hell.

340 *badana*: Asensio, 66, sees the cobbler's oath regarding *badana* and *cordovam* an allusion to the *Danza de la Muerte* in which Death says to a cobbler, 'O, çapatero, no me hagas creer/que no vendiste cordobán y es badana' [O, cobbler, don't make me think/that you did not sell cordovan leather that was in reality sheepskin]. However, the cobbler's oath is not close enough to the *Danza* to show a clear influence, and both invocations of *badana* and *cordovam/cordobán* are more likely to reflect a common background in the tools of the cobbler's trade than dependence of Vicente upon the *Danza*.

343 *traquitana* would seem to have the sense of 'a rickety cart' (cf. *GEPB* 32, 573a) *Janatam*: Jonathon. *D* changes the name to *Janantam* (i.e., *João Antão*), which Braga, II, 56, considered to be the cobbler's name; μ has 'Ioam Antam' (Quintela, 161). Quintela, 275, noted that a parallel name, *Janafonso*, occurs in the *Templo de Apolo* (*Copilaçam*, f. 162 v° - 164 v°).

347 *cárrega*: load (Moura, *Teatro*, 167).

349 *u*: 'where', common in mediæval Portuguese, the word was passing out of use at the beginning of the sixteenth century, and consequently had a distinctly popular flavour (Teyssier, *La Langue de Gil Vicente*, 483). μ has 'isto onde que se yrá' (Quintela, 162).

351 *de praça*: 'in public. An expression that is very common in writers of the fifteenth century' (Quintela, 275).

μ & *D* both omit scene of the friar in its entirety (Quintela, 56, 124-5).

355 The lasts are meant to signify the cobbler's thefts which he committed as part of his profession.

360-63 These lines depend upon a pun on *coser*, to sew (leather) or to cook. The cobbler intends the first meaning, whereas the Angel takes up the second. I have attempted to reproduce the pun (which is, after all, the most important feature of the lines) with similar puns in the English ('fixed', 'soul/sole', 'repair'). A more literal translation of these lines would be: 'COBBLER: And so you've made up your mind/that I should sew (leather) [or cook] in Hell./ANGEL: Your name's written down/in the menus of Hell'. There is an implied contrast between the cobbler's being written down in the 'menu (or book) of Hell' and the saints, whose names are written in the Book of Life, whch is a means of expressing their entry into Heaven.

364 (*C*): 'Well, devils, what are you waiting for?'

stage direction *frade*: Gil Vicente delighted in presenting friars as being far too fond of secular enjoyments. The friar of the *Frágua do Amor* complains bitterly about the discomforts of religious life, preferring to dance and to eat the food his mistress prepares for him. The frair of the *Auto das Fadas* preaches on the theme, *Amor vincit omnia*, love conquers all.

baixa: this dance for couples was at the height of its popularity in the first half of the sixteenth century. The friar is therefore presented as being extremely *à la mode*. It was called in Italy the *bassadanza* and the *basse danse* in France, whence the English adopted the words. It was characterized by its dignified, graceful motion. The steps of the dance 'were supposed to be performed in four motions of equal duration. Yet the accompaniment consisted of six beats, divided usually into 3 + 3; i.e., the dancers had to move in two against the music's three'; its difficulty led it to be called the 'queen of measures' (Stanley Sadie, ed., *The New Grove Dictionary of Music and Musicians* (London: Macmillan, 1980) II, 257a-259a). As in this play, the basse danse was usually followed by the 'tordion', which was played at twice the speed of the basse danse.

373 *tordiam*: see above.

381 *grosa*: censure, criticism (Moura, *Teatro*, 167).

397 *namorado*: according to Teyssier (*La Langue de Gil Vicente*, 470), this word has highly favourable connotations, like the French *galant*, and so was thought to describe a virtuous quality.

406 Spina, *Gil Vicente*, 79, n. 61 (bis), suggests another possible interpretation, 'The explanation offered by P. Quintela and reproduced by Révah is not satisfactory. Quintela glossed the verse: Today one would say, 'It's that!', or: 'Now this!' Both punctuate the phrase with an exclamation. I would prefer a question mark and another interpretation of the passage: the pronoun *ela* (her) should refer to the *sentença* (sentence), as if the the Friar had said, 'Then the sentance is that? – not to go in the same boat as my Florence'.

417 The friar is referring to his 'crown' or tonsure, as symbol of his authority (Braga, II, 60).

421-22 *rolão* and *roloa*: words that are probably to be connected to the celebrated French epic hero, Roland. It may be that the friar has given names to his sword and buckler (*Roloa* and *Rolam* respectively), on the model of the names given to weapons in epic poetry.

425 *demos caçada*: according to Morais, '*dar caçada*' means, simply, to fence.

426 *contra sus*: cp. line 446.

427 *fendente*: a cut delivered downwards (E. D. Morton, *Martini A-Z of Fencing* (London: Macdonald, 1988), 63A).

428 *levada*: a lunge and parry; cp. Révah, *Recherches*, 173.

430 *talho*: a cut (i.e., a blow with the edge of the sword; see Morton,46B), the sword being moved from right to left.

430 *revés*: a cut from left to right.

436 *guarda*: 'It should be understood that *guardia* were not positions in the modern sense, i.e., identical with the parry in that particular line. In [the sixteenth century], parrying was still performed with a buckler. These *guardia* were supposed to be the best positions from which a time action could be launched on an offensive move by the adversary from any given position' (Morton, 79C).

444 *esto* (*M*): a Hispanism due to the printer, according to Paul Teyssier, 'Le système des deictiques spatiaux en portugais aux XIVe, XVe et XVIe siècles', *Études de littérature et de linguistique* (Paris: Fondation C. Gulbenkian, 1990), 161-98, at 188. *Esto* was a mediæval form in Portuguese.

457 Ley, 70, 'It is odd to note that this line, without the three verses ... [in *C*], rhymes with no other.'

465 *Andar*: Gil Vicente often used the infinitive as an imperative: see Quintela, 283, and Révah, *Recherches*, 173-4.

466 *trincham*: derived from *trinchar*, to cut into small pieces, the word would seem to mean a 'tasty piece', i.e., the friar's mistress (see *GEPB* 32, 863A).

stage direction *Brísida Vaz*: Dean W. McPeeters, 'La *Celestina* en Portugal en el siglo XVI', in *'La Celestina' en su contorno social*. *Actas del I Congreso Internacional sobre 'La Celestina'*, Colección Summa, 2 (Barcelona: Borras, 1977), 367-76, at 368, suggests that the figure of the Vicentine bawd is inspired by Rojas' Celestina, a character from the *Tragicomedia de Calixto y Melibea* which appeared in the first years of the sixteenth century, immediately became a 'best seller', and exerted a tremendous influence upon subsequent literature. Brísida's character is also discussed by Nelly Novaes Coelho, 'As alcoviteiras vicentinas', *Alfa*, 4 (1963), 83-105, at 98.

473-76 *C*: 'DEVIL: Father, you have to come now./FRIAR: Yes, take Florence there for me,/and let's fulfil this sentence/and let's order that we leave!'

479 *μ* has 'Ora acabay dom mangàs' (Quintela, 56).

481 Whilst *M*, *C*, and *D* all attribute this comment to Brísida Vaz, *μ* places it in the cobbler's mouth (Quintela, 57), and modern editors attribute it to the devil's mate. Another candidate would be the usurer, who previously swore by 'Sancta Joana de Valdes' (l. 240). The mate's speech has, up to now, been of a rigidly repetitive and formulaic character.

486 *catar*: although the modern usage of this word gives it the meaning of 'to look for fleas', in Vicente's day it was used by all levels of society and meant, in a broad sense, 'to look for' (Teyssier, *La langue de Gil Vicente*, 81).

490 This verse was prohibited by the 1624 *Index* of the Portuguese Inquisition. It is presumably meant to recall the literary figure of Celestina (see Fernando de Rojas, *Comedia o tragicomedia de Calisto y Melibea*, ed. Peter E. Russell (Madrid: Castalia, 1991), 245 and note 165).

μ has 'Seiscentos modos postiços' (Quintela, 57).

491 *feytiços*: Celestina was also famed for her use of spells (see Russell, 245-47, 292-95).

500 *embayr*: 'to fool, trick or fill someone's understanding with false ideas .... It is an ancient word, more Castilian than Portuguese' (Santa Rosa de Viterbo, II, 211A). The alteration is, according to Révah, *Recherches*, 92, to be ascribed to Luis Vicente.

μ has 'com dous coxins de fingir' (Quintela, 57).

509 *martella*: It may be that Gil Vicente has developed this feminine form, *mártella*, from the rustic '*mártel*'(for *mártir*) to gain a comic effect, rather than that it was a pre-existent rustic word as Révah thought (*Recherches*, 175).

μ has 'Es sou hũa martelada'.

516 *mais real*: Morais, II, 557A, describes a 'galé real' as being the largest in the fleet. Brísida Vaz is therefore making a comparison between the size of the two ships.

523-4 *preciosa*: μ has 'piadosa'. The change wrought by C may be a printer's error, mistaking the idiomatic phrase 'a molhos' for '*os* molhos', or, what is more likely, it may be an attempt to remove part of the more risqué elements of the play, probably carried out by the Inquisition.

526 μ has 'para os de boa relé'; *D*, 'para as vender muyto bem' (Quintela, 172).

527 *D* 'passayme ora la alem' (Quintela, 172).

529-40 this passage is suppressed in *D* (Quintela, 289).

529 Quintela, 289, writes, *pèrlinhas*, 'to respect the pronunciation of the time, as expressed in the spelling provided by *C*.'

530-33 μ has 'que eu são assas enfadada/engelhada, & martelada/& fiz bem sempre as vizinhas' (Quintela, 172).

533-40 Censored by the Inquisition in μ (Quintela, 289).

533 *Santa Úrsula*: the legend of Ursula was highly embroidered throughout the mediæval period. The saint was supposedly martyred in Cologne with eleven thousand virgin companions by the Huns; in some accounts these women were waiting-women of Ursula, in others, they were women she had converted by her preaching. See D. H. Farmer, *The Oxford Dictionary of Saints* (Oxford: Clarendon Press, 1978), 386B-87B. The reference to Ursula is not without contemporary resonance: Queen Lianor had acquired and translated the relics of one of Ursula's virgin companions to a side altar in her conventual foundation of Madre de Deus in 1509. The triptych which adorned the altar can be seen in the Museu de Arte Antiga in Lisbon.

540 *ponto*: Teyssier, *La Langue de Gil Vicente*, 483, points out that negations using *ponto* (or *C*'s *ponta*) have a distinctly popular air. Spina, *Gil Vicente*, 70, translates, 'no time was lost at all'.

542 *emportunar*: this word is the normal form of literary language, whilst popular forms existed (Teyssier, *La Langue de Gil Vicente*, 163).

551-552 *C*: 'and such a fairy told my fortune/that I seem ill outside'. Cp. 'más fadas que vos fadaram', *Quem Tem Farelos* l. 431.

552 This line may represent the idea that, as Brísida's body decomposes, so her soul, reflecting the state of the body, appears worse and worse.

555 *μ* has 'se fizestes santa vida' (Quintela, 174).

564 *escusado*: cp. *Exortação da Guerra*, l. 501.

stage direction: the goat is a complex symbol, drawing on imagery from the Old and New Testaments. It is the 'scapegoat', the animal driven out into the wilderness on the Day of Atonement with the sins of Israel upon itself (Leviticus 16: 21-22). The scapegoat is, however, a type of Christ, who took the sins of the world upon himself. Vicente is pointing to the Jew's blindness in not seeing Christ reflected in the Old Testament scapegoat. The goat is, however, also associated with those damned at the Last Judgement (Matthew 25: 33). The appearance of the Jew, with the goat on his shoulders, is further intended to evoke memories of Christ as the good shepherd, carrying a sheep on his shoulders: the Jew brings his own damnation upon his shoulders; Christ brings salvation upon his.

565 *cabrões*: a pun, meant to indicate the goat and also the Jew, who is a goat in that he is 'horned', i.e., cuckolded.

567 One *tostão* is equivalent to one hundred reais which represented four times the daily pay of a carpenter or stonemason in 1531 (Maria Lourdes Saraiva, 56); in 1515, a kid cost between twenty-five and thirty reais.

576 *meirinho*: The Jew comically mistakes the noble for a bailiff, magistrate and colonel. The Jew's invocations of the noble, however, presage the appearance of the magistrate upon the stage.

577-78 *μ* has 'Dia. E o nome quem lho deu. / Judeu. / Ou mayoral do batel' (Quintela, 175).

581 *Azará*: a rendition of the Hebrew, *ha-sarah*, 'distress, affliction, misfortune' (Révah, *Recherches*, 175, citing J. Fuerst, *A Hebrew and Chaldee Lexicon to the Old Testament* (Leipzig-Londres, 1867), 1209).
Berardinelli, *Antologia*, 158, suggests that the Jew's *pedra miúda* might refer to the small stones used in calculation, known in Latin as *lapilli*. There was an ancient tradition of using such stones to mark days, a white one for a good day, a black stone for a day of affliction. The Jew would then be wishing a time of affliction upon the devil. A work attributed to Bede, *De computo dialogus* (*PL* 90, 650D), contains the following: 'Antiqui enim ante inventionem numeri nescientes numerare, ex lapillis sua tempora suosque dies numerabant: in prosperitate candidis, in adversitate nigris'. Reference to such a stone would seem to have had a semi-proverbial resonance in the late Middle Ages: Reimerus Sancti Laurentii Leodinensis, *De claris scriptoribus monasterii sui*, PL 204, 34C, 'Hæc quidem ineptiæ quasi nigro calculatæ sint lapillo'. *Lapillus* was used by Hildegard of Bingen, in her *Subtilitates diversarum naturarum creaturum* (*PL* 197, 1185AB) to describe the gallstone: the Jew might be wishing such a painful malady upon the devil. Having in mind the scatalogical

content of the Jew's expression, it is possible that *pedra miúda* refers to the *lapis judaicus*, or Jewstone (*OED* 8, 232B: 'the fossil spine of a large sea urchin, found in Syria') which Sir Thomas Browne described as 'diureticall' (*OED* 8, 649A).

582 *chanto*: a clear marker of Jewish speech in Vicentine theatre. Its meaning is 'lamentation', and hence 'misfortune, catastrophe' or 'distress' (Teyssier, *La Langue de Gil Vicente*, 219).

lodo: a synonym of *chanto*, from the expression *pôr de lodo*, 'ruin', 'dishonour', 'make unhappy' (*Ibid.*, loc. cit.).

581-82 *μ* has 'Granizo pedra miuda/lodo, cinza, fogo, lenha' (Quintela, 60).

585 Révah, *Recherches*, 176, notes that *Par el Deu* was calqued on the archaic expression *par Deos* (cf. v. 70). Whilst Spanish Jews said *el Dio* in place of *Dios*, Portuguese Jews said *o Deu* or *el Deu* (by anology with *el-Rei*).

μ has 'juro a deu que te sacuda'.

589 *μ* has 'Furtaste a chiba ladram'.

591 *guafanhoto*: perhaps the intent in calling the Jew a 'locust' is to identify him with a plague.

Almerim was the location of the palace in which Dom Manuel was accostomed to spend the winter months (*GEPB* 2, 79B).

Alcoutim (*C*): one of the titles of the Marquês of Vila Real was 'Conde de Alcoutim'; Vicente is perhaps referring to Dom Fernando de Meneses (†1523) or his son, Pedro de Meneses (†*c*. 1543).

592 *seirão* would seem to be an augmentative of *seira*, 'wicker or rush basket' (*T* 573); *μ* has 'ceiram.'

593 The devil refers to the Angel's boat as willing to take the Jew across — which, of course, is not true.

596 *n'ergueja*: cp. line 281. The evolution of the popular form *ergueja* from *ecclesia* is normal: see Teyssier, *La Langue de Gil Vicente*, 132.

597-99 It is difficult to assess exactly what the insult thrown at the Jew is meant to signify. 'The day of our Lord' may mean the Sabbath, which would then mean that the Jew cooked on the Lord's day. If the 'day of our Lord' is understood as the *dies dominica*, i.e., domingo, Sunday, it is hard to see why the Jew should not eat meat, for Christians were explicitly forbidden fasting on Sundays; Friday was the day on which no meat could be eaten by Catholics.

μ, ever keen to remove inconsistencies, has, for lines 597-600, '& comia a carne da panela/em inuerno, & veram,/sus andar com teu cabram/pera essoutra carauela'.

599 *salvanor* is not used here in the sense of 'excuse the word', but rather means, in the words of Correas' *Vocabulario*, 'el trasero' (Révah, *Recherches*, 114).

602 *a toa*: the Jew is to be dragged behind. Whilst *à toa* can mean 'aimlessly' (*A* 1683C), the repetition of the word at line 752 leaves little doubt of the meaning intended. The devil informs the Jew he may not travel with the

other sinners because the fool has foretold that he would urinate on the boat.

stage direction: the magistrate's rod is the sign of his authority in administering justice.

607 *amador de perdiz*: 'judges were easily bribed by presents, amongst which partridge is much cited in the theatre of Vicente and his followers' (Berardinelli, *Antologia*, 159). Cp. l. 719.

608 *C*: 'how may processes you've brought!'

610 *C*: 'that they haven't come how I'd like'; μ has 'que não he ella de meu geito' (Quintela, 61).

611 *dereito*: the modern form is *direito*, which *C* adopts.

614 *papel*: the paper referred to is probably the material of the legal processes (*feitos*) (Révah, *Recherches*, 176).

616 *poeremos*: *poer* is an archaic form of *pôr*.

619 μ has 'Alto descorregedor' (Quintela, 61).

622 *de regule juris*: according to the rule of law.

623 The Latin words, *Ita, ita*, would seem to mean 'indeed! indeed!'.

627 *barzoneiro*: See Teyssier, *La langue de Gil Vicente*, 405. The sense of the Spanish word, *barzonar*, is to refuse work. μ has 'malhadeiro' (Quintela, 62).

634 *hoc non potest esse*: this cannot be.

636 *linguagem*, according to Morais, II, 227B, is the native, or romance language, opposed to Latin.

638 'You don't know for whom you are asking'. The Latin may allude to Jesus' reply to the mother of the sons of Zebedee, James and John, who asked that they be given the places of honour in heaven: *Nescitis quid petatis* (Matthew 20: 22, Mark 10: 38), 'You don't know for what you are asking'. See Michaëlis, 314.

639 'Is your power above the king's law?' Berardinelli, *Antologia*, 160, comments, 'The magistrate invokes the *jus majestatis* which made the representatives of the King immune from prosecution'. The irony implicit in the statement is that the Devil represents an expression of the divine law, the law of the eternal king, not that of an earthly sovereign.

638 μ has 'Ou atentay, quid petatis'.

641 *ouvidor*: a judge similar in powers to the *corregedor* (*GEPB* 19, 816).

642 *nonne accepistis rapina*: did you not accept bribes?
μ has 'non aceptaueis rapina' (Quintela, 62).

644 Berardinelli, *Antologia*, 160, comments, 'The devil uses the formula, "It is our mercy that ..." (i.e., "it is our pleasure that ..."), proper to royal authority, which contrasts with the *jus maiestatis* invoked by the magistrate.'
mei: pronounced 'á portuguesa', to rhyme with 'sey', rather than as two syllables in the Latin. *Domine, memento mei*: Lord, remember me.

648 *Nom* is Portuguese, 'not'; *es* is probably the misspelt Latin, *est*, 'is', rather than the Spanish *es*, 'is'; *tempus* is Latin, 'time'; *bacharell* is Portuguese, referring to the magistrate's qualifications in Law.

649 *imbarquemini* is a form invented by Vicente to sound like Latin.

650 'because you judged through malice'.

651-52 'I always acted in justice'. There is perhaps a pun intended: the magistrate did or acted 'in justice' or he performed 'injustice'.

652 *per nivel* would seem to be a set phrase applied to the working of justice: Morais records the phrase, 'governar por nivel'. The stress should fall upon the final syllable, *nivél*; the modern form is *nível*. For *per*, see at line 234.

656 *percalços*: profit or wages gained from an employment. It is perhaps an ironic choice of word, for 'percalçar direito' meant 'to have justice done with equality and rectitude' (Santa Rosa de Viterbo, II, 537B).

657-58 *pec(c)atus meus / peccavit uxore mea*: 'my sin, my wife sinned.' These lines are perhaps meant to recall Adam's blaming of Eve for their eating of the forbidden fruit (cf. Genesis 3: 12, 'The woman, said Adam, whom thou gavest me to be my companion, she it was who offered me fruit from the tree, and so I came to eat it', Knox, *The Holy Bible*, 3A).

659 'And to you also with her'.

660 *temuisitis deus*: 'you feared God'.

661-668 'you acquired/of the blood of the labourers/the ignorant of sins/so that you did not hear them'. The general sense is probably that, by denying justice to the poor who were ignorant (or, perhaps, innocent) of sin, the magistrate grew rich. See Spina, *Gil Vicente*, 80, n. 10.

665 *nonne legistis*: 'did you not read?' Michaëlis, 279, suggests that the form of the reproof was suggested by the fomula with which Jesus often confounded the Pharisees and Sadducees, *Non legistis...? Nunquam legistis...?*

666 The phrase is proverbial: 'Dádivas quebrantan peñas' Correas, *Refranes*, 509B, i.e., 'Gifts break stones'.

668 *sed aliquid tradidistis*: 'but [that] you brought something'; *C*'s version, *si aliquid tradidistis*, is more correct, meaning 'if you brought something'.

669 *negros*: 'black' has the connotation of evil, suffering, ugliness, and of damnation (Teyssier, *La Langue de Gil Vicente*, 430). See *Auto da Índia*, ll. 31, 377, 420.

670 *lago dos cães*: cp. l. 313, 'lago dos demos'. Mediæval visionary literature abounded in descriptions of the 'geography' of Hell; one of the punishments often depicted would be that of souls immersed in lakes that held serpents or other animals to torture them (see Alison Morgan, *Dante and the Medieval Other World* (Cambridge, 1990), 29). It is exceedingly odd, however, to find a *lake* full of dogs, rather than such water-dwelling creatures as serpents and dragons, which are hinted at in *Exortação da Guerra*, ll. 118-19. Luiz da Cunha Gonçalves, 'Gil Vicente e os homens do fôro', in *Gil Vicente: vida e obra* ... (Lisboa, 1939), 205-55, at

252, relates the *lago dos cães* to Dante's *Inferno*, canto XIII, line 124-6: 'Di rietro a loro era la selva piena/di nere cagne, bramose e correnti/come veltri ch'uscisser di catena' (*La Commedia secondo l'antica vulgata*, ed. Giorgio Petrocchi (Torino: Einaudi, 1975), 56). ['Behind them, the wood was filled with black braches, eager and fleet, as greyhounds that have escaped the leash' (*The Inferno of Dante Alighieri* (London: J. M. Dent, 1906), 143.

671 Braga, II, 73, comments on this passage, 'In Spanish literature [of the time], references to the morality of scribes abound, emphasizing that they should go to Hell' and quotes Mateo Alemán, *Guzmán de Alfarache*, I, i, "Y así, me parece que cuando alguno se salva..., al entrar en la gloria dirán los ángeles unos a otros, llenos de alegría: '*Lætamini in domino*: ¿Escribano en el cielo? Fruta nueva, fruta nueva." [And so, it seems to me that when a scribe is saved..., and enters into glory, the angels will say, one to the other, full of joy, '*Lætamini in domino*, let us rejoice in the Lord! A scribe in Heaven? A thing never seen before, never seen before!] (ed. Benito Brancaforte (2 vols.; Madrid: Catedra, 1979), 113).'

672 *coma*: this form, although modernized in this instance by *C*, is found elsewhere in Vicente's work: e.g., *Exortação da Guerra*, l. 370.

674 *evangelistas*: The word is most probably a pun, 'evangelist' being a term of slang for public notaries, although there is no evidence beyond the text for such a meaning.

674-76 *µ* has 'estam os trampistas./Di. Os mestres das burlas vistes/la estam bem refregados' (Quintela, 63).

676 *fragoados* may well be another pun; *fraguar* can mean to forge (in the sense of falsify: *A* 807C) or to beat into shape. The punishment depends on images of Hell in which devils treat souls as metal in a furnace.

684 *jogatais*: the modern form is *joguetear*.

685 *gente* may be synonymous with 'crew' (see António Marques Esparteiro, *Dicionário ilustrado de marinharia* (Lisboa: Livraria Clássica, 1943), 108B).

695 *extremo*: final, mortal, in the sense of *extrema unctio*, anointing on the last point of life.

696 *dor*: the pain which announced death was a commonplace from at least the thirteenth century onwards. The uncertainty of death was of particular concern in the late Middle Ages: 'death ever necessitated an adequate preparation so that it might be understood as a "good death", given man's not knowing the day of his passing' (Pimenta Ferro Tavares, 77).

706 'for we hope in God': a conflation of two biblical phrases from Psalm 49, 'Spera in Deo' (Trust in God) and I Timothy 4: 10, 'speramus in Deum vivum' (we hope in the living God).

707 *Imbarquimini*: cp. l. 649.

713 *µ* has 'como vindes ociosos'

715 *abeatis*: 'have' (imperative). *Clemencia*, the Portuguese word, is used instead of the Latin *clementia* — which would have had to have been *clementiam* in its use as object of the verb.
   μ has 'Oo habete aqui clemencia'.

717 *briviairos*: probably a reference to the canon law collection of Bernadus Papiensis (Bernard of Pisa), the *Breviarium extravagantium*, compiled between 1187 and 1191.

718 *rapinastis*: 'you stole'; *coelhorum*: mock-Latin, calqued on *coelho*, the Portuguese word for 'rabbit'; *cuniculus* is the respective Latin word.

719 *pernis perdiguitorum*: 'the legs of partidges', but the Latin is very far from
   . being correct.

720 μ has '& subis nos campanairos'

722 Braga, II, 76, understood the verse to mean, 'Where are the sheriffs (who are to hand over the magistrate and advocate to the Pilot of the boat)'. The fool may be mocking the magistrate and the advocate: although protected by their officials upon earth, they are now deprived of any such protection after death. *Beleguynis* is a mock-Latin word, calqued from the Portuguese *beleguim*; *ubi sunt*: where are they?

723 *macairus* is a word of uncertain sense. It is used (in its Portuguese form, *macairo*) in another play by a follower of Vicente, António Prestes, *Auto dos Dois Irmãos*, f. 80v, "Ja nesta devação dou/dinheiro enterra o macairo" (quoted by Révah, *Recherches*, 177) . In this context, it may mean 'fool' or even 'corpse', perhaps connected to the French *macabré*. Certainly, in the fool's self-description, its juxtaposition to *latinus* glances at 'macaronic', although I doubt whether this is the meaning of the word.

725 Cf. line 747.

728 μ has 'no batel por vosso mal' (Quintela, 65).

729 *Malçal* is a popular form of *Marçal*. St. Martial was the first Bishop of Limoges, a missionary sent from Rome to preach the Gospel in Gaul in the middle of the third century (*The Book of Saints* (London: A & C Black, 1934), 183).

735-6 Whilst Sardoal is a town mentioned in Vicente's *O Juiz da Beira* famed for dancing, I side with Ley's interpretation (75-6): 'I think that in the text we are not dealing with a toponym, but rather that *sardoall* signifies "a place covered by *sardões*". ... The sense would then be, "that you seem to be a fearful falcon, sent into the undergrowth".'
   nebri: Antonio de Nebrija, *Vocabulario de romance en latín: transcripción crítica de la edición revisada por el autor (Sevilla, 1516)*, ed. Gerald J. MacDonald (Madrid: Castalia, 1973), 140B, gives to 'nebli (especie de halcon)' the meaning 'accipiter columbarius', which is probably to be identified with the *falco columbarius*, or merlin. See Stanley Cramp and K. E. L. Simmons, eds., *Handbook of the Birds of Europe, the Middle East and North Africa* (Oxford: OUP, 1980), II, 308-16. Calisto's loss of his 'neblí' was the cause of his entry into Melibea's garden (and so the beginning of his perdition) in *La Celestina* (see Russell, 274). Mr M. Dalton of the

Cotswold Falconry Centre has informed me that falcons will not pursue quarry into a wood, and will indeed become afraid if taken into a wooded area.

737 Another example of the fool's 'dog-latin'; *zambuquis* is a Latinization of the Portuguese *zambuco* (cp. l. 261), which I have again rendered as sampan.

738 *cá*: I follow Révah, *Recherches*, 177, in disregarding *M*'s *aca*, since it is more likely to be one of the printer's hispanisms rather than the archaic form, *aca*.

740 *degredo*: the *Concordantia discordantium canonum* (usually known as the *Decretum*), compiled and edited *circa* 1140 by the Camaldolese monk, Gratian of Bologna. 'Although Gratian's work was not an "official" collection, it became almost immediately upon its appearance the fundamental and universally used canonistic collection, upon which all subsequent studies of the canon law depended': Brundage, *Medieval Canon Law*, 39.

744 *siquer*: the modern form is *sequer*.

746 *encoroçada* is an addition to the text to increase its visual power. Presumably, Brísida would have appeared on the stage with a *coroça* on her head, which was the usual punishment for any woman convicted of prostitution (cf. *Ordenações Manuelinas*, book v, title 29, where the *polaina* or *emxaravia vermelha* are prescribed).

747 Quintela, 301, 'It was the formula which began the town-crier's address that announced the execution of a sentence'.

749 omitted by *D*.

750 *dizede*: this form of the imperative was limited in use to the 'commères' (in Teyssier's elegant word) of Vicentine drama. It is the only occasion that Brísida Vaz gives voice to such a form, indicating that, now she is damned, she no longer need maintain the *persona* which she projected in her attempt to be received onto the heavenly boat. See Teyssier, *La Langue de Gil Vicente*, 184-85 and 198 where he comments that the form of the imperative with an intervocalic 'd' has a both a feminine and popular stylistic value.
   µ has 'Dizei bom Iuyz dalçada'

751 *Pero de Lisboa* was a scribe in the treasury (Braamcamp Freire, 118-9).

754-825 ommitted in *D* (Quintela, 135-6).

759 *buiz*: the modern form is *aboiz*.

764-65 *µ* has 'Nã he essa a nao queu governo/Oo rapaz./Diabo./Oo cara dinuerno/digote eu que a queiras'

766 Carolina de Michaëlis, 381, suggested that *Barrabas* was a corruption of *Barnabas*. However, the Barrabas in question must refer to the man freed in the place of Jesus by Pontius Pilate who "was a robber" (John 18:40).

776 *latins*: incomprehensible terms (see Braga, II, 80).

777 *C*'s emendation, '*como seu latim soubera*', may be a change wrought by Gil Vicente, for Moniz corresponded with the Italian humanist, Cataldus

Siculus, in Latin; the change would only make sense if the audience were familiar with Garcia Moniz (Costa Ramalho, 'A "feia acção"', 126).

778 *no paʃʃo ∂erra∂eiro*: 'at the moment in which they were hanging me' (Braga, II, 80).

782 *moeʃteiro*: the modern form is *moʃteiro*.

784 *Affonʃo Valente*: there are two figures known with this name. The first was gaoler in the Limoeiro, the prison in Lisbon (Braamcamp Freire, 86). Quintela, 303, pointed to another, a poet in the *Cancioneiro geral*, who was resident in the monastery of Tomar. The passage is thus a joke, built on the homonymous names: one would expect *ʃancta gente* in Tomar, not the Limoeiro.

798 *jentar*: the modern form is *jantar*.

804 *barqueiro nem barqueira*: an invention of Gil Vicente's on the model of popular expressions characterised by internal rhyme, e.g., *não ter eira nem beira* (Teyssier, *La Langue ∂e Gil Vicente*, 501).

811-17 *μ* has 'Disse que era o limoeyro/onde esteue preso primeiro,/& o pregam o mortuorio,/& que era tam notorio/como diciprinados,/& as oras dos finados,/& missas de San Gregorio.' (Quintela, 69).

813 *pregam vitatorio*: the final address made before the convict was hanged.

817 *miʃʃaʃ ∂e Sam Gregorio*: a set of thirty masses said for a departed soul to assist with its passage through purgation of its sins. It was named after Pope Gregory the Great (†604), after whose example the practice was initiated. See Farmer, 177B-79B.

818-25 *C*: 'DEVIL: Now board, since you have to./Don't wait for your father./THIEF: I'll board, since it's like that./DEVIL: That was good to embark./Ho, everyone, get off,/the ferry's stranded:/doctor, push out the boat,/noble, jump into the sea!'

824 *Babriel*: in the *Auto ∂aʃ Fa∂aʃ*, a sorceress invokes a Frey Gabriel thus: 'Praza à conjunçam carnal / de Frey Graviel com Marta / sua filha espiritual' [May it please the carnal conjuction of Fray Gabriel with Marta, his spiritual daughter]. A figure known to the court is presumably implied.

μ has 'say vos frey bacharel' (Quintela, 69).

stage direction I follow Révah, *Rechercheʃ*, 162, in modifying 'outorgados *por* todos' for the more usual *per*. See at line 234.

837 *∂eʃpoiʃ*: the modern form is *∂epoiʃ*.

838 *ventura*: on the meaning of this word in the middle ages, and for further bibliographical references, see Joy E. Wallace, 'Transposing the Enterprise of Adventure: Malory's "Take the Adventure" and French Tradition', in *Shiftʃ an∂ Tranʃpoʃitionʃ in Me∂ieval Narrative: a feʃtʃchrift for Dr. Eʃlpeth Kenne∂y*, ed. Karen Pratt (Cambridge: D. S. Brewer, 1994), 151-167.

843 *paʃʃeacʃ* would seem to be a reference back to line 164.

847 'There is a sign at the beginning of this verse which is difficult to understand, but one can suppose that a new character speaks. *C* helps us in this difficulty by introducing here a character that is called "Outro"' (Ley, 79).

μ has 'Ca. quê morre por Iesu Christo'

850 *queraes*: the modern form is *queirais*.

863 instead of the stage direction, μ has in the middle of the two columns (Quintela, 71),

LAVS DEO

Visto pello D. Iorge Cabral.

Vista a conferencia pode correr. Em Lisboa.

Gaspar Pereira. Francisco Barreto.

printer's note: *Cancioneiro Gèral*: reference is made to Garcia de Resende's collection of poetry from varied authors, which was also printed with permission from Dom Manuel, which set a fine of two hundred *cruzados* and the confiscation of all copies should anyone print anything from the *Cancioneiro*; the same fine was also established should the work be printed outside Portugal and sold within the kingdom (see the *Cancioneiro Geral de Garcia de Resende*, ed. Aida Fernanda Dias (4 vols.; Lisboa: Imprensa Nacional-Casa da Moeda, 1993), IV, 353).

Introduction to the *Auto da Índia*

The *Auto da Índia* is one of Vicente's most justly celebrated plays. It is set during the two-and-a-half year absence of the fleet that sailed out to India under the command of Tristão da Cunha (†1514) in 1506. The farce shows how the feckless wife of one of the sailors 'plays around' with two lovers. The first lover to appear is a Spaniard, overflowing with false valour; the second is Lemos, an impecunious Portuguese who had courted the wife on a previous occasion. The wife's attempts at juggling these two admirers is the subject of the comedy. The play ends with the return of the trusting husband, who knows nothing of his wife's infidelity and whom she easily deceives.

The circumstances of the performance

The rubric in the *Copilaçam* informs us that this play was performed in Almada before Queen Lianor in 1509. The title, *Auto da Índia*, does not seem to have been that originally given to the play by Gil Vicente, since the *Copilaçam* calls the play as 'Farsa que chamam Auto da Índia', *Farce which they call India Play*. It may well be that the play was, at first, merely called by its generic title, 'farsa', as it acted as an end to the celebrations held in Almada for the the return of da Cunha's fleet, marking the point at which the assembled revellers should make their courtly way, following the husband and wife of the farce, down to the harbour to see the ships.[1] The farce, therefore, makes ribald fun at the expense of the returning soldiers and sailors, who were teased with the possibility that 'when the cat's away, the mice will play'. Tristão da Cunha is mentioned twice in the play, yet is the butt of no merry-making. It may have been that Vicente's son, Gaspar, had been under his protection in India.[2]

As can be seen, the *farsa* fits into events of great importance for Portugal. It would therefore be desirable to establish the precise historical moment of the Discoveries in which the play was written.

The discovery of the route to India by the Portuguese

Manuel I came to the throne at a momentous point in Portugal's history. Bartolomeu Dias (†1500) had rounded the Cape of Good Hope in 1486

---

1   I am most grateful to Prof. T. F. Earle for suggesting this possibility to me.
2   Braamcamp Freire, 99.

and thereby shown that a sea-route to India was possible. Although the painstaking exploration of the African coast had finally flowered, if not quite borne fruit, another ten years were to elapse before Vasco da Gama was sent with a rather paltry fleet of three vessels to complete the journey to India. The reasons for this delay are not known, but it has been surmised that opposition in Portugal to the exploitation of the route to the Indies was the cause of such a gap.[3]

The landed nobility, whose interests were diametrically opposed to the Crown's, opposed any activity beyond their traditional military theatre of North Africa, and particularly an activity which appeared likely to swell the coffers of the King's treasury and thereby strengthen his position.[4] Commercial exploitation by Portuguese merchants of the West African coast was highly profitable and risk-free. Other European nations were forbidden by the Pope from entering the Southern Atlantic and Moors were limited to caravan routes far inland.[5] Thus the interests of an important part of the merchant classes were well-established in this region, and these merchant classes were consequently unwilling for the Guinea coast to be ignored or undermanned through any decision to send more men to trade and fight in Asia.

Against these entrenched economic interests, the Crown had a mixture of commercial and military objectives, namely those of joining the spice-trade and establishing an alliance with Prester John, legendary Christian king of Ethiopia. Under Manuel, these aims took on the aspect of a grand, Messianic strategy which would, he thought, bring about the end of Islam and the beginning of the millenium of peace, justice and tranquility.[6]

Manuel's military plan was breathtaking in its grandeur. By creating a blockade of Egypt from the Indian Ocean, he would cut the Mamluk Empire off from the wealth-giving spices of the Indies, and by opening the trade route around the Cape of Good Hope, he would prevent the Christian Mediterranean powers from becoming economically weakened by the blockade of Egypt, for they were able buy pepper and other spices in Lisbon.[7] The second purpose in seeking to command the Indian Ocean

---

3   Luis Filipe F. R. Thomaz, 'Factions, interests and messianism: the politics of Portuguese expansions in the East, 1500-1521', *The Indian Economic and Social History Review*, 28 (1991), 97-109, at 98.

4   *Idem.*, 'L'idée impériale manueline', in *La Découverte, le Portugal et l'Europe. Actes du Colloque, Paris, les 26, 27 et 28 mai 1988* (Paris: Fondation Calouste Gulbenkian, 1990), 35-103, at 58-61; Sanjay Subrahmanyam, *The Portuguese Empire in Asia, 1500-1700: a political and economic history* (London: Longman, 1993), 36, 52 and 57.

5   Thomaz, 'Factions, interests and messianism', 99.

6   *Idem*, 'L'idée impériale manueline', 50.

7   See *Ibid.*, 51 and 54.

was to establish an alliance with the king of Ethiopia. Such an alliance would allow an attack to be mounted upon Egypt from the south, whilst diversionary attacks by other Christian kings along the North African and Palestinian coasts and against the Ottoman Turks would prevent Islam from presenting a united front to this new Crusade. The goal, of course, was to reclaim Jerusalem.[8] Once Egypt had been returned to Christian rule, the need for the Cape route to India would pass away, and trade between the West and East could continue in much the same fashion that it had in Roman and Early Byzantine times.[9]

Although Manuel's reign was seen by his supporters through the glass of Messianic prophecy, the ideology of Manueline Messianism was never completely enunciated. It can be glimpsed through allusions and comments in contemporary writers, indicating that the matter was common knowledge in the court, even if it was not officially acknowledged. The project, however, gave rise to much hostility, particularly among the landed nobility and their supporters, who would seem to have done their utmost to prevent any voyage to India, and then, when Manuel's determination carried through, to have forced da Gama onto the King as commander of the fleet that left Portugal in 1497, a state of affiars which one is led to surmise by the monarch's reluctance to reward him on his return.[10]

Although da Gama had aroused little curiosity but much suspicion in India, the subsequent fleet sent from Lisbon under Pedro Álvares Cabral (†1520) in 1500 was a resounding success. The third fleet, led by Tristão da Cunha in 1506, sought to establish Portuguese control over the Indian ocean and Manuel's suzereignty over the kingdoms of the coast. Part of the fleet was under the command of Afonso de Albuquerque (†1515), a close ally of the king. Albuquerque's warfare on the coast of Arabia seems to have aroused some opposition through its barbarity, to judge from the anonymous chronicle held in the British Library.[11] The accusations levelled at Albuquerque may merely reflect how much he had become the *bête noire* of the party opposed to Manueline Messianism, for Arabic chroniclers do not mention any atrocities during this time.[12] Tristão da

---

8   *Idem*, 'Factions, interests and messianism', 98-99.

9   See *Rome and India: the ancient sea trade*, ed. Vimala Begley and Richard Daniel de Puma (Madison, Wisconsin: The University of Wisconsin Press, 1991).

10   Thomaz, 'Factions, interests and messianism', 48.

11   *Crónica do Descobrimento e Conquista da Índia pelos Portugueses*, ed. Luís de Albuquerque (Coimbra, 1974), ch. 79; see Thomaz, 'L'idée impériale', 78.

12   See R. B. Serjeant, *The Portuguese off the South Arabian Coast: Hadrami Chronicles with Yemeni and European Accounts of Dutch Pirates off Mocha in the seventeenth century* (Oxford:

Cunha's fleet returned to Lisbon in the July of 1509, having left Albuquerque as viceroy in India.

The Farce called *Auto da Índia*

The *Auto da Índia* was written, therefore, for a court riven by differing opinions on the viability of the route to the Indies. Having seen how the *Auto da Barca do Inferno* fits into Manuel's plans for a crusade, we may well wonder what political stance Gil Vicente takes regarding the Indian voyages. The husband's words at the end of the play as he describes his voyage have been taken as showing that the journey to India was unprofitable for those involved, full of dangers, bloodshed, disease and death. This is, however, due to reading Gil Vicente with the advantages of hindsight, as an analysis of the husband's rôle will show.

The first report of the appearance of the husband — given by the maid — informs the audience that he was 'so fat it was frightening' (l. 394), a sure sign that he was both healthy and wealthy. The husband, when he appears on stage, describes the storm that they first encountered (ll. 439-41), although his wife seems to outdo him in the hardships she suffered for his sake. He makes reference to reaching the Red Sea or *Rio de Meca* (l. 464), which links him to Afonso de Albuquerque's campaign, the purpose of which is summarized in line 465, 'we fought and we stole'. Slightly later, he paints a blacker picture, 'There, I tell you, are such travails,/so many deaths, so many struggles/and outlandish dangers/that we were ground down thus/sheared like sheep' (ll. 493-97). We may take this as a veiled allusion to the brutality of Albuquerque's campaign, a gesture of support from the playwright for the party ranged against the voyagers to India.

The husband goes on to complain that he would have brought back a 'million' were it not for the captain of the boat (l. 501). Such a complaint is understandable, but it is odd that it is directed at an immediate superior. Profit for those manning the fleet came from the division of booty in strictly defined percentages. The lion's share went to the Crown and Treasury ($73^1/_3\%$). The Viceroy received $6^1/_2\%$ and the captain of a *nau* would receive just below 3%. Pilots received below 1% and mariners and men-at-arms around $^1/_2\%$ each.[13] The husband's complaint would have been more realistic had it been directed at Crown and treasury rather than blaming the ship's captain. However, even if he did not bring back 'um milhão', he can still say to his wife that 'you'll see/how prettily you'll come

---

Clarendon Press, 1963), 43-46; they do mention the murder of Muslims in a mosque when Goa was taken in 1510: *Ibid*, 46

13   The details are taken from Subrahmanyam, 62.

out of this' (ll. 502-3), indicating that, despite the captain's share, what was left over for able shipmen and men-at-arms was substantial.

The husband's disenchantment with the India voyage due to the hardships he endured is also undercut: his description of labours, deaths and war comes as a reply to his wife's wondering whether he had been unfaithful thanks to the temptation provided by beautiful Indian women. His war-weariness, therefore, may well be a bluff to convince his wife, in much the same way that she convinces him, of his unyielding fidelity.

The political attitude adopted by the playwright would seem to have been finely nuanced, allowing both factions in the court to see their positions reflected in the farce: on the one hand, a seemingly veiled criticism of Albuquerque; on the other, the recognition that riches did flow from the India voyage. There is, however, no real invocation of the nationalist messianism dear to Manuel's heart and reflected in the *Auto da Fama*, written later for performance before the King himself. We may assume that Manuel did not see the *Auto da Índia*.

The farce

The generic word, farce, comes from the Latin *farcire*, to stuff. It would seem to have originally been a 'stuffing', a 'padding out' of liturgical tropes and liturgical formulæ. 'Subsequently, the Old French *farce* ... occurs as the name for the extemporaneous amplification or "gag", or the interludes of impromptu buffoonery, which the actors in the religious dramas were accustomed to interpolate into their text.'[14] Whilst this wider sense of 'low-class comedy' continued in French drama, the farce became associated most strongly with the representation of an intrigue, aptly characterized as 'un monde où les personnages se comportent comme des acteurs qui créent, assument, rejettent ou délaissent des rôles'.[15] This is the genre that we find fully fledged in Gil Vicente and which is not found in the *farsas* of Lucas Fernández published at Salamanca in 1514, which are more akin to parodic sketches.[16]

The *Farsa chamada Auto da Índia* is based around successful deceit at a number of levels. On a first level, the maid's asides, whilst providing an

---

14   *OED* 5, 272b
15   Thierry Boucquey, *Mirages de la Farce: fête des fous, Bruegel et Molière*, Purdue University Monographs in Romance Languages, 33 (Amsterdam-Philadelphia: John Benjamins, 1991), xii; see also Halina Lewicka, *Études sur l'ancienne farce* (Paris-Warszawa: Klincksieck-pnw, 1974), 13.
16   See Humberto López Morales, 'Parodía y caricatura en los orígenes de la farsa castellana', in *Teatro Cómico fra Medio Evo e Rinascimento: la farsa* (Roma: Convegno di Studi sul Teatro Medioevale e Rinascimentale, 1987), 221-226.

ironic commentary upon the action, require her to dissumulate before her mistress (ll. 63-65, 353-55 and 407).[17] Secondly, the prospective lovers themselves dissemble. The Castilian feigns bravery on the model of Centurio of the *Celestina*.[18] Although the maid sees through him, the wife is taken in, and says, 'He seems very fine to me' (l. 203). The impecunious Lemos promises to spend everything on dinner, but neither roast kid nor flounders nor oysters are bought (see lines 266-83).

The arrival of the Spaniard at the agreed time of nine in the evening demands from the wife some imposture of her own: to Lemos she explains that the stone thrown by the Spaniard against the window was due to children playing in the street below (ll. 246-7); to the Spaniard, she casts Lemos as her brother who is paying a visit (l. 256). Finally, the wife must convince her husband of her devotion; as for her husband, the possibility that he is also deceiving his wife has been mentioned above.

Only the Spaniard is humiliated, being left in the street during the long winter's night. Gil Vicente, whilst setting out the foundations of the national theatre, was careful to allow only Lemos, the Portuguese, to occupy Costança's bed, and to keep the Spaniard, Juan, outside in the cold.

Time

Perhaps the most striking element in the play is time itself. Whilst the fleet was absent from Lisbon for nearly two and a half years, the play gives the impression of taking place over one night.[19]

The fleet left on Palm Sunday, 6 April, 1506, and it is at this point in Spring that the play opens. The initial scene of the wife's despair that her husband is not to go is followed, when the maid goes to confirm the fact, by the wife's prayer that her husband not return. It ends, 'I shall sleep, I shall sleep,/be there good news when I awake:/Saint John was in the wilderness,/and the little bird did sing./God fulfil what I've dreamt!' (ll. 41-45). The invocation of Saint John and the *passarinho*, or little bird, draws on a well-known mediæval legend, a version of which features in *cantiga* 103 of the *Cantigas de Santa Maria*.[20] The story runs as follows: a

17 Two other asides are not picked up by the wife at ll. 239 and 373.
18 Thomas R. Hart, *Gil Vicente: farces and festival plays* (Eugene, Oregon: University of Oregon, 1972), 20.
19 Hart, *Farces and Festival Plays*, 19.
20 Alfonso X, *Cantigas de Santa Maria*, ed. Walter Mettmann, Clásicos Castalia, 134, 172, 178 (Madrid: Castalia, 1986-89), ii, 16-18. See also J. J. Nunes, 'Uma lenda medieval: o monge e o passarinho', *Boletim da 2ª Classe, Academia das Sciencias de Lisboa*, 12 (1917-18), 389-405; J. Figueira Valverde, *La Cantiga ciii: noción del tiempo y gozo*

monk prays to God that he might experience paradise. He enters the monastery garden and is transfixed for a moment by the song of a bird. Waking from his reverie, he returns to his monastery, only to find it utterly changed, and all the monks different to his companions. He discovers, in conversation with the abbot, that, in the space of the bird's song, three hundred years had passed. The allusion to the *passarinho* in the wife's prayer is intended to awaken the audience to a psychological aspect of the experience of time, to how intense pleasure may make time seem short. Similarly, the reference to sleeping and dreaming which follows it emphasizes another facet of time: we may think, when we awaken, that we have passed only a short space in sleep in which we find no pleasure, but in fact many hours have gone by.

The next mention of time is by the wife: 'They leave here in May' (l. 91). The statement is clearly false, and would be so perceived by the audience. The line accomplishes two things: it shows Costança deceiving herself regarding time, exaggerating the injury of her abandonment by placing it in a month associated with love;[21] the mention of May also moves the time of the action of the play along by a month or two. Costança could not mention May were that month not already come and, perhaps, gone. With this in mind, it is difficult to accept that Costança is telling the truth to the Spaniard nearly forty lines later when she says that her husband 'left the day before yesterday' (l. 128). In any case, time has not only been compressed (a month or two has become two days), but it has also been used to deceive. 'He left the day before yesterday' may well have the same force as Costança's patently false words to Lemos at lines 234-6, 'My husband's gone to India/and since then, no other man/has come where you have in mind'. The two days that had supposedly elapsed after her husband's departure would allow the Spaniard to think that he was the first to seek Costança's affections. Costança sends him away with the instruction that he should come at nine that evening.

After the Spaniard's depature, Lemos appears, and stays to dine. The season is now summer, for cherries are ripe and roast kid covered in flies (ll. 273 and 275). The Spaniard arrives, throwing stones at the window, presumably at the time arranged: nine o'clock. His subsequent outburst at

---

eterno en la narrativa medieval (Santiago de Compostela, 1936; repr. Vigo, 1982). The story originated with Bishop Maurice de Sully of Paris in the twelfth century, and is connected to Psalm 89: 4 ('In thy sight, a thousand years are but as yesterday, that has come and gone, or as one of the night-watches', Knox, *The Holy Bible*, 516a) or 2 Peter 3: 8 ('with the Lord a day counts as a thousand years, and a thousand years as a day', *Ibid.*, 252a).

21 Hart, *Farces and Festival Plays*, 69.

being ignored reveals that 'It's a night of Christmastide./It's about to dawn;/it won't take half an hour' (ll. 309-11), shifting the action from summer to winter, from after dusk to before daybreak. The wife subsequently dismisses Lemos because the sun is about to rise (ll. 348-49).

Once Lemos has gone, the maid informs her mistress that the fleet sailed on a Sunday morning two years earlier (ll. 357-362). The latter is unaware of the time that has gone past, and the maid takes advantage of this to increase her mistress's discomfort at the return of her husband, raising the time the fleet has been away to three years (l. 366), and then, when her mistress thinks it only a year and a half (l. 368), increasing the tally to three years and more. Time is again used deceptively, since the wife has no idea of the true duration of her husband's absence, and the maid exaggerates that duration for her own amusement.[22]

The husband's return provides another opportunity for falsification. The wife manages to project herself as devout and concerned for her husband's safety by establishing synchronous links between her supposed pilgrimages masses and the events of his voyage

Rather than being 'unaware of the inconsistencies of his text, or confident that his audience would not notice them',[23] Vicente's insistence on a chronological progression on two levels is an integral part of the play. The *farsa*, lasting not more than half an hour, represents a day, a night and the following morning, and in those twenty-four hours, twenty-eight months can be 'stuffed'. Time is not merely compressed, but becomes a means of delusion and deception. The audience are brought into active compliance with this deception at the very end of the play, for they go to see the ship following the wife and husband *as though* the ship had just arrived. Mediæval theories of time are employed to draw attention to the mechanics of the drama. The play is self-reflexive in a remarkable way, in that it presents the psychological experience of time through its characters, whilst the play represents that time again in a foreshortened form.

Costança

The wife is constantly on stage and dominates the action. She speaks half of the lines of the play.[24] Although farce as a genre tends to emphasize

---

22   Luís Amaro de Oliveira, *Farsa chamada Auto da Índia* (Porto-Coimbra-Lisboa: Porto Editora-Livraria Arnado-Emp. Lit. Fluminense, 1977), 77.

23   Hart, *Farces and Festival Plays*, 19.

24   The respective sizes of the parts are as follows: wife, 49%; Spaniard, 24%; maid, 15%; husband and Lemos, 6% each.

stereotypical character types, Vicente succeeded in giving to Costança a roundness usually denied to the unfaithful wife of mediæval dramatic tradition.[25]

Thomas Hart quite rightly pointed out that, at the beginning of the play, Costança is angry that her husband is leaving for India, and this anger, 'paradoxically, makes her fear that he will not really go after all'.[26] Her infidelity may then be seen as the means by which she could be revenged upon him (cf. l. 74) for leaving her against her wishes.

Although there has been a tendency amongst modern critics to condemn Costança absolutely, such an attitude would not have been entertained by those contemporaries who watched the play. Costança herself, in lines 75-6, 'that she who's young and pretty/should wait …', would seem to allude to the common mediæval folk-tale concerning a young wife who began an adulterous relationship because her husband had abandoned her for several years. The tale placed the fault of such an adulterous liason onto the foolish head of the husband.[27] This attitude was not just the amoral, unprincipled view of the folk. The mediæval canonists shared the same position. Ivo of Chartres (†1115),[28]

in a letter addressed to a nobleman who intended to participate in the crusade and who had vowed to do so, … sternly warned his correspondent that the fulfilment of his crusade obligations must take second place to the fulfilment of his marital obligations. If his wife would not consent to his absence on crusade, then he must abstain from joining the crusade in order to satisfy his wife's desire for company. Ivo further argues that his correspondent's crusade vow would be fulfilled at the expense of his wife; she would pay for his pious intentions, in other words, by being deprived of a legitimate sexual outlet because of her husband's absence. This, Ivo warned, might drive her to adultery and the responsibility for that would rest upon her absent husband, since he would have created the situation which led to this outcome.

For mediæval canonists, marriage involved a contractual relationship in which the partners' mutual consent was the crucial factor in bringing

25 Lewicka, 13: 'Pour la plupart, les personnages de la farce se ramènent à quelques modèles tirés en quantité d'exemplaires. Ainsi les maris sont généralement des imbéciles qui se laissent mener au bout du nez par leurs épouses égoïstes, rusées et infidèles sinon dans le fait du moins dans l'intention'.

26 Hart, *Farces and Festival Plays*, 25.

27 See, for example, the episode of 'Pitas Payas' in the fourteenth-century *Libro de Buen Amor*, 474-486, ed. G. B. Gybbon-Monypenny, Clásicos Castalia, 161 (Madrid: Castalia, 1988), 207-210.

28 James A. Brundage, 'The crusader's wife: a canonistic quandry', in *The Crusades, Holy Wars and Canon Law* (Aldershot: Variorum, 1991), xv 427-41, at 430-31; cf. *pl* 162: 251-53.

about the union. From this agreement, mutual obligations flowed, including that of the requirement that each partner accede to the other's desire for conjugal relations. Any agreement to limit or do away with this particular right demanded mutual consent, since neither partner could undo this essential parity in the marriage.[29]

The husband in the play, by abandoning his wife to go to India, was also depriving her of her legitimate sexual fulfilment. What happens during the play is the result of his unwise decision to leave her; her behaviour is not solely to be explained by her being a woman viciated by her carnal nature, as some critics would seem to think, but rather by her very normality. She possesses normal desires that she strives to fulfil in the wrong way, a sin for which her husband shares greatly in the blame. Yet explaining the wife's actions solely by sexual frustration would not do justice to her character. A farther motivation is her wish to be free of her husband's authority: when the maid exclaims, at the return of the husband, 'our master ...', Costança corrects her, one imagines, tartly, '*your* master ...' (ll. 416-17).

Vicente reveals the wife's name, Costança (Constance), after she lies to Lemos that no man but her husband had 'come where you have in mind' (l. 236) and as she goes on to swear that it is only because of how she remembers him that he may 'enter such privacy' (l. 241). Her inconstancy is underlined, inconstancy not only to her husband but to one of her lovers. Her promise to the Spaniard (cf. ll. 191 and 206) goes unfulfilled. Yet, together with this inconstancy, the word *certo*, 'certain', 'sure', occurs several times on her lips early in the play. It is applied by Costança to the news that the fleet was not to sail (ll. 17-18), that her desires that her husband remain in Lisbon are small (l. 24), and to indicate the certainty which the taking of pleasure provides (l. 86). The fleet sailed on time. Her expressed desires that her husband leave are contradicted shortly before he enters the stage, when she is provided with a monologue, wherein she muses, 'How funny it would be/if that accursed husband of mine/came back to Lisbon alive/to keep me company' (ll. 375-78). The wife's desire for her husband's companionship is balanced by the 'certainty' that he died at sea: 'I want to sew and sing/sure that I'll never see him again' (ll. 382-83). The invocation of certainty, therefore, and her settling upon pleasure as the means of providing that certainty, is, in part, a reaction to the very uncertainty that her husband will return from India.

The basis for Costança's election of her course of actions, the certainty of pleasure, is also brought into question, since, in the representation on

---

29   See *ibid.*, 440.

stage, Costança does not have an opportunity to commit adultery with Lemos. Although, in the words of the maid, Costança has 'one in the street, the other in bed' (ll. 355), she is caught between them both, having to silence the Spaniard and lie to Lemos. The compression of the space of two and a half years into a single night allows the adultery to be contemplated, arranged, but not represented. The audience is left uncertain as to whether the adultery happened or not, and whether Costança took any pleasure from the experience. Costança proclaims to her returned husband that her state was miserable in his absence: 'Where there's no husband/consider everything as sadness./There's no pleasure, no rest./Know that it's life gone to waste' (ll. 480-83). This could be mere bluff, but it is of a piece with Costança's not knowing how much time has passed (l. 366); life lived not in the pursuit of goodness but of evil is indeed 'vida perdida' (l. 483), lost or gone to waste. Time thus becomes empty and immesurable, like time spent unconsciously asleep. Because it is empty, it can be compressed. Unlike the experience of Saint John in the wilderness (l. 43), the pleasure (if in fact there was any) is evanescent and leads to despair: Costança cries, when she hears that her husband is to return, 'I don't know what life is for!' (l. 411).

Her husband's return does seem to hold some advantages for Costança over her dalliance with Lemos, for she orders the maid to 'go for wine/and half of a roast kid' (ll. 426-27), commodities which Lemos had refused to buy (ll. 274 and 279). The husband is blissfully unaware of his wife's behaviour, and, in the words of Paul Teyssier, 'tout se termine dans la bonne humeur. Mari et femme reprennent la vie commune, et Constance réintègre le lit conjugal sans la moindre gêne, et même avec un certain plaisir',[30] as her coquettishness in lines 420-21 ('Jesus! How black and sunburnt:/I don't love you, I don't love you') clearly indicate.

Note to the Critical Edition

The norms I have followed are identical to those of the edition of the *Auto da Barca do Inferno*, with one exception. Italic script is used to indicate the use of humanist script in the *Copilaçam*. The Spanish spoken by the Castilian has been treated in the same way as the rest of the text, since the *Copilaçam* was published with a Portuguese readership in mind, and its Spanish spelt accordingly. For example, *reis* (l. 116) is spelt 'reijs' in the *Copilaçam* whereas contemporary Spanish texts would spell the word 'reis'.

---

30   Paul Teyssier, 'L'envers de l'épopée', *Critique: revue générale des publications françaises et étrangères*, 46 (1988), 676-83

Farsa chamada

'Auto da Índia'

A Farce

called 'The India Play'

A *farsa seguinte chamão Auto da India. Foy fundado sobre que ũa molher, estando ja embarcado pera a India seu marido, lhe vieram dizer que estava desaviado, & que ja nam ia, & ella de pesar está chorando, & fala-lhe ũa sua criada.*

Foy feyta em Almada, representada à muyta catholica Rayna dona Lianor. Era de M. D IX. Annos.

¶*Entram nella estas figuras:*

¶*Ama, Moça, Castelhano, Lemos, Marido.*

	MOÇA:	¶Jesu, Jesu, que é ora isso:	[*Cf.* 195r A]
		é porque parte a armada?	
	AMA:	Olhade a mal estreada!	
		Eu hey de chorar por isso?	
5	MOÇA:	Por minha alma, que cuydey	
		& que sempre imaginey	
		que choraveis por noss' amo.	
	AMA:	Por qual demo ou por qual gamo	
		ali má ora chorarey?	

10		¶Como me leyxa saudosa!
		Toda eu fico amargurada.
	MOÇA:	Pois porque estais anojada?
		Dizey-mo por vida vossa.
	AMA:	Leyxa-m' ora, eramá,
15		que dizem que nam vay ja.
	MOÇA:	Quem diz esse desconcerto?
	AMA:	Dixeram-mo por muy certo
		que é certo que fica cá.

		¶O Concelos me faz isto.
20	MOÇA:	S'elles ja estam em Restelo
		como pode vir a pello?
		Melhor veja eu Jesu Christo:
		isso é quem porcos há menos.
	AMA:	Certo é que bem pequenos
25		sam meus desejos que fique.

---

introduction ũa · hũa ia · hia está · esta ũa · hũa catholica · cacholica

T*he following farce is called the India Play. Its plot concerns a woman, whose husband has already embarked for India, and who is told that he has changed his mind and is no longer going, and she is crying from grief, and one of her servants speaks to her.*

It was performed in Almada, for the very Catholic Queen dona Lianor, in the year of 1509.

The following characters appear:

Wife, Maid, Spaniard, Lemos, Husband.

	MAID:	Jesus! Jesus! What's this now?
		Is it because the fleet has left?
	WIFE:	Oh, look, look at my wretchedness!
		Would that make me shed tears?
5	MAID:	I thought, by my soul,
		and always supposed
		that you were crying for our master.
	WIFE:	For what devil or what hind
		would that make me damn-well cry?
10		How he leaves me with longing!
		I'm eaten up with bitterness.
	MAID:	Well, why are you upset?
		Tell me why, on your life.
	WIFE:	Leave me now, damn you,
15		for they say he's not going any more.
	MAID:	Who said such nonesense?
	AMA:	They told me it was most sure
		that it's sure he's staying here.
		It's Concelos that's doing this to me.
20	MAID:	If they're already in Restelo
		how could it come about?
		Easier to see Jesus Christ:
		you're just imagining it.
	WIFE:	Certainly, my desires
25		that he remain are very small.

1, 2 é · he 9 má · ma 4 hey · ey 18 é · he cá · ca 23 é · he há · ha 24 é · he

MOÇA: A armada está muyto a pi<u>que</u>.
AMA: Arreceo al de menos.

¶Andey na maora & nella
a amassar & biscoutar
30   pera ò demo levar
a sua negra canela.
E agora dizem que nam …,
agasta-se-m' o coraçam   [*Cf.* 195r B]
que quero sayr de mim.
35   MOÇA: Eu yrey saber se é assim.
AMA: Ajas a minha bençam.

    ¶Vay a moça, e³ fica a ama dize<u>n</u>do,

¶A sancto Antonio rogo eu
que nunca mo cá depare.
Nam sinto que nam s'enfare
40   de um diabo Zebedeu.
Dormirey, dormirey,
boas novas acharey;
sam Joam no ermo estava
& a passarinha cantava.
45   Deos me cumpra o que sonhey!

¶Cantando vem ella & leda.
MOÇA: Day-m' alvissaras senhora:
ja vay lá de foz em fora.
AMA: Dou-te ũa touca de seda.
50   MOÇA: Ou quando elle vier
day-me do que vos trouxer.
AMA: Ali muytieramá,
agora há de tornar cá?
Que chegada & que prazer!

55   MOÇA: ¶Virtuosa está minha ama!
Do triste delle hey dó.

---

35 é · he 38 cá · ca **40 um** · hum **46 lá** · la **49 touca** · toca

MAID: The fleet's about to set sail.
WIFE: That's the least of my fears!

30
In an evil hour did I
kneed and bake biscuits
for him to take his damned
cinnamon to the devil.
And now they tell me that he's not ...
— my heart's worn out,
I'm beside myself.

35
MAID: I'll go and see if that's how it is.
WIFE: My blessing go with you!

The girl goes, and the wife remains on stage and says,

Saint Anthony I beseech
never to make him appear here;
I'm not sorry for whoever's not sickened
40
by a devil Zebedee.
I shall sleep, I shall sleep,
be there good news when I awake:
Saint John was in the wilderness,
and the little bird did sing.
45
God fulfil what I've dreamt!

She's coming — singing happily.
MAID: Give me a good reward, ma'am.
It's already beyond the rivermouth.
WIFE: I'll give you a silk cap.
50
MAID: Or, when he gets back
give me something he's brought you.
WIFE: That! Oh, damn, damn, damn, and damn!
Now he's to come back here?
Oh what a return, what good cheer!

55
MAID: My mistress is being virtuous!
I'm sorry for her poor husband.

---

53 **há** · ha **cá** · ca

	AMA:	E que falas tu lá só?
	MOÇA:	Falo cá com esta cama.
	AMA:	E essa cama bem, que há?
60		Mostra-me essa roca cá,
		siquer fiarey um fio.
		Leyxou-me aquelle fastio
		sem ceytil.
	MOÇA:	Ali eramá!

[*C f.* 195v A]

65		¶Todas ficassem assi.
		Leyxou-lhe pera tres annos
		trigo, azeyte, mel, & panos.
	AMA:	Mao pesar veja eu de ti!
		Tu cuydas que nam t'entendo?
70	MOÇA:	Que entendeis? Ando dizendo
		que quem assi fica sem nada
		coma vos, que é obrigada …
		ja me vos ys entendendo?

	AMA:	¶Ha ha ha ha ha ha!
		Estará bem graciosa
75		quem se ve moça & fermosa
		esperar pola yramá.
		Hi se vay elle a pescar
		mea legoa polo mar,
		isto bem o sabes tu,
80		quanto mais a Calecu —
		quem há tanto d'esperar?

		¶Milhor senhor sé tu comigo
		à hora de minha morte.
		Que eu faça tam peca sorte,
85		guarde-me Deos de tal perigo!
		O certo é dar a prazer;
		pera que é envelhecer
		esperando polo vento?
		Quant' eu por muy necia sento

---

57 **lá** · la 58 **cá** · ca 59 **há** · ha 60 **cá** · ca 61 **um** · hum 65 **Todas** · Todos

WIFE: What are you saying there to yourself?
MAID: I'm speaking to this bed.
WIFE: And that bed — what's the matter with it?
60   Show me that distaff —
at least I can spin a thread.
That old miser left me
without a penny.
MAID: There we are, damn!

65   May they all be left like this!
He left her enough wheat,
oil, honey and cloth for three years.
WIFE: May I see when you'll rue that!
Do you think I don't understand?
MAID: What did you hear? I was saying
70   that whoever is left with nothing
(like you), is obliged ...
Now you're getting the idea.

WIFE: Ha ha ha ha ha ha!
That would be really funny.
75   That she who's young and pretty
should wait — oh damnation!
If he goes to fish here
half a league out in the sea ...
that you know very well;
80   how much more to Calicut!
Who would wait so long?

Better, Lord, be at my side,
at the hour of my death!
That I'd have such an ill betide ...
85   May God keep me from such a threat.
What's certain is the taking of pleasure:
why should you grow old
waiting for the wind?
As for me, I think she's stupid

---

71 é · he **74 Estará** · Estara **81 há** · ha **86, 87** é · he

90   a que o contrayro fizer.

              ¶Partem em Mayo d'aqui
              quando o sangue novo atiça,
              parece-te que é justiça?
              Milhor vivas tu, amem,
95   & eu comtigo tambem!
              Quem sobe por essa escada?
CASTELHANO: ¡Paz sea nesta posada!
AMA: Vos sois, cuydey que era alguem.
CASTELHANO: A segun esso, soy yo nada.

100   AMA: ¶Bem, que vinda foy ora esta?
CASTELHANO: Vengo aqui em busca mia,
              que me perdi en aquel dia
              que os vi hermosa y honesta,
              y nunca más me topé,
105   invisible me torné,   [*C f.* 195v B]
              y de mi, crudo enemigo.
              El cielo imperio es testigo
              que de mi parte no sé.

              ¶Y ando un cuerpo sin alma,
110   un papel que lleva el viento,
              un pozo de pensamiento,
              una fortuna sin calma.
              Pese al dia en que nasci,
              vos y Dios sois contra mi,
115   y nunca topo el diablo.
              ¿Reís de lo que yo hablo?
AMA: Bem sey eu de que me ri.

CASTELHANO: ¶¿Reísvos del mal que padezco?
              ¿Reísvos de mi desconcierto?
120   ¿Reísvos que teneis por cierto
              que miraros no merezco?

---

93 é · he   **104 más** · mas   **108 sé** · se   **116 Reís** · reijs

90   who'd do the opposite!

They leave here in May,
when the new blood begins to rise.
Do you think that's fair?
May you live better — amen —
95   and I with you again.
Who's coming up those stairs?
SPANIARD: Peace be unto this house!
WIFE: It's you? I thought it might be someone.
SPANIARD: By this, I am nought.

100   WIFE: Well, what have you come for now?
SPANIARD: Here come I in search of me,
for I lost myself on that day
that I saw you, honest and lovely,
and I met myself no more.
105   I turned invisible,
and my own harsh enemy.
The ruling heaven is a witness
that I do not know about myself.

I go about, a body with no soul,
110   a scrap of paper borne by the wind,
a well filled with cares,
a storm that never stills.
Curse the day of my birth!
Against me, you and God are set,
115   and the devil I've never met —
Does what I say make you laugh?
WIFE: I know what I'm laughing at.

SPANIARD: Do you laugh at the evil I suffer?
Do you laugh at my discomfiture?
120   Do you laugh because you think it certain
that I do not deserve to look at you?

118, 119, 120 **Reísvos** · Reisuos

AMA: Andar embora.
CASTELHANO: ¡Ò mi vida y mi señora,
luz de todo Portogal!
125
Teneis gracia especial
para linda matadora.

¶Supe que vuesso marido
era ydo.
AMA: Antontem se foy.
CASTELHANO: ¡Al diablo que lo doy,
130
el desestrado perdido!
Que más India que vos,
que más piedras preciosas
que más alindadas cosas
que estardes juntos los dos?

135
¶No fue el Juan de Çamora
— ¡que arrastrado muera yo! —
si por quanto Dios crió
os dexara media hora.
Y aunque la mar se humillara,
140
y la tormenta cessara,
y el viento me obedeciera,
y el quarto cielo se abriera,
un momiento no os dexara.

¶Mas como evangelio es esto,
145
que la India hizo Dios
solo porque yo con vos
pudiesse passar aquesto.
Y solo por dicha mia,
por gozar esta alegria,
150
la hizo Dios descobrir,
y no hay más que dezir
por la sagrada Maria.

---

131 **más** · mas **que** · qne 132, 133 **más** · mas 151 **hay más** · ha mas

	WIFE:	Go on.
	SPANIARD:	Oh, my life and my lady,
		light of all of Portingale,
125		you have a special grace
		to be a beautiful *assassine*.

Your husband, I heard them say,
has gone away.

	WIFE:	He left two days ago.
	SPANIARD:	Then to the devil let him go,
130		the accursed wretch!

What more India could there be,
what more precious stones than you?
What more things of beauty
than both of you to be together?

135   Juan de Zamora he was not;
drawn through the streets be my lot
if, for all things created by God's power,
I'd leave you even half an hour.
And, even if the sea be humbled
140   and the sea-storm cease,
and the wind obey me,
and the Fourth Heaven be opened,
I'd not leave you for a moment.

But as Gospel-truth is this:
145   God has made India
only so that we two
could go through this together;
and, solely for my happiness
to partake of this joy
150   God had India discovered,
and there's nothing else to say,
by God's holy mother!

	AMA:	¶Moça vay àquelle cam
		que m' anda naquellas tigelas.
155	MOÇA:	Mas os gatos andam nelas.
	CASTELHANO:	¡Cuerpo del cielo con vos!
		Hablo en las tripas de Dios
		¿y vos hablaisme en los gatos?
	AMA:	Se vos falais desbaratos,
160		em que falaremos nos?

	CASTELHANO:	¶No me hagais derreñegar
		o hazer un desatino —
		¿vos pensais que soy devino?
		Soy hombre, y siento el pesar.
165		Trayo de dentro un leon
		metido en el coraçon:
		tieneme el anima dañada
		d'ensangrentar esta espada
		en hombres, que es perdicion.

170		¶Ya Dios es importunado
		de las animas que le embio;
		y no es en poder mio
		dexar uno acuchillado.
		Dexe bivo allá en el puerto
175		un hombrazo alto y tuerto,
		y despues fuylo a encontrar:
		pensó que lo yva a matar
		y de miedo cayó muerto.

	AMA:	¶Vos quereis ficar cá?
180		Agora é cedo ainda:
		tornareis vos outra vinda
		& tudo se bem fará.
	CASTELHANO:	¿A que hora me mandais?
	AMA:	Às nove horas & no-mais.
185		E tiray ũa pedrinha
		pedra muyto pequenina

---

174 **allá** · alla 178 **cayó** · cayo 179 **cá** · ca 180 **é** · he 185 **E** · & **ũa** · hũa

	WIFE:	Maid, shoo away that dog
		that's walking among those plates.
155	MAID:	But it's the cats that are there.
	SPANIARD:	Christ's body be with you!
		I speak about God's guts
		and you talk to me of cats?
	WIFE:	If you speak nonsense
160		what will we talk about?

SPANIARD: Do not make me forswear
or commit an act of folly.
Do you think that I'm like God?
I'm a man, and I feel grief!
165 Within me, there's a lion I carry
placed within my heart;
he has damned my soul
by bloodying this sword
against other men, which means perdition.

170 God is already encumbered
by the souls I send him,
and it's not within my power
to leave anyone only wounded.
I left alive there in the harbour
175 a big man, tall and fierce,
and then I approached him again
and he thought I'd kill him
and he dropped dead through fear.

WIFE: Do you want to stay here?
180 But it's still early yet.
Come back some other time
and all will turn out well.
SPANIARD: What time do you set for me?
WIFE: Nine o'clock and no later,
185 and throw a little pebble
a teeny-weeny stone

à janela dos quintaes.

¶Entonces vos abrirey
de muyto boa vontade;
190   pois sois homem de verdade,   [C f. 196r B]
nunca vos falecerey.
CASTELHANO: Sabeis que ganais en esso
el mundo todo por vuesso,
que aun que tal capa me veis
195   tengo más que pensareis,
y no lo tomeis en gruesso.

¶Beso-os las manos señora:
voyme con vuessa licencia,
más hufano que Florencia.
200   AMA: Yde & vinde muyt' embora.
    CRIADA: Jesu, como é rebolam!
Day, day ò demo o ladram!
    AMA: Muyto bem me parece elle.
    CRIADA: Nam vos fieis vos naquelle,
205   porque aquillo é refiam.

    AMA: ¶Ja lh' eu tenho prometido.
    MOÇA: Muyto embora, seja assi.
    AMA: Um Lemos andava aqui,
meu namorado perdido.
210   MOÇA: Quem, o rascam do sombreyro?
    AMA: Mas antes era escudeyro.
    MOÇA: Seria, mas bem çafado.
Nam sospirava o coytado
senam por algum dinheyro.

215   AMA: ¶Nam é elle homem dessa arte.
    MOÇA: Pois inda elle nam esquece?
Há muyto que nam parece.
    AMA: Quant' eu, nam sey delle parte.
    MOÇA: Como elle souber, a fé,

---

187 à · a   195 más · mas   201 é · he   205 é · he   208 Um · Hum   216 Há · Ha

138

at the garden window.

Then I'll open to you
with all good will.
190   As you're a real man
I'll never fail.
SPANIARD: By this, do you know what you gain?
The world all for your own;
and although you see me in such a guise
195   I've more than you would think
and don't take it in bulk.

I kiss your hands, my lady.
I go with your leave.
Florence could not be more jubilant.
200   WIFE: Go, but come back soon.
MAID: Jesus! Jesus! What a braggart.
Oh, leave the thief to the devil!
WIFE: He seems very fine to me.
MAID: Don't you put any trust in him
205   because that one there's a pimp.

WIFE: But I've already promised.
MAID: If it's like that, that's just fine.
WIFE: Did Lemos come over,
my forsaken lover?
210   MAID: Who? The rascal in the hat?
WIFE: No, he was a squire.
MAID: Perhaps, but a threadbare one.
The poor wretch only ever sighed
for a bit of money.

215   WIFE: He's not a man of such wiles.
MAID: Well, won't you be far from his mind?
He hasn't seen you for a while.
WIFE: As for him, I don't know a thing.
MAID: When he knows, by my faith,

220   que nosso amo aqui nam é,
       Lemos vos vesitará.
  LEMOS: Hou de casa!
  AMA: Quem é lá?
  LEMOS: Subirey?
  AMA: Suba. Quem é?

  LEMOS: ¶Vosso cativo senhora.
225 AMA: Jesu, tamanha mesura!
       Sou raynha por ventura?
  LEMOS: Mas sois minha emperadora.
  AMA: Que foy do vosso passear
       com luar & sem luar
230   toda a noyte nesta rua?
  LEMOS: Achey-vos sempre tam crua
       que vos nam pude aturar.   *[C f. 196v A]*

       ¶Mas, agora, como estais?
  AMA: Foy-se à India meu marido,
235   & depois homem nacido
       nam veo onde vos cuydais.
       E por vida de Costança
       que se nam fosse a lembrança ...
  MOÇA: Dizey ja essa mentira!
240 AMA: ... que eu vos nam consentira
       entrar em tanta privança.

  LEMOS: ¶Pois que agora estais singela
       que ley me dais vos, senhora?
  AMA: Digo que venhais embora.
245 LEMOS: Quem tira àquella janela?
  AMA: Meninos que andam brincando,
       & tiram de quando em quando.
  LEMOS: Que dizeis, senhora minha?
  AMA: Metey-vos nessa cozinha
250   que me estam ali chamando.

---

220 é · he 222 Hou · Ou é lá · he la 223 é · he 250 AMA · Bma.

220   that our master isn't here,
Lemos will come a-visiting.
LEMOS: Anybody home?
WIFE: Who's there?
LEMOS: Shall I come up?
WIFE: Come up. Who is it?

LEMOS: Your captive, my lady.
225   WIFE: Jesus! What a bow!
By any chance, am I a queen?
LEMOS: But you are my Empress.
WIFE: What happened to your walking
with the moon or without moon-light
230   in this street every night?
LEMOS: I always found you so severe
that I could not persevere.

Yet, now, how are you?
WIFE: My husband's gone to India,
235   and since then, no other man
has come where you have in mind.
And I, Costança, by my own life,
if it were not for the memory …
MAID: Now, tell this fib!
240   WIFE: … I would not permit
you to be taken into such privacy.

LEMOS: Well now that you are alone
what command will you give me, my lady?
WIFE: I'll say that you came at a good time.
245   LEMOS: Who's throwing stones at that window?
WIFE: It's only children out to play:
they throw stones now and again.
LEMOS: What do you say, lady mine?
WIFE: Go there, into the kitchen,
250   they're calling me from outside.

	CASTELHANO:	¶ ¡Abrame, vuessa merced,
		que estoy aqui a la verguença!
		¡Esto usasse en Siguença!
		Pues prometeis, mantened.
255	AMA:	Calay-vos, muytieramá,
		até que meu yrmão se vá.
		Dissimulay por hi em tanto:
		ora vistes o quebranto?
		Andar, muytieramá!

260	LEMOS:	¶Quem é aquelle que falava?
	AMA:	O castelhano vinagreyro.
	LEMOS:	Que quer?
	AMA:	Vem polo dinheyro
		do vinagre que me dava.
		Vos querieis cá cear
265		& eu nam tenho que vos dar.
	LEMOS:	Vá esta moça à ribeyra
		& traga-a cá toda enteyra,
		que toda s' há de gastar.

	MOÇA:	Azevias trazerey?
270	LEMOS:	Dá ò demo as azevias!
		Nam compres, ja m'enfastias.
	MOÇA:	O que quiserdes comprarey.
	LEMOS:	Traze ũa quarta de cereyjas
		& um ceytil de briguigões.
275	MOÇA:	Cabrito?
	LEMOS:	Tem mil barejas.

	MOÇA:	¶E ostras? Trazerey dellas?
	LEMOS:	Se valerem caras, nam —
		antes traze mais um pão
		& o vinho das estrelas.
280	MOÇA:	Quanto trazerey de vinho?
	LEMOS:	Tres picheis deste caminho.
	MOÇA:	Dais-me ũ cinquinho no-mais?

---

256 vá · va **260** é · he **264** cá · ca **266** Vá · Va **267** cá · ca **268** s' há · sa

142

	SPANIARD:	Open up to me, madam,
		for I stand here ashamed.
		Is this what they do in Spain?
		Since you've promised, now fulfil.
255	WIFE:	Shut up, damn it,
		just until my brother goes.
		In the meantime, just dissemble.
		Now do you see the misfortune?
		Go on, damn you!

260	LEMOS:	Who was that who was speaking?
	WIFE:	The Spaniard who sells vinagre.
	LEMOS:	What does he want?
	WIFE:	To be paid
		for the vinegar he gave.
		You'll want to have your dinner
265		and I've nothing to give you.
	LEMOS:	Let this maid go to the river
		and bring it all together
		for we'll spend everything.

	MAID:	Shall I bring flounders?
270	LEMOS:	Flounders? To the devil with 'em;
		don't buy any; you've begun to annoy me.
	MAID:	I'll buy whatever you wish.
	LEMOS:	Bring a quarter of cherries
		and a penny's worth of cockles.
275	MAID:	Roast kid?
	LEMOS:	Covered in blue-bottles.

	MAID:	What about oysters: should I bring any?
	LEMOS:	If they're expensive, no.
		But rather, bring back a loaf
		and the wine from the stars.
280	MAID:	How much wine should I bring?
	LEMOS:	Three pitchers of about this size.
	MAID:	Are you only giving me a farthing?

---

273 ũa · hũa 274, 278 um · hum 282 ũ · hũ

LEMOS: Toma ahi mais dous reais.

¶Vay & vem muyto emproviso.
285 "Quem vos anojou meu bem,
bem anojado me tem."
AMA: Vos cantais em vosso siso?
LEMOS: Deyxay-me cantar, senhora.
AMA: A vezinhança, que dirá
290 se meu marido aqui nam está
& vos ouvirem cantar?
Que rezam lhe posso eu dar
que nam seja muyto má?

CASTELHANO: ¶¡Reniego de Marenilla!
295 ¡Esto es burla, o es burleta!
¿quereis que me haga trompeta
que me oyga toda la villa?
AMA: Entray-vos ali senhor,
que ouço o corregedor.
300 Temo tanto esta devassa!
Entray-vos ness' outra casa
que sinto grande rumor.

¶*Chega à janella.*

¶Falay-vos passo, micer.
CASTELHANO: ¡Pesar ora de san Pablo:
305 esto es burla, o es diablo!
AMA: E eu, posso-vos mais fazer?
CASTELHANO: ¿Y aun en esso está aora?
¡La vida de Juan de Çamora!
Son noches de Navidá,
310 quiere amanecer ya,
que no tardará media hora.

AMA: ¶Meu yrmão cuydey que se ia.
CASTELHANO: ¿Ah, señora, y reísvos vos?

---

294 **Marenilla** · Marenilha **302 que** · qne **304 san Pablo** · sam palo

	LEMOS:	Here, take another tuppence.

LEMOS: Go, but come back quickly.
285 "Whosoever grieveth thee, my love,
has sorely grievèd me."
WIFE: You're singing — are you mad?
LEMOS: Let me sing, my lady!
WIFE: The neighbours — what will they say?
290 If my husband is away
and they hear you singing,
what reason can they be given
that won't look very bad?

SPANIARD: Oh, I forswear Marenilla,
295 is this a joke or is it a jest?
Do you want me to sound
like a trumpet to wake the town?
WIFE: Go in there, sir, go in there,
I can hear the corregidor.
300 I'm so afraid of enquiry!
Go into this other room,
for I can hear a lot of noise.

¶*She goes to the window.*

Speak quietly, messieur!
SPANIARD: Curses now upon Saint Paul!
305 Is this a trick or is it the devil?
WIFE: What can I do for you more?
SPANIARD: Now are you still playing at that?
By Juan de Zamora's life!
It's a night of Christmastide,
310 it's about to dawn
in less than half an hour.

WIFE: I thought that my brother was going.
SPANIARD: Ah, lady, can you laugh!

---

309 Navidá · nauida **312 ia** · hia **313 Ah, señora** · Aa señora **reísvos** · reisuos

145

		¡Abrame, cuerpo de Dios!

315 AMA: Tornareis outro dia.

CASTELHANO: Assosiega coraçon,
adormientate, leon,
no heches la casa en tierra,
ni hagas tan cruda guerra

320 que mueras como san Son.

¶¡Esta burla es de verdad,
por los **hue**ssos de Medea,
sino que arrastrado sea
mañana por la ciudad!

325 ¡Por la sangre soverana
de la bata**l**la troyana!
Y juro a la casa sancta ...

AMA: Pera que é essa jura tanta?

CASTELHANO: Y aun vos estés hufana?

330 ¶Quiero destruyr el mundo,
quemar la casa, es la verdad,
despues quemar la ciudad.
Señora, en esto me fundo.
Despues, si Dios me dixere

335 quando allá con el me viere,
que por sola una muger...
bien sabré que responder,
quando a esso viniere.

AMA: ¶Isso sam rebolarias.

340 CAST.: Sea me Dios testigo,
que vos vereis lo que digo
antes que passen tres dias.

AMA: Má viagem faças tu,
caminho de Calecu,

345 praza à Virgem Consagrada.

LEMOS: Que é isso?

AMA: Nam é nada.

---

322 huessos · ossos **326 batalla** · batalha **328 é** · he **329 estés** · estes

		Open up to me, by the body of Christ!
315	WIFE:	You'll come back some other time.
	SPANIARD:	Oh, my heart, be at peace!

Open up to me, by the body of Christ!

315 WIFE: You'll come back some other time.

SPANIARD: Oh, my heart, be at peace!
Oh, lion, return to sleep!
Do not pull down the house,
do not wage such cruel war
320 that you die like Sam's son.

This trick is for real,
by Medea's bones!
If not, may I be drawn
through all the town,
325 by the sovereign blood
of the Trojan war.
And I swear by the holy house ...

WIFE: Why are you making all these oaths?

SPANIARD: And are you still disdainful?

330 I would destroy the world,
burn down the house, that's the truth,
after that, burn down the city,
that's what I think, my lady.
After that, if God said to me
335 when I go to be with him,
that for only one woman ...
I'd well know what to reply
when it came to that.

WIFE: These are idle threats.

340 SPANIARD: May God be me witness,
that you'll see what I say
before the end of three days!

WIFE: May yours be a bad journey
on the way to Calicut.
345 May that please the Virgin Mary!

LEMOS: What was that?

WIFE: It was nothing.

---

335 allá · alla 345 é · he (twice) 337 sabré · sabre

LEMOS: Assi viva Berzabu!

AMA: ¶Y-vos embora, senhor,
que isto quer amanhecer.
350 Tudo está a vosso prazer,
con muyto dobrado amor.
Ò que mesuras tamanhas!

MOÇA: Quantas artes, quantas manhas
que sabe fazer minha ama:
355 um na rua, outro na cama!

AMA: Que falas, que t'arreganhas?

MOÇA: ¶Ando dizendo entre mi
que agora vay em dous annos
que eu fuy lavar os panos
360 alem do cham d'Alcami.
E logo partio a armada,
domingo de madrugada.
Nam pode muyto tardar
nova se há de tornar
365 noss' amo pera a pousada.

AMA: ¶Asinha?

MOÇA: Tres annos há
que partio Tristam da Cunha.

AMA: Quant' eu, anno & meo punha.

MOÇA: Mas tres, & mais averá.

370 AMA: Vay tu comprar de comer.
Tens muyto pera fazer:
nam tardes.

MOÇA: Nam senhora.
Eu virey logo ness' ora,
375 se m' eu lá nam detiver.

AMA: ¶Mas que graça que seria
se este negro meu marido
tornasse a Lixboa vivo

---

355 um · hum 354, 356 há · ha 368 Quant' eu · Canteu 375 lá · la

148

	LEMOS:	Then long live Beelzebub!
	WIFE:	Go in good time, my lord,
		for it's just about to dawn.
380		All lies here at your pleasure
		with much redoubled love!
		Oh, how many bows!
	MAID:	How many wiles, how many deceits
		can my mistress perform!
355		One in the street, the other in bed!
	WIFE:	What do you say? Why are you grinning?

	MAID:	I was saying to myself
		that it's been two years
		that I went to wash clothes
360		beyond the chão d'Alcami.
		And then the fleet left,
		early on a Sunday morning.
		It can't be much longer
		for news about whether our master
365		will return to his own home.

	WIFE:	Really?
	MAID:	It's three years
		since Tristão da Cunha left.
	WIFE:	I'd say a year and a half.
370	MAID:	Three, and more, it'll be.
	WIFE:	Go and buy something to eat.
		You've got a lot to do,
		don't take your time.
	MAID:	No, ma'am.
		I'll be back straightaway,
375		if I don't make myself late.

	WIFE:	But how funny it'd be
		if that accursed husband of mine
		should come back to Lisbon alive,

380 | pera minha companhia!
Mas isto nam pode ser,
que elle havia de morrer
sòmente de ver o mar.
Quero fiar & cantar
segura de o nunca ver.

385   MOÇA: ¶Ay, senhora, venho morta:
nosso amo é hoje aqui!
AMA: Má nova venha por ti,
pera escomungada torta!
MOÇA: A Garça em que elle ia
390 vem com muy grande alegria.
Per Restelo entra agora,
por vida minha, senhora,
que nam falo zombaria

¶E vi pessoa que o vio,
395 gordo que é pera espantar.
AMA: Pois, casa, se t' eu cayar:
mate-me quem me pario!
Quebra-me aquellas tigelas,
& tres ou quatro panelas,
400 que nam ache em que comer.
Que chegada & que prazer!
Fecha-me aquellas janelas.

¶Deyta essa carne a esses gatos,
desfaze toda essa cama.
405 MOÇA: De merces está minha ama:
desfeytos estam os tratos.
AMA: Por que nam matas o fogo?
MOÇA: Rayvar, qu' este é outro jogo!
AMA: Perra, cadela tinhosa!
410 MOÇA: Digo que o matarey logo.

---

381 **havia** · auia 386 **é hoje** · he oje 389 **ia** · hia 403 **a om.** *C* 408 **é** · he

380		to keep me company!
		But that cannot be —
		he would have died
		as soon as he'd seen the sea;
		I want to sew and sing
		sure that I'll not see him again.
385	MAID:	Oh, ma'am, I'm frightened to death!
		Our master's here today!
	WIFE:	May you always bring ill tidings,
		you wicked excommunicate!
	MAID:	The *Garça*, that he sailed in,
390		has come, with great joy.
		Now it's coming in by the Restelo.
		On my life, ma'am,
		I'm not saying it for fun!
		And I saw someone who'd seen him,
395		so fat, he was frightening.
	WIFE:	Well, house, if I whitewash you,
		may she who bore me strike me dead.
		Break those plates for me,
		and three or four pots.
400		He mustn't find anything to eat.
		Oh what a coming, what good cheer!
		Shut those windows!
		Throw that meat to those cats.
		Unmake all of that bed.
405	MAID:	My mistress is most polite!
		Our intimacy's at an end.
	WIFE:	Why don't you put out that fire?
	MAID:	Rave on, that's another game.
	WIFE:	She-dog, mangy bitch,
		what are you grumbling about, traitoress?
410	MAID:	I was saying, I'll put it out straightaway.

AUTO DA ÍNDIA

AMA:	¶Nam sey per que é viver.
MARIDO:	Houlá!
	Ali maora este é!
AMA:	Quem é?
MARIDO:	Homem de pé!
AMA:	Gracioso se quer fazer.

415   Sobi, sobi pera cima!

MOÇA: É noss' amo, como rima.

AMA: Teu amo — Jesu, Jesu!
Alvissaras pedirás tu!

MARIDO: Abraçay-me minha prima!

420   AMA: ¶Jesu! Quam negro e tostado!
Nam vos quero! Nam vos quero!

MARIDO: E eu a vos, si, porque espero
serdes molher de recado.

AMA: Moça, tu que estás olhando?

425   Vay muyto asinha saltando:
faze fogo, vay por vinho,
& ametade dum cabretinho
emquanto estamos falando.

AMA: ¶Ora, como vos foy lá?

430   MARIDO: Muyta fortuna passey.

AMA: E eu, ò quanto chorey
quando a armada foy de cá!
E quando vi desferir
que começastes de partir,

435   Jesu!, eu fiquey finada:
tres dias nam comi nada,
a alma se me queria sayr.

MARIDO: ¶E nos, cem legoas d'aqui,
saltou tanto sudueste,

440   sudueste & oest-sudueste
que nunca tal tromenta vi.

AMA: Foy isso à quarta feyra,

411 é · he 412 Houlá · Oula é · he 413 é · he 418 pedirás · pediras

152

WIFE:	I don't know why I should live!
HUSBAND:	Hello!
WIFE:	There, damnation, it's him.
	Who's there?
HUSBAND:	A foot sold-ier!
WIFE:	He wants to be funny.
415	Come up, come up, up here.
MAID:	It's our master, by his rhyme!
WIFE:	Your master. Jesus, Jesus!
	You'll ask for a good reward!
HUSBAND:	Embrace me, my darling!
420 WIFE:	Jesus! How black you are, and tanned!
	I don't love you, I don't love you!
HUSBAND:	And I do love you, for I hope
	you've been a prudent woman.
WIFE:	Maid, what are you staring at?
425	Jump to it, quickly,
	light a fire, go get some wine
	and half a roast kid
	while we are talking.
	Now, how were you over there?
430 HUSBAND:	I went through many dangers.
WIFE:	And me, how much I cried
	when the Armada sailed from here!
	And when I saw you striking off,
	that you were beginning to leave,
435	Jesus, I almost died!
	For three days, I didn't eat a thing,
	I thought I was about to die!
HUSBAND:	And us, a hundred leagues from here,
440	there rose up such southwesterlies,
	southwest and west-southwesterlies
	such that I'd never seen such storms.
WIFE:	Was that on the Wednesday,

aquella logo primeyra?

MARIDO: Si, & começou n'alvorada.

445   AMA: E eu fuy-me de madrugada
a nossa Senhora d'Oliveyra.

¶ E com a memoria da cruz
fiz-lhe dizer ũa missa,
& prometi-vos em camisa

450   a Sancta Maria da Luz.
E logo à quinta feyra
fuy ao Spirito Sancto,
com outra missa tambem,
chorey tanto que ninguem

455   nunca cuydou ver tal pranto.

¶ Correstes aquella tromenta?
Andar.

MARIDO: Durou-nos tres dias.

AMA: As minhas tres romarias
com outras mais de quarenta.

460   MARIDO: Fomos na volta do mar,
quasi, quasi, a quartelar;
a nossa Garça voava
que o mar se espedeçava.

¶ Fomos ao rio de Meca,

465   pelejamos & roubamos
& muyto risco passamos,
a vella, arvore seca.

AMA: E eu **cá a** esmorecer,
fazendo mil devações,

470   mil choros, mil orações.

MARIDO: Assi **havia** de ser.

AMA: ¶ Juro-vos que de saudade
tanto de pam nam comia,
a triste de mi cada dia.

---

445 AMA om. *C.* E · & 448 ũa · hũa 468 **cá a** · ca 471 **havia** · auia

the very first, after you left?
HUSBAND: Yes, and it began at dawn.
445 WIFE: I went, early in the morning
to Our Lady of Oliveira.

And, keeping in mind the cross,
I had them say a mass
and, in only my shift, I commended
450 you to Our Lady of Light;
and then on the Friday,
I went to the Church of the Holy Ghost,
with another mass as well.
I cried so much that no-one
455 could ever think of seeing such tears.

Did you run through that storm?
Go on.
HUSBAND: It lasted three days.
WIFE: My three pilgrimages,
with the forty more that I did.
460 HUSBAND: We went out into the ocean
almost, almost changing direction,
our *Garça* flew along
and the sea split asunder.

We went to the Red Sea —
465 we fought and we robbed,
and we passed many dangers,
driven along by the gales.
WIFE: Me, here, fading away,
performing a thousand devotions,
470 a thousand tears, a thousand prayers.
HUSBAND: That's the way it ought to be.

WIFE: I swear to you that with longing
I did not eat so much bread,
sad little me, every day.

475   Doente, era ũa piedade.
           Ja carne nunca a comi,
           esta camisa que trago
           em vossa dita a vesti,
           porque vinha bom mandado.

480   ¶Onde nam há marido,
           cuyday que tudo é tristura;
           nam há prazer nem folgura;
           sabey que é viver perdido.
           Alembrava-vos eu lá.
485 MARIDO: E como?
     AMA: Agora aramá,
           lá há Indias muy fermosas,
           lá farieis vos das vossas,
           & a triste de mi cá,

           ¶encerrada nesta casa,
490   sem consentir que vezinha
           entrasse por ũa brasa
           por honestidade minha.
     MARIDO: Lá vos digo que há fadigas,
           tantas mortes, tantas brigas,
495   & perigos descompassados
           que assi vimos destroçados,
           pelados como formigas.

     AMA: ¶Porem vindes vos muyto rico?
     MARIDO: Se nam fora o capitam,
500   eu trouxera a meu quinham
           um milham vos certifico.
           Calay-vos, que vos vereis
           quam louçam aveis de sayr.
     AMA: Agora me quero eu rir
505   disso que me vos dizeis.

_____

475 **ũa** · hũa 480 **há** · ha 481 **é** · he 482 **há** · ha 483 **é** · he

475	Sick — it was so pitiful;
	now, meat I never ate.
	This blouse that I'm wearing
	I put on in your honour
	because good news had come.
480	When no husband is there,
	consider everything as sadness.
	There is no pleasure, no joy.
	Know that it's life gone to waste.
	Did you remember me out there?
485 HUSBAND:	And how!
WIFE:	Now, now, damnation,
	out there, there are beautiful Indian women:
	you'll have been up to your tricks,
	and poor, sad me here,
	locked up inside this house
490	not even allowing a neighbour
	to come in for a light for the fire
	so that I'd keep my reputation.
HUSBAND:	There, I tell you, there are many labours,
	so many deaths, so many battles,
495	and outlandish dangers
	that we were ground down thus,
	sheared like sheep.
WIFE:	But, have you come back very rich?
HUSBAND:	If it were not for the captain,
500	I would have brought back as my share,
	I assure you, a million.
	Now don't say another word, for you'll see
	how prettily you'll come out of this.
WIFE:	Now I'd like to laugh
505	at what you tell me.

---

486 **lá há** · la ha   487 **lá** · la   491 **ũa** · hũa   493 **Lá** · La **há** · ha   496 **destroçados** · destrocados   499 **MARIDO** · Mo.

¶Pois que vos vivo viestes,
que quero eu de mais riqueza?
Louvado seja a grandeza
de vos, Senhor, que mo trouxestes!
510   A nao vem bem carregada?

MARIDO: Vem tam doce embandeyrada.

AMA: Vamo-la — rogo-vo-lo — ver.

MARIDO: Far-vos-ey nisso prazer?

AMA: Si, que estou muyto enfadada.

Fim.

¶*Vam-se a ver a Nao & fenece esta primeyra farsa.*

		Since I see you alive,
510		what do I want with more riches?
		Praised be your greatness,
		Lord, you who brought him back to me!
		Is the ship well laden?
	HUSBAND:	She's decked out so sweetly.
515	WIFE:	Let's go there, I implore you, to see it.
	HUSBAND:	Would you be pleased by this?
	WIFE:	Yes, because I'm much out of sorts.

THE END.

They go to see the ship and so ends this first farce.

NOTES TO THE *AUTO DA ÍNDIA*

1 The same line is found at *Auto da Barca do Purgatório*, line 593.

2 *armada*: sixteen ships sailed in the fleet that left under the command of Tristão da Cunha, five of which were under the command of Albuquerque.

3 *Olbade*: see Teyssier, *La Langue de Gil Vicente*, 184. The modern Portuguese form would be *olbai*; the form given in this line had already passed from educated speech by 1425 (*ibid.*, 196). Cp. *Auto da Barca do Inferno*, l. 750.

   estreada: Morais, I, 728A, gives the following definition for '*Bem, ou mal estreado*; por bem parecido, bem dotado ao nascer da natureza, naquilo que ella então dá' [*Well, or ill starred* for well-seeming, gifted by nature in that which nature gives].

8 *gamo*: 'stag', but by extension, 'cuckold' because of the horns both possessed. The devil, too, who was often given horns in popular iconography, was also associated with cuckoldry (cp. the fool's insults to the devil in the *Auto de Inferno*, ll. 282-86), and, because the devil was coloured black, 'negro' was also a colour to be associated with cuckolds (cf. ll. 40 and 129-30 for the equivalence of the husband with the devil; ll. 376 and 421, for the husband being 'negro', black). The same unholy trinity was employed by Shakespeare in *Othello*.

17 *dixeram*: although this pronunciation is now confined to rustic speakers of Portuguese, it was common to all levels of society when Vicente wrote (Teyssier, *La Langue de Gil Vicente*, 82, note 2).

19 *O Concelos*: Jorge de Vasconcelos (†1525) was in charge of the arming and provisioning of the fleet from 1501. He was a poet who featured in the *Cancioneiro Geral*. See Braamcamp Freire, 143-44, and Michaëlis, 394-95.

20 *Restelo*: The *praia de Restelo*, near Belém, was the beach whence boats left and whither they returned. See Adrien Roig, 'Le théâtre de Gil Vicente et le voyage aux Indes', *Quadrant*, 7 (1990), 5-23, at 7.

21 *vir a pello*: to come on purpose or on time (cf. Morais, II, 424A).

23 The first half of a common proverb. Osório Mateus, *India*, Vicente: colecção dirigida por Osório Mateus (Lisboa: Quimera, 1988), 5, gives, 'Quem porcos acha menos, as moitas lhe roncam' [When your pig is missing, every thicket oinks at you], or, in other words, 'Whoever lacks something, thinks he sees it everywhere'.

31 *canela*: cinnamon, along with other spices, was one of the objects sought after in trading with India.

37 *Santo Antonio*: Saint Anthony, born in Lisbon in 1195, became a Franciscan in 1220 and died in Padua in 1231. His cult received (and still does) enormous popularity. The invocation of the saint is humorous because it inverts the usual pattern of such prayers: the wife prays not that her husband be safely returned to her, but that he be lost at sea. In Portugal and southern Brazil, Anthony is nowadays regarded as a 'matchmaking saint', which, if this were also the case in sixteenth-century Portugal, would add a certain piquancy to the request.

38 Morais, I, 531B, *'deparar.* Dar, apresentar sem ser esperado', i.e., to present someone with something unexpectedly.

40 *Zebedeu* is perhaps the husband's name. The line was changed in the 1586 edition of the *Copilaçam* to 'de um diabo como o meu'. *Zebed* is the name given to one of the devils in the list of *Interlocutores* in the *Exortação da Guerra*, although the character is called Zebrom throughout that play. *Zebedee* was the name of the father of the apostles James and John.

41-2 A proverbial phrase, found in Gonzalo Correas, *Vocabulario de refranes y frases proverbiales (1625)*, ed. Louis Combet (Bordeaux: Institut d'Études Ibériques et Ibéro-Américaines de l'Université de Bordeaux, 1967), 332B, 'Dormiré, dormiré, buenas nuevas hallaré'. Correas goes on to note that it is a proverb 'Kontra los floxos ke se fían mucho de la ventura, o fortuna i tienpo' [against the weak who trust themselves to chance, or fortune and time]. It's appearance on the wife's lips is therefore ironic.

47 *alvissaras*, a word from the Arabic *al-bushāra*, 'a gift to a bringer of glad tidings' (Hans Wehr, *A Dictionary of Modern Written Arabic*, ed. J. M. Cowan (4th edn.; Wiesbaden: Otto Harrassowitz, 1979), 73B). See José Pedro Machado, *Influência arábica no vocabulário português* (Lisboa: Álvaro Pinto, 1958), 290, *s. v. alvissaras*.

48 Morais, II, 53A, '*De foz em fóra*; i.é., fóra do rio, ou barra para o alto'.

50-51 The maid's refusal of a silk headpiece in favour of a share in the husband's spoils from India is not only designed to tease her mistress, but to indicate an expectation that great wealth would flow from the east. The *alvissaras* are referred to again as the play draws to a close, at l. 418.

54 The wife repeats this line when she learns of her husband's arrival, at l. 401.

63 The *ceitil* was, according to Morais, I, 370B, a coin from the time of João I, worth one sixth of a *real*. It was also spelt *seitil*.

68 Morais, II, 441B, cites the phrase 'mao pesar veja eu do demo', indicating that *pesar* was pronounced with the stress falling on the first syllable, i.e., *pêsar*.

77-8 These lines have at times been taken to show that Costança had adulterous liasons before the action of the play takes place (e.g., Castro Osório, 180-81). Such an inference is not quite supported, for the phrase remains unfinished. It is more likely that the lines refer to the number of opportunities which presented themselves to Costança when her husband was away for only a short time, and these opportunities would be manifestly more frequent now. It is not at all certain that she availed herself of such opportunities in the past, since Lemos says that he stopped roaming in the street below her house because he always found her so cruel (ll. 231-32), presumably an indication that she did not grant him the object of his desires.

88 *vento*: the wind provides a triple image. In the first sense, it refers to the return of her husband whose travel was dependent upon the right winds. In the second, it characterizes such a wait as futile, for the wind is empty (cp. Morais, II, 841A, where *vento* is synonymous with vanity). Thirdly, the blowing of the wind is a folkloric image of se:.. l intercourse (see Stith

Thompson, *Motif Index of Folk Literature* (6 vols.; Compenhagen: Rosenhilde & Bagger, 1955-1958), V, 394, at T524.

89   *Quant'eu*: probably pronounced *cant'eu* (cf. line 368, and *Auto da Barca do Inferno*, line 71).

90   *contrairo*: 'contrário', a common form in Vicentine Portuguese.

92   *sangue novo*: it was thought that with the heat of spring and summer, the body produced new blood and the humours were more active. See Hart, *Farces and Festival Plays*, 69.

96   The Spaniard comes up the stairs without being asked to ascend, the contrary of both Lemos and the husband (cp. ll. 221-223 and 412-15).

97   Cp. Matthew 10:12, 'Intrantes autem domum, salutate eum dicentes: pax huic domui' [When you go into a house, greet it saying: peace be to this house].

103 *honesta*: a word with a dual meaning. The Spaniard clearly intends it as a synonym for *hermosa*, although it also meant chaste, which adds to its irony. Antonio de Nebrija (ed. MacDonald, 146A), gives 'honestus, pulcher' as the meaning for *honesto*; Morais, II, 118B, gives 'casto, pudico'.

108 Cp. l. 218. Compare also ll. 104 and 217. A parallel is being drawn between the Spaniard's professed feelings for Costança and hers for Lemos.

112 *fortuna*: 'storm' (Martín Alonso, *Diccionario medieval español: desde la Glosas emilianenses y Silenses (s. X) hasta el siglo XV* (2 vols.; Salamanca, Universidad Pontificia, 1986), 1166A, 'Borrasca, tempestad en mar o tierra'. Cf. line 430, 'Muita fortuna passei'.

114 The 1596 edition of the *Copilaçam* substituted 'señora sois contra mí' for this line.

115 Cp. l. 104.

130 *desestrado*: Nebrija, 71B, gave 'infelix, infortunatus' [unhappy, unfortunate] as the meaning of *desastrado*. Cp. l. 3.

134 *estardes juntos los dos*: 'the use of the inflected infinitive is common in Vicente's Castilian texts' (Hart, *Farces and Festival Plays*, 70).

135 *Juan de Zamora*: the Spaniard's own name. *Juan* may be an ironic epithet: *Jean* in French farce usually signifies that the character is a fool or a cuckolded husband (see Lewicka, 78-84). The Spaniard's lack of success with Costança may be foretold in his name. Braga, V, 96, thought that the Spaniard's name was perhaps suggested by the poet who composed the *romance* of the *Bela Mal Maridada*, a tale of adultery.

142 i.e., that the sun should shine.

143 *momiento*: a comic exaggeration of the Castilian tendency to form the dipthong '*ie*' from the stressed Latin '*e*'. The true Castilian form of the word is *momento*.

144 The second edition of the *Copilaçam* (1586) has 'mas la verdad es aquesto' in place of this line.

153-55 The wife attempts to prevent the maid listening to the Spaniard's declaration of love by sending her to shoo away a dog that is sniffing around the crockery; the maid refuses to go, since cats are there, not dogs.

157 The *Copilaçam*'s second edition in 1586 has 'hablo en las cosas de Dios'.

184 *no-maiʃ*: the modern form is *não maiʃ*.

188 *Entonceʃ*: this form of the word is less common in the *Copilaçam* than *então*, but is used by all levels of society (Teyssier, *La Langue de Gil Vicente*, 140).

195 The allusion would seem to be to the proverb found in Correas, 34B, 'Aunke me veis kon este kapote, tres ovexas tengo en el monte: las dos no son mías, la otra es de un onbre' [Although you see me with this cloak, I have three sheep on the mountain: two are not mine, the other belongs to someone else].

199 *Florencia*: a reference to the glories of the Italian city-state.

201 *rebolam*: the Spaniard, on the model of Centurio from the *Celeʃtina*, lives at the expense of the women he seduces. Nebrija, 171B, gives as the Spanish form 'rofian o alcahuete' and glosses the word as 'leno'. Morais, II, 658A, '*Rufião*. Homem que traz consigo meretrizes para ganhar por ellas' or 'o que as desfruta de graça, e talvez é mantido por ellas'.

202 *ò* seems to be the form preferred in phrases such as 'dou ò demo', but, on other occasions, the more modern *ao* seems to have been slightly more favoured by Vicente and his subsequent editors.

216-7 an allusion to the proverb, 'Quem não aparece, esquece', he who doesn't come calling, forgets, or, perhaps, 'Out of sight, out of mind', an allusion I have attempted to repeat in the translation.

225 *meʃura*: cf. l. 352.

232 As occured with the Spaniard (ll. 127-28), the courtly rhetoric drops to a more prosaic exchange.

242 *ʃingela*: apart from meaning 'single' (i.e., deprived of her husband: cp. Morais, II, 702B), the word can, by extension, mean 'not double or duplicitous', 'frank', 'innocent' (*Ibid.*, 702A). It is thus as ironic a word upon Lemos' lips as *honeʃta* was upon the Spaniard's (l. 103).

244 *embora*, ie., *em boa ora*. The literal truth of the welcome Costança gives to Lemos, 'You come at a good hour', is immediately thrown into doubt, for the hour is nine and the Spaniard has begun throwing stones at the window.

248 Amaro de Oliveira, 76 comments that Lemos seems to disbelieve what Costança says, and so she is forced to change tactics.

253 *Siguença*: a Spanish town, reconquered from the Moors in 1124, presumably chosen to rhyme with *verguença*. The Spaniard's being left out in the street may have led him to remember that, in 1465, the dean of Siguenza fortified himself in the town square whilst he disputed the bishopric with the cardinals Juan de Mella and Pedro González de Mendoza (*Enciclopedia universal iluʃtrada europeo-americana* (Madrid-Barcelona: Espasa-Calpe, 1927), 56, 114B).

254 *prometeiʃ*: cf. l. 206.

257 *Diʃʃimulai*: it is perhaps significant that this verse, in which Costança orders another character to play a rôle, should be exactly half-way through the play (the entire play has 514 lines).

259 Cp. l. 122.

261 *vinagreiro*: a vinegar-seller (Morais, II, 853B); vinegar had the meaning of 'ill-humour, bad temper' (*Ibid.*); cf. *Auto da Barca do Inferno*, l. 270, 'Pero Vinagre beyçudo'.

264 *cear*: Lemos has just come out of the kitchen (cf. l. 249).

274 *briguigões*: the modern form is 'berbigões'.

277 Oysters, of course, are always expensive.

275 *barejas*: 'varejas'.

282 *cinquinho*: according to Santa Rosa de Viterbo, 103A, a *cinquinho* was worth five silver *réis*, and was minted during the reigns of João II and Manuel I. The name had a popular flavour (*Ibid.*, 662B), for the coins were always called 'cincos' in Law codes and by the Treasury.

285-6 These lines are sung by Lemos, and perhaps refer back to ll. 261-263.

289 Cf. l. 490.

292 *rezam*: the modern form is 'razão'.

lhe: '*Lhe* for *lhes* is common in classical Portuguese, as is *le* for *les* in sixteenth-century Castilian' (Hart, *Farces and Festival Plays*, 76).

294 Carolina de Michaëlis commented (*Notas Vicentinas*, 429) that this line was 'a burlesque form of an oath'. However, there does not seem to have been anywhere actually called Marenilla by which the Spaniard might curse. There may be a printer's error, 'n' being printed for 'u' (i.e., 'v') and that 'Marevilla (=Maravilla)' was meant. The Spaniard may then be referring to a place near Frías, in the department of Choya, province of Santiago (*Enciclopeida universal ilustrada*, 32, 1295A); 'de maravilla' may also be taken as 'marvellously, greatly, to excess', although it would seem that mediæval Castilian only used 'a maravilla' in this context (see Alonso, II, 1359B). Otherwise, 'marinilla' may be the deminutive of *marina*, which, according to Alonso, II, 1361B, meant the coast or a region near to the sea — perhaps indicating that the Spaniard was cursing Lisbon, and implying a contrast with his native Castile. A final suggestion is that the word should be spelt 'morenilla', and taken as a diminutive of *morena* which, in the fifteenth century, meant 'an argument' (*Ibid.*, II, 1411A). As it seems impossible to choose between possible mis-readings and printer's errors, I have left the text as it appears in *C*.

Reniego: the Spaniard's exclamation is perhaps meant to recall Ecclesiasticus 19: 2, rendered twice into Spanish in *La Celestina*: 'las mugeres y el vino hazen a los hombres renegar' [women and wine make man apostasize himself] (Russell, 225, 227).

296 The wife, having silenced Lemos for fear of the neighbours, is faced with the Castilian threatening to wake all of the town.

301 *outra casa*: this, we later learn, is the bedroom (l. 355).

303 *micer* 'is a borrowing from Italian *messer*, or, rather, from a dialectal form *misser*, perhaps by way of Catalan *misser*. In Castilian, *micer* was often used in the fifteenth and sixteenth centuries to refer to Italians and Catalans; it may be significant that Costança uses it in addressing the Castilian Juan de Zamora' (Hart, *Farces and Festival Plays*, 77).

309 *Navidá*, a form representing the pronunciation of the Castilian, 'Navidad'.

313 Cf. ll. 116 and 118-121.

314 Cf. l. 181.

315-6 Cf. ll. 165-6.

320 *san Son* probably a joke at the Spaniard's expense. Juan thinks that *Sansón* was really two words, *san Són*, i.e., *saint Són*. Such comic misundertanding of names is found in the *Celestina*: 'Minerva con el can', *el can*, the dog, rather than *Vulcan*, the god (Russell, 223). Samson died when he pulled down the Philistine's temple whilst he was also inside (Judges 16: 23-30)

322 *ossos*: As Vicente otherwise uses the correct Castilian form(*Barca da Gloria*, 25; *Auto de los cuatro tiempos*, 53, 134), one must surmise that this Portuguese form of the word is the result of a printer's error.

Medea: a figure from classical legend, who was connected strongly to magic and indomitable passion. She assisted Jason to escape with the golden fleece from her father; later in life, however, on learning of Jason's infidelity, she slew all of their children (cp. Maria Helena da Rocha Pereira, 'O mito de Medeia na poesia portuguesa', sep. de *Humanitas*, 15 (1963), 6).

The references to the stories of Samson (and Delilah: cp. Judges 16: 4-21) and of Medea would bring to the contemporary audience's mind the treacherous nature of women. Medea killed her brother, and so may have been used by the Spaniard to express his frustration and his wish that Costança would get rid of her 'brother'.

323 *arrastrado*: cf. l. 135

327 *casa santa*: the holy house of Loreto, claimed in the Middle Ages to have been the house in which Jesus grew up, and to have been miraculously transferred to Loreto in Italy. The Italian parish church in Lisbon, founded in 1518, was dedicated to the Madonna di Loreto. The oath is perhaps designed to further characterize the Spaniard as a foreigner (cf. l. 304).

334 *me fundo*: see *Auto da Barca do Inferno*, at line 225.

342 A reference to John 2: 19, 'Jesus answered, Destroy this temple, and in three days I will raise it up again' (Knox, *The Holy Bible*, 88A).

344 *Calecu*: cf. l. 80. The oath equates the Spaniard with Costança's husband, for Costança is glad to be rid of both of them.

345 Cp. ll. 445-46.

352 This line, in lieu of a stage direction, indicates both *that* Lemos has left (the wife exclaims to herself), and also *how* he leaves (bowing); cf. l. 225.

353 *artes*: cf. l. 215.

360 *Chã d'Alcamí*: Michaelis, 370, identifies it as the former 'rossio' of Lisbon, in the parish of S. Cristóvão, although Braga, V, 108 situates it above the small building of St. Mamede's Church.

370 Cf. ll. 266 and 426. The concentration upon the maid's going for food which we never see consumed — and the food that is present on stage is thrown away (ll. 399 and 402) — is perhaps designed to contrast with the husband's being 'fat' (l. 394) when he returns.

377 Beelzebub is a reference to the Devil.

381 Cp. ll. *77-78*, where it is revealed that the husband is a fisherman. Costança is again deceiving herself.

382 Cp. l. 61.

388 *Garça* was the name of one of the ships in Tristão da Cunha's fleet. It was also written *Graça* (Michaëlis, 409).

395 Berardinelli, *Antologia*, 285, explains that the wife's refusal to whitewash the house should be understood as a metaphorical refusal to show any joy or celebration at her husband's return.

402 Cf. l. 155.

416 According to Mateus, 19, the maid's statement may refer to the rhyme that exists between 'amo' (master) and 'gamo' (stag) — a reference to his being cuckolded: cf. l. 8.

426 Cp. l. 407.

446 *Nossa Senhora da Oliveira*: a shrine situated in the churchyard of S. Julião (Braga, V, 113). S. Julião is mentioned in the *Auto da Barca do Inferno*, l. 596.

449 *em camisa*: three interpretations are equally possible: first, that the wife went to the sanctuary dressed only in a shift to commend her husband to Our Lady, and thereby guarantee his safety: it would be normal to make a subsequent pilgrimage of thanks on his safe return; secondly, that the wife means that she offered the equivalent weight of wax to that of her husband's weight when dressed only in a shirt (Braga, V, 113); thirdly, Berardinelli, *Antologia*, 287, suggested that the wife had promised to take him to the shrine, dressed only in a shirt, as part of a thanksgiving pilgrimage. The first explanation fits in well with the wife's (false) enumeration of her sufferings on her husband's behalf. Braga's explanation fits in well with the tradition of making *ex-votos* from wax in the image of something which had been lost and presenting it to the shrine of the Blessed Virgin. If this is the case, the wife's lie contrasts strongly with the sentiments expressed in ll. 37-38.

452 *Spirito Santo*: Amaro de Oliveira, 78, suggests that the church referred to in this line is to be identified with one in Santa Cruz do Castelo. Churches of the Holy Spirit would seem to have been particularly associated with the exploration of Africa (see Thomaz, 'L'idée impériale', 94), and hence a suitable destination for the wife's devotion.

461 *quartelar*: to change direction (Moura, *Teatro*, 162). António Marques Esparteiro, *Dicionário ilustrado de Marinharia* (2nd edn.; Lisboa: Livraria Clássica, 1943), 21 B, gives the following definition: 'Alçar a barlavento as escotas das velas de proa ou dos latinos, a fim de obrigar o navio a ceder à manobra que se quer executar.'

465 *roubamos*: 'roubar' is a word used by Afonso de Albuquerque in his letters' (Mateus, 21).

467 *a vela árvore seca*: cf. *correr em árvore seca*, 'to scud, to be driven swiftly before a gale' (Hart, *Farces and Festival Plays*, 83).

475 *carne*: cp. ll. 402 and 275.

476 The wife's abstaining from meat is in part as an expression of grief, in part a harking back to her religious and penitential pilgrimages and vows on her husband's behalf.

478 *ðita*: cp. l. 148.

484 Cp. l. 216.

498 Although the verse is one syllable too long, this feature may be a deliberated device on the part of the playwright to draw attention to the question the wife asks and the sentiments that lie behind it.

510 *ðoce* is an adverb here, signifying 'richly', 'prettily' (Moura, *Teatro*, 162).

513 *prazer*: cf. ll. 54, 86, 350, 401 and 482.

fenece eʃta primeira farʃa: This designation at the end of the play would seem to indicate that the work was the first farce that Gil Vicente wrote. It is preceded in the *Copilaçam* by *Quem tem farelos?*, but this work is generally accepted as being ten years later than the date of 1505 that Luis Vicente gave to it. In the *Auto ða Índia*, therefore, Vicente used Portuguese as his dramatic language for the first time. Claude-Henri Frèches thought that the relative perfection of the play indicated that Vicente must have seen farces or mystery plays 'digne de ce nom, dans la Péninsule Ibérique, sinon en France, dans la Flandres ou en Allemagne' (*Le Théâtre neo-latin au Portugal (1550-1745)* (Paris-Lisbonne: Librairie A. G. Nizet-Librairie Bertrand, 1964), 30).

INTRODUCTION TO THE *EXORTAÇÃO DA GUERRA*

The *Exortação da Guerra* has a processional format. A cleric is the first character to appear. He mocks his own necromantic powers, and summons two devils from Hell. The devils, although unwilling, are forced to carry out the cleric's wishes, which are to bring a series of figures from Classical legend and Roman history out of Hell to speak to the audience, praising both king and court and inciting the audience to support the martial intentions of the king. First to appear is Polixena, daughter of Priam, king of Troy. After her appears Panthesileia, Queen of the Amazons, then Achilles, Hector, Hannibal and Scipio. The play closes with the characters dancing and singing whilst Hannibal tells the audience that Portuguese victory over the Moors is assured.

The date and circumstances of the perfomance

The *Exortação da Guerra* is, like the *Auto da Índia*, preserved only in the *Copilaçam*'s version of its text. It is unlikely that it was ever published separately. Again, like the *Auto da Índia*, it is court entertainment, but of a very different type. Rather than being a farce to celebrate the arrival of a fleet, the *Exortação da Guerra* is the play of Gil Vicente's which most approximates itself to the earlier 'momos' or mimes that were the established entertainment of the Portuguese court. The *Copilaçam* describes the *Exortação* as having been performed in 1513 on the occasion of the departure of Dom Jaime, Duke of Bragança, for Azamor, a stronghold on the Morrocan coast. As we have seen with the *Auto da Barca do Inferno*, the assertions of the *Copilaçam* regarding the dates of the plays it contains must be taken with some caution, for it is patently clear that the text of the *Exortação*, as we have it in the *Copilaçam*, is not a record of the play that was performed in 1513. Numerous allusions in the text point to events that occurred after the expedition to Azamor. There may well be a central kernel of the play that does date to 1513, although it would be difficult to identify exactly which parts are original.

Braamcamp Freire showed that certain of the cleric-necromancer's prophecies were the product of a later revision. Isabel married Charles V in November of 1520 (ll. 259-65); Beatriz married the Duke of Savoy (see l. 278) eight years after the performance of the play; and Dom Fernando married 'rich and prosperous' (l. 270) in 1530. However, the latter's marriage was dissolved in 1534 after the death of all of the children, and so Braamcamp concluded that the additions must have been carried out between 1530 and 1534.[1] It may well be that Gil Vicente was already preparing a *Copilaçam* of his works before João III 'commissioned' one from him.

Some allusions at the beginning of the play also refer to events which occurred after the conquest of Azamor. The devils taunt the cleric with the elephant sent to Rome as part of the embassy of Tristão da Cunha in 1514 (ll. 195-96). This part of the play would seem to have been written shortly after the embassy's success, for the right to the *terças* that the pope had conceded to him was eventually exchanged by Manuel I for a lump sum from the clergy. Aubrey Bell thought that the the 'exhortations of l. 351 *et seq.* and l. 559 *et seq.* are better suited to a time when more men and money were needed actively to continue the war than when an army of 18,000 was equipped and ready to leave', as would have been the case in 1513.[2]

The difficulty in ascribing a date to the play would, it seems, only be solved by the necromantic summoning of Gil Vicente's shade to testify. Indeed, it is very possible that the text of the play as we have received it from the *Copilaçam* is the end of a process by which its literary aspect was worked up from the notes made for the staging of a court 'momo'. This reworking, coming a year later than the performance, would explain the presence of allusions to events after the taking of Azamor. The reworking was then further revised between *c.* 1530 and 1534.

Genre

Although the *Copilaçam* lists the play amongst the tragicomedies, both its themes and form place it within the ambit of courtly mime or 'momo'. The cleric necromancer who conjures up all of the other characters that appear on the stage acts as a means of explanation for the appearance of figures from classical epic and provides a 'frame' in which the play might evolve. The characters, in turn, praise the sovereign and the court before beginning their exhortation to war against the Muslims. Little evidence regarding the entertainments in the Portuguese court before Gil Vicente's activity has survived, apart from the valuable testimony of the Spanish

---

1   Braamcamp Freire, 104.
2   Aubrey F. G. Bell, *Four Plays of Gil Vicente. Edited from the* editio princeps *(1562), with translation and notes* (Cambridge: CUP, 1920), 75.

ambassador to Lisbon in 1500 who reported a courtly entertainment to his sovereigns.[3]

According to this description of the mime of 1500, an allegorical frame of an 'enchanted orchard of love' enclosed the drama. Characters were played by court figures, who appeared in a sequential, processional form, saluting Queen or King and speaking mainly of love. They bore texts which they presented to the Queen or King (which the ambassador copied in his letter), and other texts which were presented to the ladies of the court. The celebration ended with a dance in which[4]

> el Señor Rey danzó con todos los momos en una danza que dicen acá Serau y despues subieron el Rey y la Reyna a sua Camara con mucho placer e triunfo y asentaronse en la Camara y cenaron juntos muy alegremente.
> *the lord King danced with all the actors in a dance which is here called 'Serau' and afterwards the King and Queen went up to their chamber with much pleasure and triumph and they sat down in their chamber and they dined together very joyfully.*

The *Exortação* also ends with a dance among all the actors. We may say with confidence that the play was written to be recognisable as a type of 'momo', a form of official court celebration. However, rather than the more diffuse and ponderous court mime, Vicente produced a concentrated and coherent structure, and, what is more, a focus that encompassed the polite, courtly concern of love yet went beyond it in an argument for war in Africa.

The structure of the play

The cleric opens the play with a monologue that makes burlesque claims for necromancy by emphasizing that it can bring about nothing but what is natural. Gil Vicente, as with his presentation of astrology through Mercury in the *Auto da Feira*, rejects the possibility that 'occult' arts may bring any power to their devotees, but rather asserts the Christian faith as the means of controlling devils. Zebrom and Danor are brought to heel by the invocation of Christ and the Virgin, and two of the cleric's pseudo-Greek invocations end with the words 'ò filui soter' (ll. 95 and 97); *soter* is reminiscent of the Greek 'sotiros', Saviour, and *filui* would seem to be a compression of the Latin '[In nomine patris et] *fil*i et spirit*ui* [sancti]', [*In*

---

3 The text of the letter referring to the 'momo' was transcribed by Fidelino de Figueiredo, *A Épica Portuguesa no século xvi: subsídios documentares para uma theoria geral da epopêa*, Separata do boletim ci — Letras — n°. 6 (São Paulo: Faculdade de Filosofia, Ciências e Letras da Universidade de São Paulo, 1950), 126-132.

4 *Ibid.*, 132.

the name of the Father and] *of the Son and of the* [*Holy*] *Spirit*. The assertion of
Christianity as the provider of true power over the underworld is a direct
parallel to the later assertion that Manuel's Christianity is the reason for
his military success over the Muslims.

Polixena is summoned, and, true to the courtly form of the play, praises
the king, queen and court, and is questioned about love. She presents
military involvement as the most fitting activity for a lover, and valour as
outweighing even physical uncouthness (cp. ll. 342-50). Polixena
describes the ladies of the Trojan court to which she belonged as being
concerned not with the demands of fashion but with those of supporting
the men at war by beautifying their standards and flags and by giving
away their necklaces and jewels (ll. 351-363). She encourages the women
of the Portuguese court to take part thus in the war effort, and, as a
comparision, calls upon the warlike Panthesileia, Queen of the Amazons,
who fought the Greeks outside the walls of Troy.

The cleric seizes on Polixena's suggestion, and orders that the devils
bring her. Panthesileia arrives immediately and launches into an eulogy of
the king, and encourages Portugal to put all of its energies into warfare
rather than aiming at profit through mercantile activity (ll. 404-12). She
then suggests that Achilles should be called, so that he might also tell the
same truth to the assembled court.

Achilles is duly called for, recites a long eulogy of Manuel and his
Queen by stressing the favourable horoscope that marked their births. He
appeals to the nobles to continue their victorious path, and to the clerics
that they might contribute financially to the war so that their 'contraries'
(l. 485), the Muslims, be defeated. Should Achilles not provide authority
enough, then he himself suggests Hector, Scipio and Hannibal, who are
immediately summoned to the stage. Again, they compliment the court,
saying that their presence is not needed amongst such company. Hannibal
recapitulates the message of the previous figures, stressing the importance
of the financial contribution from ladies and churchmen.

Running throughout the play is a contrast between the glory of the
Manueline court and the classical world. Polixena can exclaim that 'The
palace of Troy/was not worthy of your perfection'; Panthesileia can
contrast the meaningful wars of Manuel with the 'phantom' or 'empty
wars' that she fought (cp. l. 394); Achilles is 'blessed' to see Portugal's
glory (l. 463). The final comparison, provided by Hector, Hannibal and
Scipio, is perhaps the greatest. Whilst Polixena had encouraged the
women of the court to support the war effort, and Panthesileia had wished
to take part in the war herself, Achilles was content to behold Portuguese
honour, and the final trio confessed that they would be surplus to

requirements in Manuel's court (ll. 501-5), presumably because the martial standing of the nobles and king was so great. The alternating appeals to noble women and clergy to fund the wars also provides a unity, the seriousness of the appeals being mirrored in the devils' taunting of the necromantic priest over his payment of the *terças*. All of the disparate appeals are woven together in Hannibal's address which marks the end of the play.

The ideology of the play

The crusade that is so insistently preached in the play is one curiously distant from a traditionally religious perspective such as one finds in the *Auto da Moralidade*. Rather, one finds a chivalric conception of holy war, in which fighting for the faith was one aspect of the comportment of the ideal knight. The ideal of battle with the infidel was linked more closely to aristocratic conceptions of the value of martial activity than to the spiritual ideals put forward by the Church. As Maurice Keen could write,[5]

> the knightly life, with all its violence and with all the richness and decor of its aristocratic trappings, is within its own terms a road to salvation. The idea here is one that looks back, through the colour and overlay of the fashions, phrases and moods of the late twelfth and early thirteenth centuries, to the conception of the religious worth that kingship (modelled on Christ's kingship) confers on service rendered to it, rather than any ideal of knighthood serving the *sacerdotium*. This is typical of the attitude that underpinned the conception of chivalry as a Christian vocation.

An aristocratic, martial ethic pervades the play, as the playwright presents a plan for society which would turn Portugal into a completely crusading nation. Sobriety in dwellings and dress are put forward as the national characteristic, as distinct from the showy Italians (ll. 404-12; cf. ll. 351-59). There is an implicit rejection of the mercantile activity which was so important in the trade with India in Pantasileia's advice, 'Gain the fame of fearsomeness/not of riches, for that's dangerous' (ll. 413-14).

Following Gil Vicente's habitual procedures, the clergy are singled out for criticism, particularly from the ghostly mouths of Achilles and Hannibal. Vicente, through Achilles, expresses his wish that the very ecclesiastical structure of the Church be transformed, and its wealth 'nationalized', put at the service of the wars for the defeat of the prelates' 'opposites' (l. 485). Christianity is presented by Vicente as locked into a

---

5   Maurice Keen, *Chivalry* (New Haven-London: Yale University Press, 1984), 62-63.

binary opposition with Islam, in a struggle which represents the archetypal struggle between good and evil. Any sacrifice, therefore, ought to be contemplated to remove the Muslims, even to the extent of pawning prayer-books (l. 482), of setting aside what was necessary for ceremonial religious observance in order to destroy the foe. Any independence which the institutional Church enjoys ought to be surrended, since clerics should cease to appeal to Rome for protection (ll. 479-80).

Through Hannibal, the message to the clergy is even more uncompromising. The money they gain is spent neither on church upkeep nor on the poor, but for their own enrichment (ll. 540-44), and so should be given to assist the war. Similarly, the wealth of priories should be used to reward soldiers and men-at-arms, since this action would be true evangelical charity deserving the reward promised by Christ to his disciples, that they would receive a hundred-fold what they gave up for his sake (ll. 536-39). Vicente proposes a radical change to his society, in which the monasteries could be broken up and distributed to those who fought against Islam in the service of the king. Rather than knighthood being at the service of the *sacerdotium*, the Church should be placed at the service of the knights.

Manuel is the central figure of the play's rhetoric. He is hailed by Polixena as 'one greater than Priam, a most sovereign Cesar' (ll. 242-43); by Panthesileia as 'King of great marvels/who with small companies/vanquish whom you wish' (ll. 383-85); and laden with astrological praise by Achilles. It is, however, in Hannibal's words that the king's rôle becomes clear.

God 'holds the king's heart in his hand' (ll. 584-85), and thus He has inclined it to war against the infidel so that Fez may be conquered and its mosque be turned into a Cathedral. Aspects of Manuel's messianic rôle are certainly depicted, particularly by the conquest of North Africa being placed in the context of Manuel's domination of the globe (ll. 579-82; cp. ll. 396-98). Yet the goal depicted is only Fez, and not Jerusalem. The prosecution of crusading in Morocco did suit Manuel's global strategy, for this was seen as one of the routes by which Jerusalem might be reached, although the crusade, as it is presented by Gil Vicente, is not explicitly about the retaking of Jerusalem at all. It was, however, precisely in the military theatre of North Africa that Manuel and his leading nobles saw eye-to-eye, all parties being convinced of the importance of fighting there. Whilst Gil Vicente was prepared to acknowledge that Manuel was inspired by the Holy Spirit (ll. 583-85),[6] his inspiration is limited to a field in which the nobility were already committed, and the crusade itself is presented not in religious but in chivalric terms. The play provides neither messianic preaching nor political opposition to the king. Rather it focuses on the area which had historically served to emphasise unity within the court and to diffuse the serious internal conflict between the Crown and the fractious landed nobility.[7]

Note to the Critical Edition

The norms I have followed are identical to those of the edition of the *Auto da Barca do Inferno*, with one exception. Italic script is used to indicate the use of Roman type in the *Copilaçam*.

---

6   Thomaz, 'L'idée impériale manueline', 92, comments that the same reference to Proverbs 21:1 was made by an ideologue of Manueline messianism, Duarte Galvão, to stress the illumination that God provided for the monarch.

7   Thomaz, 'Factions, interests and messianism', 97: 'we have good reasons to believe that, at least in the fifteenth century, external expansion itself was carried out as a means to diffuse an internal crisis in Portugal.'

Exortação

da Guerra

The Exortation

to War

A Tragicomedia *seguinte, seu nome é Exortação da Guerra. Foy representada ao muyto alto & nobre Rey dom Manoel o primeyro em Portugal deste nome na sua cidade de Lixboa na partida pera Azamor do illustre & muy magnifico senhor dom Gemes Duque de Bargança & de Guimarães, &c. Era de M. D. xiiij. annos.*

¶*Interlocutores:*

¶*Nigromante, Zebed, Danor (Diabos), Policena, Pantasilea, Archiles, Anibal, Eytor, Cepiam.*

¶*Entra primeyramente um clerigo nigromante, & diz:*

	¶Famosos & esclarecidos	[C f. 156r A]
	principes muy preciosos,	
	na terra vitoriosos	
	& no ceo muyto queridos,	[C f. 156r B]
5	sou clerigo natural	
	de Portugal;	
	venho da cova Sebila	[C f. 156v A]
	onde se esmera & estila	
	a sotileza infernal.	
10	¶E venho muy copioso	
	magico & nigromante	
	feyticeyro muy galante	
	astrologo bem avondoso.	
	Tantas artes diabris	
15	saber quis	
	que o mais forte diabo	
	darey preso polo rabo	
	ao iffante dom Luis.	
	¶Sey modos d'encantamentos	
20	quaes nunca soube ninguem,	
	artes pera querer bem,	
	remedios a pensamentos.	
	Farey de um coraçam duro	

---

introduction é · he ¶Interlocutores: · Inrerlocutores. um · hum

The name of the Tragicomedy which follows is the Exhortation to War. It was performed before the very highly-born and noble King dom Manuel, the first of that name in Portugal, in his city of Lisbon, on the departure for Azamor of the illustrious and most magnificent Lord dom Gemes, Duke of Bragança, and of Guimarães, etc., in the year, 1514.

Speakers:

¶Necromancer, Zebed, Danor (Devils), Polixena, Pentasilea, Achilles, Hanibal, Hector, Scipio.

A cleric necromancer enters first, and says:

Famous and learnèd,
highly-prized princes,
on earth victorious,
in heaven belovèd,
5   a priest am I, born
in Portugal;
I come from the Sybil's cave
where hellish subtlety
is refined and esteemed.

10   I come to you a highly-skilled
magician, necromancer,
a very galant sorcerer,
a highly-gifted astrologer.
I've gained knowledge
15   of so many devilish arts
that I'll take the strongest devil
by his tail and give him
to our Prince, dom Luis.

I know means of enchantments
20   such as no-one's ever known:
arts to have true love,
remedies for its cares.
I'll make the heart harder

---

23 um · hum

177

mais que muro
25   como brando leytoayro,
& farey polo contrayro
que seja sempre seguro.

¶Sou muy grande encantador
faço grandes maravilhas:
30   as diabolicas silhas
sam todas em meu favor.
Farey cousas impossiveis,
muy terriveis,
milagres muy evidentes
35   que é pera pasmar as gentes
visiveis & invisiveis.

¶Farey que uma dama esquiva,
por mais çafara que seja,
quando o galante a veja
40   qu'ella folgue de ser viva.
Farey a dous namorados
muy penados
qu' estem cada um per si,
& cousas farey aqui
45   que estareis maravilhados.

¶Farey por meo-vintem   [C f. 156v B]
que ũa dama muyto fea
que de noyte, sem candea,
nam pareça mal nem bem.
50   E outra fermosa & bella
como estrella,
farey por sino forçado,
que qualquer homem honrrado
nam lhe pesasse com ella.

---

30 **silhas** · sillas **33 terriveis** · terribeis **35 é** · he **37 ũa** · hũa

than the city wall
25   soft as an opiate,
and I'll do the opposite,
that it may always be secure.

I am a great enchanter,
great wonders I perform:
30   the devilish swarms
are all found in my favour.
I'll do things impossible,
things most terrible,
most evident miracles
35   to astound all peoples,
visible and invisible.

I'll make a haughty lady,
however shrewish she be,
when seen by an admirer
40   feel pleased to be alive.
I'll make two lovers,
much pained by love,
love each other,
and I'll do such things here
45   that will make you all amazed.

I'll make, for a halfpenny,
a very ugly woman,
at night, without a candle,
look neither fair nor foul.
50   And another, beautiful and lovely
as a star,
I shall force her fate
so that any gentlemen
would suffer in love for her.

---

43 **um** · hum 47 **ũa** · hũa

55 ¶Far-vos-ey mais pera verdes
— per esconjuro perfeyto —
que caseis todos a eyto
o milhor que vos poderdes.
E farey da noyte dia
60 — per pura nigromancia —
se o sol alumear,
& farey yr pollo ar
toda a vam fantesia.

¶Far-vos-ey todos dormir
65 em quanto o sono vos durar,
& far-vos-ey acordar
sem a terra vos sentir.
E farey um namorado
bem penado
70 se amar bem de verdade
que lhe dure essa vontade
até ter outro cuydado.

¶Far-vos-ey que desejeis
cousas que estam por fazer,
75 & far-vos-ey receber
na ora que vos desposeis.
E farey que esta cidade
esté pedra sobre pedra,
& farey que quem nam medra
80 nunca tem prosperidade.

¶Farey per magicas rasas
chuvas tam desatinadas
que estem as telhas deytadas
pelos telhados das casas.
85 E farey a torre da sé   [C f. 157v A]
assi grande como é,
per graça da sua clima

---

60 **nigromancia** · nigromanciia **68 um** · hum

55   I'll do more for you to see
through this perfect spell
that you'll each in turn marry
as well as you are able,
and I'll make night into day
60   through pure necromancy
(if the sun would only shine),
and I'll make fly out and away
all vain fantasy.

I will make you all be asleep
65   as long as your sleeping should last,
and I'll make you wake up
without the world hearing a sound.
And I'll make a lover,
in much pain,
70   —if he loves truly and well —
remain in his affection
until he thinks of another.

I will make you wish
for things yet to happen,
75   and I'll have you receive gifts
at the moment that you wed.
And I will make this city
stand stone upon stone,
I'll make sure he who grows not rich
80   never has prosperity.

I'll make, through magical means
such unreasonable rains
that tiles will be lying
on the roofs of houses.
85   And I'll make the cathedral tower
just as high as it is,
thanks to its inclination;

que tenha o alicesse ao pé
& as ameas em cima.

90 ¶Nam me quero mais gabar,
nome de sam Cebriam!
Esconjuro-te, Satam!
Senhores, nam espantar.
Zét zeberet zerregud zebet,
95 ó filui soter
Rehe, zezegot relinzet
ó filui soter.

¶Ó chaves das profundezas,
abri os porros da terra!
100 Princepes da eterna treva,
pareçam tuas grandezas!
Conjuro-te, Satanás,
onde estás,
polo bafo dos dragões,
105 pola yra dos liões,
polo vale de Jurafás,

¶polo fumo peçonhento
que sae da tua cadeyra,
& pola ardente fugueyra,
110 polo lago do tormento.
Esconjuro-te, Satam,
de coraçam,
zezegot selvece soter.
Conjuro-te, Lucifer,
115 que ouças minha oraçam.

¶Polas nevoas ardentes
que estam nas tuas moradas
pollas poças povoadas
de bibaras & serpentes.

---

102 **Satanás** · Satanas 104 **dragões** · dragoes 106 **jurafás** · jurafas

at its foot, shall be its base,
and its battlements on top.

90   I don't want to praise myself any more,
by the holy name of Cyprian.
I conjure you, Satan
(my lords, be not afraid!):
Zet, zeberet, zerregud, zebet,
95   *oh filui soter.*
Rebe, zezegot relinzet,
oh filui soter.

Oh, keys of the depths,
open the pores of the earth!
100   Great lords of eternal darkness,
now appear!
I conjure you, Satan,
where you stand,
by the breath of dragons
105   by the rage of lions
by the valley of Josaphat,

by the poisonous smoke
that comes from your throne,
and by the burning furnace,
110   and by the lake of torment.
I conjure you, Satan,
from the heart:
zezegot selvece soter.
I conjure you, Lucifer,
115   to hear my prayer,

by the burning mists
that inhabit your mansions,
by the pools haunted
by vipers and snakes,

---

113 **selvece** · seluece   117 **estam nas** · estannas   118 **poças** · pocas

120 E pello amargo tormento
muy sem tento
que dás aos encarcerados,
pollos grytos dos danados
que nunca cessam momento.   [*C f. 157r B*]

125 ¶Conjuro-te, Berzebu,
pola ceguidade Hebrayca,
& pola malicia Judayca
com a qual te alegras tu.
Rezégut Linteser
130 zamzorep, tisal,
siro ofé, nafezeri.

¶Vemos os diabos, Zebron & Danor, & diz Zebron.

¶Que hás tu, escomungado?
CLERIGO: Ó, yrmãos, venhaes embora!
DANOR: Que nos queres tu agora?
135 CLERIGO: Que me façaes um mandado.
ZEBRON: Polo altar de Satam,
dom vilam!
DANOR: Tomo-o por essas gadelhas
& cortemos-lhe as orelhas
140 qu' este clerigo é ladram.

CLERIGO: ¶Manos, nam me façaes mal,
compadres, primos, amigos.
ZEBRON: Não te temos em dous figos.
CLERIGO: Como vay a Belial?
145 Sua corte está em paz?
DANOR: Dá-lhe aramá um bofete!
Crismemos este rapaz
& chamemos lhe Zobete?

CLERIGO: Ora, falemos de siso:
150 estais todos de saude?
ZEBRON: Fideputa, meo almude,

---

122 **encarcerados** · encacerados   **stage direction**   **Vemos os diabos** · Vemos

120 and by the bitter torment,
without pareil,
that you give those imprisoned,
by the screams of the damned
that never cease for an instant.

125 I conjure you, Beelzebub,
by the Hebraic blindness,
and by the malice of the Jews
that so delights you,
Rezegut, Linteser,
130 *zamzorep, tisal,*
siro ofe, nafezeri!

The devils Zebron and Danor appear, and Zebron says,

What's the matter, excommunicate?
PRIEST: Oh, brethren, you are welcome!
DANOR: What do you want us for now?
135 PRIEST: That you obey my command.
ZEBRON: By the altar of Satan,
Sir Villein!
DANOR: I'll grab him by his mop
and then let's cut his ears off,
140 for this cleric is a thief.

PRIEST: Brothers, do me no harm,
companions, cousins, friends.
ZEBRON: We don't care two figs for you.
PRIEST: How's Belial getting on?
145 His court — is it in peace?
DANOR: Damn it, sock him one!
Let's christen this lad
and call him Zobete.

PRIEST: Now, now, let's talk sense:
150 are you all in the best of health?
ZEBRON: Whoreson half-a-pint,

---

diabos **132 hás** · has **135 um** · hum **140 é** · he **146 Dá** · Da **um** · hum

		que te<u>ns</u> tu de ver co' isso?	
	CLERIGO:	Minhas potencias relaxo	
		& me abaxo:	
155		falay-me doutra maneira.	
	DANOR:	Sois bispo de Landeyra	
		ou vigayro no Cartaxo?	

	ZEBRON:	¶É cura do Lumear,	
		sochantre da Mealhada,	
160		acipreste de Canada:	[*C f.* 157v A]
		bebe sem desfolegar.	
	DANOR:	É capelã terrantés,	
		bó Ingrés,	
		patriarca em Ribatejo,	
165		beberá sobre hum cangrejo	
		as guelas dũ Francés.	

	ZEBRON:	¶Danor, di-me, é cardeal
		d'Arruda ou de Caparica?
	DANOR:	Nenhũa cousa lhe fica
170		senam sempre o vaso tal.
		Tem um gra<u>n</u>de Arcebispado
		muyto honrrado
		junta da Pedra da Estrema,
		onde põe a diadema
175		& a mitara o tal prelado.

	ZEBRON:	¶Ladram, sabes o Seyxal
		& Almada, & pereli?
		Ó fideputa alfaqui,
		albardeyro do Tojal!
180	CLERIGO:	Diabos, quereis fazer
		o que eu quiser
		per bem, ou doutra feyçam?
	DANOR:	Ó fideputa ladram
		avemos-te d'obedecer.

---

158 ¶É · ¶He   162 É · He   163 **Ingrés** · Ingres

		what business is that of yours?
	PRIEST:	I let my powers loose,
		and I lower myself:
155		speak to me another way.
	DANOR:	Are you the bishop of Orvieto
		or the vicar of Barbaresco?
	ZEBRON:	He's a priest from Jerez,
		sub-cantor of Chianti,
160		arch-priest of Alicante,
		he'll drink without stopping for breath.
	DANOR:	He's a chaplain from Bordeaux:
		an Englishman, good-oh.
		Patriarch of Vouvray,
165		he'll drink on a crab
		the gills of a *français*.
	ZEBRON:	Danor, tell me, is he cardinal
		of Hautes Sauternes or Alsace?
	DANOR:	He's been left with nothing
170		more than a glass.
		He has an archbishopric, pretty large,
		of great renown,
		next to the Hermitage,
		where he puts his crown
175		and mitre, does this prelate.
	ZEBRON:	Thief, do you know La Rioja,
		and Navarra, and round there?
		O whoreson ayatollah!
		Packsaddler from Anjou!
180	PRIEST:	Devils, will you do
		what I wish
		with good will, or another way?
	DANOR:	Oh, whoreson thief,
		we're forced to obey.

---

166 francés · Frances **167 é** · he **172 um** · hum

185 CLERIGO: ¶Ora vos mando & re-mando
              pollas virtudes dos ceos,
              polla potencia de Deos
              em cujo serviço ando.
              Conjuro-vos da sua parte,
190   sem mais arte,
              que façais o que eu mandar
              polla terra & pollo ar,
              aqui & em toda a parte.

     ZEBRON: ¶Como te vay com as terças?
195   É vivo aquella alifante
              que foy a Roma tam galante?
     DANOR: Amargam-te a ti estas verças?
     CLERIGO: Esconjuro-te, Danor,
              por amor de sam Paulo,   [C f. 157v B]
200   & de sam Polo.
     ZEBRON: Tu não tens nenhum miolo.
     CLERIGO: Eu vos farey vir a dor,

              ¶por esta madre de Deos
              de tam alta dinidade,
205   & polla sua humildade
              com que abrio os altos ceos;
              pollas veas virginaes
              emperiaes
              de que Christo foy humanado.
210 ZEBRON: Que queres, escomungado?
              Manda-nos, nam digas mais.

     CLERIGO: ¶Minha merce manda & ordena
              que tragais logo essas oras
              diante destas senhoras
215   a Troyana Policena
              muyto bem ataviada
              & concertada,
              assi linda como era.

---

194 ¶ om. *C* 195 É · He 197 **Amargam** · Amarga 213 **oras** · horas

185	PRIEST:	I order and order you again now,
		by the heavenly powers,
		by the might of God
		in whose service I stand,
		I conjure you for His part,
190		by no other art,
		that you do what I command,
		by earth and by air,
		here and everywhere.
	ZEBRON:	How do you find the terce?
195		Is the elephant still alive
		that went to Rome and looked so spry?
	DANOR:	Do you find this food bitter?
	PRIEST:	I conjure you, Danor,
		by love of Saint Paul
200		and Saint Pole —
	ZEBRON:	You've got no brain.
	PRIEST:	I will bring you pain:
		by this mother of God
		of such high dignity,
205		and by her humility
		through which she opened the Heavens,
		by the virginal,
		imperial veins
		by which Christ was made man —
210	ZEBRON:	What do you want, excommunicate?
		Say no more, but command.
	PRIEST:	I myself command and order,
		that you bring with no delaying
		before these ladies
215		Polixena of Troy,
		well-accoutered
		and serene
		as beautiful as she was.

	DANOR:	Quanta pancada te dera
220		se podera,
		mas tens-m' a força quebrada.

	CLERIGO:	¶Venha por mar ou por terra
		logo muyto sem referta.
	ZEBRON:	E a terça da offerta
225		tambem pagas pera a guerra?
	CLERIGO:	Trazey logo a Policena,
		muy sem pena
		com sua festa diante.
	ZEBRON:	Inda yrá outro alifante:
230		pagarás quarto & vintena.

	POLICENA:	¶Eu, que venho aqui fazer?
		Ó, que gram pena me destes
		pois per força me trouxestes
		a um novo padecer.
235		Que quem vive sem ventura
		em gram tristura
		ver prazeres lh' é mais morte.
		Ó belenissima corte, [Cf. 158r A]
		senhora da fermosura.

240		¶Nam foy o paço Troyano
		dino do vosso primor,
		vejo um Priamo mayor,
		um Cesar muy soberano,
		outra Ecuba mais alta
245		muy sem falta
		em poderosa, doce, humana,
		a quem por Febo & Diana
		cada vez Deos mais esmalta.

250		¶E vos, Principe excelente,
		day-me alvissaras liberais,
		que vossas mostras sam tais

234, 243, 244 um · hum   250 alvissaras · alvisaras

	DANOR:	What a beating I'd give you,
220		if I could,
		but you've shattered my strength.
	PRIEST:	Come by land or sea,
		right now, without a pause.
	ZEBRON:	And the terce of the collection:
225		do you also pay it for the war?
	PRIEST:	Bring Polixena right away,
		with no pain,
		and her fête before her.
	ZEBRON:	Another elephant'll be sent —
230		then you pay the quarter and twentieth.
	POLIXENA:	What have I come here to do?
		Oh, what great pain you gave me,
		since you took me by force
		to a new suffering.
235		For she who lives without fortune,
		in great sadness,
		to see pleasures brings her more death.
		Oh, most beautiful court,
		very queen of loveliness.
240		The palace of Troy was not worthy
		of your perfection.
		I see one, greater
		than Priam, a most sovereign Cæsar,
		another, higher-born Hecuba,
245		most faultless
		in her power, her sweetness and humanity,
		to whom, through Phœbus and Diana,
		God ever more grants lustre.
		And you, excellent Prince,
250		give me a generous boon,
		for such is your appearance

que todo mundo é contente.
E aos planetas dos ceos
mandou Deos
255   que vos dessem tais favores
que em grandeza sejais vos
prima dos antecessores.

¶Por vos muy fermosa flor,
iffanta dona Isabel,
260   foram juntos em torpel
per mandado do Senhor
o ceo & sua companha,
& julgou Jupiter juiz
que fosseis Emperatriz
265   de Castella & Alemanha.

¶Senhor iffante dom Fernando,
vosso signo é de prudencia,
Mercurio por excelencia
favorece vosso bando.
270   Sereis rico & prosperado
& descansado,
sem cuydado & sem fadiga,
& sem guerra & sem briga,
isto vos está guardado.

275   ¶Iffante dona Breatiz,
vos sois dos sinos julgada
que aveis de ser casada
nas partes de flor de lis.
Mais bem do que vos cuydais
280   muyto mais
vos tem o mundo guardado:
perdey senhores cuydado,
pois com Deos tanto privais.

---

252 é · he 267 **vosso** · vasso é · he

that everyone is happy.
And God commanded
the planets of the heavens
255   to give you such favours
that you might be the first
in greatness among your ancestors.

For you, most beautiful flower,
Princess dona Isabel,
260   through our Lord's command,
Heaven and its company
joined in a throng,
and Jupiter, the judge, decreed,
that you should be Empress
265   of Castile and Germany.

Lord Prince dom Fernando,
your sign is that of prudence,
Mercury, *par excellence*,
takes your part.
270   You will be rich and prosperous,
and at rest,
without worry, without weariness,
without war, without conflict;
for you, all this is kept.

275   Princess dona Beatriz,
for you the fates decreed
that you are to be married
in the land of the fleur-de-lis.
Far better than you think,
280   much more,
does the world hold for you all.
Do not worry, my lords,
since you are so close to God.

	CLERIGO:	¶Que dizeis vos destas rosas,
285		deste val de fermosura?
	POLICENA:	Tal fora minha ventura
		como ellas sam de fermosas.
		Ó que corte tam lozida
		& guarnecida
290		de lindezas pera olhar:
		quem me podera ficar
		nesta gloriosa vida!

	DANOR:	¶Nesta vida lá acharás.
	POLICENA:	Quem me trouxe a este fado?
295	DANOR:	Esse zote escomungado
		te trouxe aqui onde estás.
		Pergunta-lhe que te quer
		pera ver.
	POLICENA:	Homem, a que me trouxeste?
300	CLERIGO:	Qué? Ainda agora vieste,
		& hás-me de responder.

		¶Declara a estes senhores,
		pois foste d'amor ferida,
		qual achaste nesta vida
305		que é a mór dor das dores.
		E se as penas infernaes
		se sam às do amor yguaes,
		ou se dam lá mais tormentos
		dos que cá dam pensamentos
310		& as penas que nos daes.

	POLICENA:	¶Muyto triste padecer	
		no inferno sinto eu	
		mas a dor que o amor me deu	
		nunca a mais pude esquecer.	
315	CLERIGO:	Que manhas, que gentileza,	[C f. 158v A]
		há de ter o bom galante?	

---

293 lá · la   301 hás · has   305 é · he   308 lá · la   309 cá · ca

	PRIEST:	What do you say of these roses,
285		of this vale of beauty?
	POLIXENA:	Such was also my fortune,
		to be as beautiful as they.
		Oh, what a court, that shines
		and is adorned
290		with beauties to regard.
		Would that I could remain
		in this glorious life!

	DANOR:	In this life there, you'll find that out.
	POLIXENA:	Who brought me to this enchantment?
295	DANOR:	That excommunicate sot,
		brought you here to where you are.
		Ask him what he wants
		to see from you.
	POLIXENA:	Man, why did you summon me?
300	PRIEST:	What? You've only just arrived,
		and you are to reply to me.

		Declare to these lords,
		since you were struck by love,
		which suffering in this life
305		you found to be the greatest;
		and whether the pains of Hell
		are equal to those of love,
		or if they give more torment there
		than those that here give cares,
310		and sufferings that you give us.

	POLIXENA	Very gloomy suffering
		I feel in Hell,
		but the pain I had from love
		I never could forget.
315	PRIEST:	What appearance, what finesse
		should a good beau have?

---

316 há · ha

POLICENA: A primeyra é ser constante
fundando todo em firmeza.

¶Nobre, secreto, calado,
320   sofrido em ser desamado,
sempre aberto o coração
pera receber payxão,
mas nam pera ser mudado.
Há de ser muy liberal,
325   todo fundado em franqueza,
este é a mór gentileza
do amante natural.

¶Porque é tam desviada
ser o escasso namorado,
330   como estar fogo em geada,
ou ũa cousa pintada
ser o mesmo encorporado.
Há de ser o seu comer
dous bocados ospirando,
335   & dormir meo velando
sem de todo adormecer.

¶Há de ter muy doces modos,
humano, cortés a todos,
servir sem esperar della,
340   que quem ama com cautela
nam segue a tençam dos Godos.
CLERIGO: Qual é a cousa principal
por que deve ser amado?
POLICENA: Que seja muy esforçado,
345   isto é o que mais lhe val.

¶Porque um velho dioso
feo & muyto tossegoso,
se na guerra tem boa fama
com a mais fermosa dama

---

317 é · he **320 desamado** · desañado **324 Há** · Ha **326, 328 é** · he

POLIXENA: The first of all is constancy,
founded all on determination.

Noble, secret, silent,
320 patient when unrequited,
his heart always open
to receive passion,
but not to any change.
He must be generous,
325 founded all on liberality.
This is the greatest finesse
of the natural lover,

for it is something quite astray
for a lover to be mean,
330 like fire being frozen over
or a painted thing
being also embodied.
His eating should be
two mouthfuls of air,
335 and his sleeping, half-awakenings,
yet never falling fully asleep.

He should have fine manners,
courteous to all, humane.
He should serve without hope of gain
340 for he who loves with caution
follows not the Goths' way.
PRIEST: What is the principle reason
for which he should be loved?
POLIXENA: That he be very brave:
345 this serves him best,

for if an old, old man,
prone to cough, quite foul,
in war has won renown,
he deserves good fortune

---

331 ũa · hũa 333, 337 Há · Ha 342, 345 é · he

350   merece de ser ditoso.

¶Senhores, guerreyros, guerreyros,
& vos, senhoras guerreyras,
bandeyras & nam gorgueyras   [*Cf.* 158v B]
lavray pera os cavaleyros.
355   Que assi nas guerras troyãs
eu mesma & minhas yrmaãs
teciamos os estandartes,
bordados de todas partes
com devisas muy louçãs.

360   ¶Com cantares & alegrias
davamos nossos colares
& nossas joyas a pares
per essas capitanias.
Renegay dos desfiados
365   & dos pontos enlevados:
destrua-se aquella terra
dos perros arrenegados.

¶Ó, quem vio Pantasiléa,
com quarenta mil donzellas,
370   armadas coma as estrellas
no campo de Palomea.
CLERIGO: Venha aqui! Trazey-ma cá.
ZEBRON: Deyxa-nos, yeramá!
CLERIGO: Ora, sus, que estais fazendo?
375 DANOR: O diabo que t' eu encomendo
& quem tal poder te dá.

¶*Entra Pantaſilea, & ðiz:*

¶Que quereis a esta chorosa
Raynha Pantasilea,
à penada, triste, fea
380   pera corte tam fermosa?

---

372 cá · ca **375 diabo** · diado

350   with the most beautiful lady.

Lords, warriors, warriors,
and you, ladies, warriors all,
prepare for your knights
banners and not lace collars,
355   for thus, in the Trojan wars
my sisters and myself
wove the standards
embroidered on every part
with highly elegant devices.

360   With songs and cheers
we gave our necklaces
and our jewels together
for these captaincies.
Renegue on ravelling
365   and on raised stitches:
may destruction fall
on that land of renegade dogs.

Oh, would that you'd seen Penthesilea
with forty thousand maidens
370   armed like the stars
in the field of Palomea.

PRIEST: Come on, here, bring her to me here.
ZEBRON: Leave us alone, damn you!
PRIEST: Now, courage, what are you up to?
375   DANOR: I commend you to the devil
and whoever gives you such power.

Penthesilea enters and says:

What do you want from this tearful
Queen, Penthesilea?
From one pained, sad and ugly
380   for such a beautiful court.

Porque me quereis vos ver
diante vosso poder,
Rey das grandes maravilhas,
que com pequenas quadrilhas
385   venceis quem quereis vencer?

¶Se eu senhor fora, me vira
do inferno solta agora,
& fora de mi senhora,
meu senhor, eu vos servira.
390   Empregara bem meus dias   [*Cf.* 159r A]
em vossas capitanias,
& minha frecha dourada
fora bem aventurada
& nam nas guerras vazias.

395   ¶Ó, famoso Portugal!
Conhece teu bem profundo,
pois até o Polo segundo
chega o teu poder real.
Avante, avante, senhores,
400   pois que com grandes favores
todo o ceo vos favorece,
el Rey de Fez esmorece
& Marrocos dá clamores.

¶Ó, deyxay de edificar
405   tantas camaras dobradas
muy pintadas & douradas,
que é gastar sem prestar.
Alabardas, alabardas,
espingardas, espingardas,
410   nam queyrais ser Genoeses,
senam muyto Portugueses
& morar em casas pardas.

---

386 fora · forra **407 é** · he

Why do you wish to see me
before your throne,
King of great marvels,
who with small companies
385   vanquish whom you wish?

If I were a lord, I'd come
released from Hell right now,
and if I were mistress of myself,
my lord, I would serve you.
390   I would spend my days well
in your captaincies,
and my golden bow
would be well-favoured
and not in phantom wars.

395   Oh, famous Portugal,
know your greatest fortune,
since your regal power
stretches to the second pole.
Onward, ever onward, my lords,
400   since with great favours
all Heaven favours you.
The king of Fez melts away,
and Morroco cries out aloud.

Oh, stop building
405   so many redoubled rooms,
hightly painted, highly gilded,
which are wasteful, not useful.
Halbards, halbards,
muskets, muskets!
Do not seek to be Genoese,
but rather very Portuguese
and live in sober houses.

¶Cobray fama de ferozes,
nam de ricos, que é perigosa.
415   Douray a patria vossa
com mais nozes que as vozes.
Avante, avante, Lixboa,
que por todo o mundo soa
tua prospera fortuna,
420   pois què ventura t' emfuna,
faze sempre de pessoa.

¶Archiles que foy d'aqui,
de perto desta cidade,
chamay-o, dirá a verdade
425   se nam quereis crer a mi.
CLERIGO: Ora, sus, sus, digo eu!
ZEBRON: Este clerigo é sandeu,
onde estou que o nam crismo?
Ó fideputa judeu,
430   queres vazar o abismo?

¶*Vem Archiles, & diz:*

¶Quando Jupiter estava
em toda sua fortaleza
& seu gram poder reynava
& seu braço dominava
435   os cursos da natureza;
quando Martes influya
seus rayos de vencimento
& suas forças repartia;
quando Saturno dormia
440   com todo seu firmamento;

¶& quando o sol mais lozia,
& seus rayos apurava,
& a lũa aparecia
mais clara que o meo dia;

---

414 é · he **420 sem** · tem **427 é** · he 441 ¶& · ¶E

Gain the fame of fearsomeness,
not of riches, for that's dangerous;
415   gild your own country
with more profit than loss.
Onward, ever onward, Lisbon,
that through the world resounds
your prosperous fortune,
420   since chance rushes you on,
you always appear well.

Achilles was from here,
from close to the city:
call him, he'll tell the truth
425   if you don't want to believe me.
PRIEST: Now, courage, courage, say I!
ZEBRON: This priest is quite foolish!
What am I about, that I don't crown him?
Oh, whoreson Jew,
430   do you want to empty the abyss?

Achilles enters, and says,

When Jupiter stood
in all his might
and his great power reigned
and his arm held sway
435   over the course of nature;
when Mars poured
his conquering rays
and shared out his strength;
when Saturn slept
440   with all of his firmament;

and when the sun shone more
and cleansed with his rays;
and the moon appeared
clearer than the mid-day;

445   & quando Venus cantava;
            & quando Mercurio estava
            mais pronto em dar sapiencia;
            & quando o ceo se alegrava,
            & o mar mais manso estava,
450   & os ventos em clemencia;

            ¶& quando os sinos estavam
            com mais gloria & alegria,
            & os polos s'emfeytavam,
            & as nuvens se tiravam
455   & a luz resplandecia;
            & quando a alegria vera
            foy em todas naturezas;
            nesse dia, mes, & era,
            quando tudo isto era,
460   naceram vossas altezas.

            ¶Eu Archiles fuy criado
            nesta terra muytos dias
            & sam bem aventurado
            ver este reyno exalçado
465   & honrrado per tantas vias.
            Ó, nobres, seus naturaes,
            por Deos nam vos descudeis,
            lembre-vos que triumphaes!
            Ó, prelados, nam durmais,   [C f. 159v A]
470   clerigos, nam murmureis!

            ¶Quando Roma a todas velas
            conquistava toda a terra,
            todas donas & donzelas
            davam suas joyas belas
475   pera manter os da guerra.
            Ó, pastores da ygreja,
            moura a ceyta de Mafoma!
            Ajuday a tal peleja

---

446 & · E   451 ¶& · ¶E   453 **polos** · poolos   456 & · E

445 and when Venus gave forth song;
and when Mercury
was readier to give wisdom;
and when Heaven was happy
and calmer was the sea
450 and the winds more kind;

and when the fates had
more glory and delight,
and the poles were adorned
and the clouds pulled asunder,
455 and the light shone brightly,
and when all existence
was possessed of true cheer:
in that day, month and year,
when all this came to pass,
460 your Highnesses were born.

I, Achilles, was raised
in this land for many days;
and I am blessed
to see this realm, eminent
465 and honoured in so many ways.
Oh, this nation's nobles,
be not, by God, forgetful of yourselves,
remember that you are victors!
Oh, prelates, do not slumber!
470 Oh, clerics, do not grumble!

When Rome, at full sail,
conquered all the earth,
all the ladies and the maidens
gave their pretty jewels
475 to keep men in the wars.
Oh, shepherds of the church,
death to Mohammad's sect!
Lend your aid to such a struggle,

| | | que açoutados vos veja |
| 480 | | sem apelar pera Roma. |

¶Deveis de vender as taças,
empenhar os breviayros,
fazer vasos de cabaças,
e comer pão de rabaças
485   por vencer vossos contrayros.

ZEBRON: Assi, assi, aramá,
      dom Zote que te parece.
CLERIGO: E a mi que se me dá
      quem de seu renda nam há
490   as terças pouco lh' empece.

ACHILES: ¶Se viesse aqui Anibal
      & Eytor & Cepiam,
      vereis o que vos diram
      das cousas de Portugal
495   com verdade & com rezam.
CLERIGO: Sus, Danor, & tu, Zebram,
      venham todos tres aqui.
DANOR: Fideputa, rapaz cam,
      perro clerigo ladram!
500 ZEBRON: Mao pesar vej' eu de ti

¶*Vem Anibal, Eytor, Cepiam, e͛ ∂iz Anibal:*

      Que cousa tam escusada!
      É agora aqui Anibal,
      que vossa corte é afamada
      per todo mundo em geral.
505 EYTOR: Nem Eytor nam faz mister.
CEPIAM: Nem tam pouco Cepiam.   [*C f.* 159v B]
ANIBAL: Deveis, senhores, esperar
      em Deos, que vos há de dar
      toda Africa na vossa mão.

---

489 há · ha   **502** É · He   **503** é · he   **508** há · ha

		that it may see you whipped
480		without appealing to Rome.

You ought to sell your cups
and pawn your prayer-books,
use gourds as glasses
and eat bread made with turnips,

485		that your opponents may be vanquished.
	ZEBRON:	Just like that, damn it,
		you seem like Lord Zot!
	PRIEST:	And what does that matter to me?
		The terce is a small inconvenience
490		to he who has no income.

	ACHILES:	If Hector and Hanibal
		and Scipio came here,
		you'll see what they say
		about the things of Portugal
495		with truth and with reason.
	PRIEST:	Courage, Danor, and you, Zebron,
		bring all three here!
	DANOR:	Whoreson young pup!
		Thieving hound of a priest!
500	ZEBRON:	I foresee an evil sorrow from you.

Hannibal, Hector and Scipio enter, and Hannibal says,

		How unnecessary to have come:
		here, now, stands Hanibal,
		for your court is famed
		through all the world in general.
505	HECTOR:	Nor is there any need for Hector.
	SCIPIO:	Nor even for Scipio the African.
	HANIBAL:	My lords, you must place
		your hope in God, who'll put
		all of Africa into your hands.

510 ¶Africa foy de Christãos,
Mouros vo-la tem roubada,
capitães, ponde-lh' as mãos,
que vos vireis mais louçãos
coṁ famosa nomeada.

515 Ó, senhoras portuguesas,
gastay pedras preciosas,
donas, donzelas, duquesas,
que as taes guerras & empresas
sam propriamente vossas.

520 ¶É guerra de devaçam
por honrra de vossa terra,
cometida com rezam
formada com descriçam
contra aquella gente perra.

525 Fazey contas de bugalhos
& perlas de camarinhas,
firmaes de cabeças d'alhos:
isto sim, senhoras minhas
& esses que tendes, day-lhos.

530 ¶Ó que nam honrram vestidos
nem muy ricos atavios,
mas os feytos nobrecidos,
nam briaes d' ouro tecidos
com trepas de desvarios.

535 Day-os pera capacetes.
E vos, priores honrrados,
reparti os priorados
a soyços e a soldados,
& centum pro uno accipietis.

540 ¶A renda que apanhais
o milhor que vos podeis
nas ygrejas nam gastais,

---

511 **roubada** · ronbada 515 **senhoras portuguesas** · senhores Portugueses

510 Africa was held by Christians,
Moors have stolen it from you.
Set your hands to work, captains,
and you will become more elegant
with fame and renown.

515 Oh, ladies of Portugal,
spend your precious stones,
ladies, maidens, duchesses,
for such undertakings and such wars
are most properly yours.

520 It is a war in God's service
for the honour of your land,
undertaken with reason,
planned with good sense,
against that race of curs.

525 Make your accounts with nuts,
and pearls from berries,
make your seals from garlic bulbs
— yes indeed, my ladies, —
and those that you wear, give them up.

530 Oh, no honour can come from gowns
nor the richest dresses,
but only from noble deeds,
not garments of cloth of gold
with embroidered fripperies.

535 Give them up for helmets,
and you, honoured priors
share out your priories
to soldiers and men-at-arms
and for one, receive a hundredfold.

540 The income that you grasp
as well as you are able,
you don't spend it on churches,

---

520 ¶É · He 523 descriçam · descrjçam 528 sim · si 536 E · &

aos proves pouca dais:
eu nam sey que lhe fazeis.
545 Day a terça do que ouverdes
pera Africa conquistar,   [*C f.* 160r A]
com mais prazer que poderdes
que quanto menos tiverdes,
menos tereis que guardar.

550 ¶Ó, señores cidadãos,
fidalgos & regedores,
escutay os atambores
com ouvidos de Christãos.
E a gente popular,
555 avante, nam refusar,
ponde a vida & a fazenda,
porque pera tal contenda
ninguem deve recear.

¶Todas estas figuras se ordenaram em caracol,
& a vozes cantaram & representaram
o que se segue cantando todos:

Ta la la la lam, ta la la la lam.

560 ANIBAL: Avante, avante, senhores,
que na guerra com razam
anda Deos por capitam.

Cantam: Ta la la la lam, ta la la la lam.

ANIBAL: Guerra, guerra, todo estado,
565 guerra, guerra muy cruel,
que o gram Rey dom Manoel
contra Mouros está yrado:
tem prometido & jurado
dentro no seu coração
570 que poucos lh' escaparão.

to the poor you give but little,
I don't know what you do with it.
545   Give the terce that you get
for the conquest of Africa,
with as much gusto as you manage,
for the less you've got
the less need you look after.

550   Oh, my lords, burghers,
nobles and rulers,
harken to the drums
with Christian ears.
And you, the common people,
555   onward, do not shy,
put forth wealth and life,
for, in such a fight
no-one ought to fear.

*All these characters arrange themselves
in a ring and sing in parts
and perform what all continue singing:*

Ta-la-la-la-lam, ta-la-la-la-lam.

560   HANIBAL: Onward, ever onward, lords,
for with good reason in the war
God goes forth as captain.

They sing: Ta-la-la-la-lam, ta-la-la-la-lam.

    HANIBAL: To arms, to arms, each estate,
565   to war, to war, to war most cruel,
for the wrath of great King Manuel
is kindled 'gainst the Moors.
He has promised and has sworn
within his heart
570   that few will escape him.

Cantam: Ta la la la lam, ta la la la lam.

Anibal falando

¶Sua alteza detremina
por acrecentar a fé
fazer da mesquita sé
575 em Fez por graça divina.
Guerra, guerra muy contina,
é sua grande tençam.

Cantam: Ta la la la lam, ta la la la lam.

Anibal falando

¶Este Rey tam excelente
580 muyto bem afortunado,
tem o mundo rodeado
d'Oriente ao Ponente.
Deos muy alto omnipotente
o seu real coraçam
585 tem posto na sua mão.

¶*E com esta soyça se sayram,*
e³ fenece a susodita Tragicomedia.

---

577 é · he 582 d'Oriente · Doriente

Ta-la-la-la-lam, ta-la-la-la-lam.

Hanibal, speaking:

His Highness has decided
to magnify the faith
to make the Mosque of Fez
575   a cathedral by God's grace
War, war, without cessation,
is his great intention.

Ta-la-la-la-lam, ta-la-la-la-lam.

Hanibal, speaking:

This king of such excellence,
580   by such good fortune blessed,
has enclosed the world
from sunrise to sunset.
God most high and almighty
keeps his royal heart
585   within his own hand.

*And with this soldier's song they leave the stage,
and so ends the aforesaid Tragicomedy.*

NOTES TO THE *EXORTAÇÃO DA GUERRA*.

introduction

Tragicomedia: probably not the original designation of the genre of the play; it is a *tragicomedy* in the sense that it combined courtly earnestness with comic banter. As I pointed out in the introduction to the *Auto da Barca do Inferno*, Vicente claimed that he wrote only 'farces, comedies and moralities' when in the service of Dona Lianor; tragicomedies were written only during João III's reign.

Azamor: 'The expedition to capture from the Moors the important town of Azamor in N. W. Africa consisted of over 400 ships ... and a force of 18,000 soldiers, of which 3000 were provided by James, Duke of Braganza, who commanded the expedition. It set sail from Lisbon on the 17th of August, 1513 .... It was entirely successful and the news of the fall of Azamor caused great rejoicings both at Lisbon and at Rome' (Bell, *Four Plays*, 75).

Zebed: this devil, in the rest of the play, is called Zebrom.

7   *cova de Sebila*: The Cumæan Sibyl 'lived in a grotto beside the town of Cumæ, in the Campania of Italy.' The element of prophecy concerning national greatness witnessed in the play, and the equation of Portugal's imitation of Rome in its establishment of an empire in Africa, is foreshadowed in this reference to the Cumæan Sibyl, since 'it was from her that Tarquin the Proud, the last king of Rome, acquired the three Sibylline books which contained important prophecies concerning the fate of Rome which ... were preserved carefully in the Capitol down to the time of Sulla, when they perished in a fire': Alexander Stuart Murray, *Who's Who in Mythology: classic guide to the ancient world* (2nd edn.; London: Bracken, 1874; repr. 1994), 103.

18   *O iffante dom Luis*: (1506-1555), the fourth child of Manuel I by his second wife, Maria.

25   *leytoayro*: a form of the word *electuario*, opiate (cf. Morais, I, 651A).

30   *silha*: 'chair' or 'series of beehives' (*A* 1300B).

32   It was generally accepted that, although necromancy might, through the power of demons, produce effects beyond human ability, these effects were still always within the boundaries of natural causation. Devils were constrained to work within the general laws governing natural events, hence the necromantic cleric's enumeration of the natural occurences which he presents as marvels. See Stuart Clark, 'The scientific status of demonology', in *Occult and Scientific Mentalities in the Renaissance*, ed. Brian Vickers (Cambridge: CUP, 1984), 351-74, esp. 360-62.

38   *çafara*: Morais, II, 655A, gives for *safáro*, 'bravio, esquivo, difficil de amansar'.

46   *meo-vintem*: according to *GEPB* 16, 747A, the *meio-vintém* was a silver coin from the reign of D. Sebastião, equivalent to ten silver *reais*. The *vintém*, equal to twenty silver *reais*, was first used in Manuel's reign (*GEPB*, 36, 258B). The line, as it presently stands, may be a 'correction' by Luis Vicente, perhaps from a verse that originally read 'Farei por huũ vintem'.

91   Two Saint Cyprians are probably being referred to here. The first (†258) was a bishop of Carthage in North Africa (cp. ll. 510-11), a martyr and the author of various works. The mention of his name would recall the Christian presence in Africa. The second saint Cyprian († *c.* 300) was, with Justina, a martyr of Antioch. 'A worthless Legend made Cyprian a magician who tried to seduce the Christian Justina, but was converted by her: he later became a bishop and she an abbess; both were beheaded at Nicomedia, and sailors brought their relics to Rome' (Farmer, 99A). It is presumably because of this second saint that, according to Correas, 647A, the name of Cyprian was attached to the cave in Salamanca famed as a centre of necromancy: 'La Kueva de Salamanka ... es la Universidad i estudio xeneral ke akí ai; i sobre esta verdad an finxido patrañas para hazer maravillar a los ke vienen de nuevo: i mostravan una ke era sakristía de la parrokia de San Zebrian, debaxo de la kapilla i altar mayor, i dezían ke allí se leía en sekreto nigromanzia...'.

94   The magical words recited by the necromancer are, most probably, nonsensical; however, as some of the forms do at least seem to indicate pagan gods or have links with Arabic or Greek, it may be that Vicente has taken a spell from one of the numerous occult works then in circulation, perhaps of German origin.

Zet: given as a member of the twenty-third dynasty of Egypt, in some manuscripts of St. Jerome's *Interpretatio Chronicæ Eusebi Pamphili*, PL 27, 96B. *Zet* is also the name given to a woman with whom Mohammed committed adultery, at least according to Petrus Alfonsus, a Spanish Jew who converted to Christianity in the twelfth century (see *Dialogus*, PL 157, 1601BC).

zerregut: Carolina de Michaëlis, *Notas Vicentinas*, 501, linked this word to the German 'sehr gut'. Cp. 'Rezegut', l. 129. She also remarked that this verse was very like a toungue-twister she and her sister would repeat in Berlin: 'Zet Zeberet zetzemini/Zeb zebereb zebzemini' (*loc. cit.*).

zebet: according to Haymo of Halberstat, *Expositio in D. Pauli epistolas*, PL 117, 375A, Zebet was a god of the Philistines, the equivalent of Baal or Beelzebub.

95   *soter*: Cp. Sicard of Cremona, *Mitrale*, PL 213, 229A, 'dicitur *Jesus* Hebraice, *soter* Græce, *Salvator* Latine' [*Jesus* in Hebrew is said *soter* in Greek and *Salvator* in Latin], i.e., Saviour. *Soter* was also a Ptolomaic ruler of Egypt (Petrus Comestor, *Historia Scholastica*, PL 198, 1498C).

96   *Rehe*: According to Saint Jerome, *Quæstiones Hebraicæ in Genesim*, PL 23, 997A, *ree* is the Hebrew word meaning 'friend'. Cp. Rabanus Maurus, *Commentariuim in Genesim*, PL 107, 262C.

relinzet: a partial anagram of *linteser* (l. 129).

98   *chaves*: the word has several meanings beyond that of keys. Morais, I, 385B, records for *chave* 'poder, faculdade, dominio' [power, ability, dominion]; Santa Rosa de Viterbo, II, 98A, records one meaning of *chave* as being a measurement of land.

106 *Jurafás*: the valley of Josaphat, where it was thought that the Last Judgement would take place (Michaëlis, 421).

119 *bibaras*: i.e., *víboras*.

130 *zamzorep*: *zorep* may be linked to the Arabic verb, *zariba*, 'to flow' (Wehr, 435B).

131 *siro* is perhaps to be taken as meaning Syrian.
nafezeri may be linked to the Arabic *fazara*, 'to tear, rend, burst' (*Ibid.*, 833A).

140 *ladram*: the severing of a theif's ears was a common punishment throughout Europe; according to Santa Rosa de Viterbo, 450B, it was decreed in 1499 for *peões* found stealing purses in Portugal.

148 *Zobete*: seemingly a nonce-word. *Zote* is discussed at line 487, and *Zobete* would seem to be a variant upon that insult. The *OED* 20, 815B, gives as the meaning for the U. S. slang, *zob*, whose origin is unknown, 'a weak or contemptible person; a fool'. *Zobete* may be linked to the Greek Διο-, *of Zeus*, e.g., Διοπαιζ, *son of Zeus*. Cp. l. 94, 'zebet'.

151 *almude*: equal to twelve gallons (Bell, *Four Plays*, 76).

156-179 This section is thick with the names of Portuguese wine-producing areas. As many of the wines mentioned are little known beyond Portugal, and in order to add some zest to the translation, I have preferred the names of European wines.

156 *Landeira* is a village in the diocese of Évora, on the Marateca river. It possessed a chapel of the Order of Santiago (*GEPB* 14, 657B).

157 *Cartaxo*: a town in the Ribatejo, famed for its wines.

159 *Lumear* (nowadays, Lumiar): a wine-producing district very close to Lisbon.

159 *Mealhada*: a town in the Bairrada region of Portugal, famous for its wines.

160 *Canada*: GEPB 5, 677A-78B, gives numerous places as having this name; a 'canada' was also a measure of liquids, being a twelfth of an *almude*, equivalent in Lisbon to 1·4 litres.

162 *terrantés*: an indigenous grape variety. Correas, 180B, has the following, 'Uva torrontrés, ni la komas ni la des, para vino bueno es...' [Torrontres grape, don't eat it or give it, good for wine it is].

163 Both the English and the French were famed for their immoderate consumption of alcohol. See Braga, IV, 135; Michaëlis, 416.

168 *Arruda*: probably Arruda dos Vinhos, Estremadura.
Caparica: a village four kilometres from Almada, a kilometre and a half from the Tejo.

173 *Pedra da Estrema*: situated near Lisbon, celebrated for its wines. It was more usually written *Pedra do Extremo*. See José Pedro Machado, *Dicionário Onomástico Etimológico da Língua Portuguesa* (3 vols.; Lisboa, Editorial Confluência, 1984), 611A.

176 *Seixal*: a town seventeen kilometres from Barreiro and twenty-nine from Setúbal, situated near the Tejo.

177 *Almada* is close to Seixal and Caparica.

178 *alfaqui*: Morais, I, 90A, 'o mestre, ou Sabio da Lei, titulo usado dos Africanos'. The word is derived from the Arabic *al-faqīH* (Machado, *Dicionário Etymologico*, 191A). Cp. l. 485.

179 *Tojal*: Pedro Machado, 1416A, records a document of 1444, 'No tojall termo desta çidade de lixboa'; Bell, *Four Plays*, 179, situates it near Olivais, in the Lisbon district. Tojal means 'whin-moor, gorse-common'.

194 *terças*: a contribution for the crusade levied from the clergy. It was a third of the clergy's income, usually destined for the upkeep of churches (Giles Constable, *Monastic Tithes from their Origins to the Twelfth Century* (Cambridge: CUP, 1964), 47). The first gift of the 'terce' to a king in the Iberian peninsula had been made to Fernando III, king of Castile and León, by Innocent IV in 1247 for the campaign against Sevile: Peter Linehan, *The Spanish Church and the Papacy in the Thirteenth Century*, Cambridge Studies in Medieval Life and Thought, 3rd. Series, 4 (Cambridge: CUP, 1971), 111.

195 *alifante*: the elephant sent by Dom Manuel to Pope Leo X as part of the embassy of Tristão da Cunha in 1514. The pope was delighted by the gift and granted Manuel the *terças* to be used in crusades against the infidel, as well as indulgences to all those who contributed to the North African war. See Bell, *Four Plays*, 75.

200 *sam Polo*: *Polo* is the Venetian form of *Paulo*, to whom a major church is dedicated in that city. The name may have been transmitted as part of the nautical terminology the Portuguese adopted (cf. *caro*, at line 3 of the *Auto da Barca do Inferno*, which also came from a Venetian source) — oaths invoking saints were a key part of the sailor's trade. I presume the use of *Polo* and *Paulo* is meant to be taken as comic ignorance, in that the names refer to the same saint.

215 *Policena*: Polixena, the daughter of Priam, king of Troy, and Hecuba. She fell in love with Achilles and, after his death, was sacrificed upon his tomb on the instruction of the latter's ghost: N. G. L. Hammond and H. H. Scullard, *The Oxford Classical Dictionary* (2nd edn.; Oxford: The Clarendon Press, 1970), 856A.

229 'In 1517 among other exotic presents a rhinoceros was sent to the Pope. It was, however, shipwrecked and drowned on the way. It had the honour of being drawn by Albrecht Dürer' (Bell, *Four Plays*, 76).

238 *bellenissima*: a nonce-word, coined by Vicente.

242 Priam, king of Troy.

243 *Cesar*: Julius Cæsar (†31 B.C.). Both Priam and Cesar refer to Manuel.

244 *Ecuba*: Hecuba, wife of Priam. Here referring to Manuel's queen, Dona Maria.

246 *Febo & Diana*: the gods of sun and moon, Phœbus and Diana.

249 The following lines refer to the future João III (born 1502, reigned 1521-1557).

257 This 'prophecy' may well be a later addition to the play, perhaps when Gil Vicente was compiling his works at the end of his life, for here he indicates that João was to be superior to Manuel.

259 The Infanta Isabel (1503-1539) married the Habsburg Emperor Charles V (†1558). Charles, born in 1500, became king of Spain in 1516. However, he was not elected Emperor until 1519 (see John Lynch, *Spain under the Habsburgs* (2 vols.; New York: OUP, 1965), I, 31-42). This stanza, therefore, must have been written after the 1513/1514 date of the play.

266 The stanza alludes to a marriage of Dom Fernando (1507-1534) to Dona Guiomar Coutinho, daughter of the Count of Marialva, Dom Francisco Coutinho, in 1530. It was therefore written slightly before 1530 but not later than 1534, when the marriage was dissolved.

275 The Infanta Dona Beatriz (1504-1521) married Carlos, Duke of Savoy, in 1521.

284 *rosas*: the ladies of the court (Braga, IV, 141).

306 It was a commonplace in *Cancioneiro* poetry to contrast the *pena* of love with that of Hell or Purgatory. See Jane Yvonne Tillier, *Religious Elements in Fifteenth-Century Spanish Cancioneros* (unpublished PhD. thesis, Cambridge, 1985), 133-138.

311-318 This stanza is one line too short in comparison to the others. Given that the shortness of Polixena's reply (cp. ll. 316-341 and 346-371), it may be surmised that the Inquisition has excised a passage it found theologically suspicious: there may well be a lacuna in the text of around 21 lines; both of Polixena's other speeches are twenty-five lines long.

313-14 Cp. Dante, *Inferno*, V, 103-6, 'Amor, ch'a nullo amato amar perdona,/mi prese del costui piacer sí forte,/che, come vedi, ancor non m'abbandona' (*La Commedia*, 23). ['Love, which to no loved one permits excuse for not loving, took me so strongly with delight in him, that, as thou seest, even now it leaves me not' (*The Inferno*, 55).]

320 *desamado*: the *Copilaçam* gives *desañado*, which might conceal an original which read either *desamado* or *desdenhado* (disdained), although the *m* of *desamado* would be more likely to give rise to the *ñ* of *desañado* than would *desdenhado*; the acceptance of the latter would imply the change of three letters.

341 Bell, *Four Plays*, 76, suggests the 'Godos' should be taken as meaning 'of ancient race, "Norman blood"'.

345 *dioso* was a contemporary form of *idoso*, aged, elderly.

367 *perros*: Muslims.

368 *Pantisilea*: Penthesilea, Queen of the Amazons, who, according to the *Æthiopis* (a lost epic poem composed as a sequel to the *Iliad* and ascribed to Arctinus of Miletus), attacked the Greeks at Troy after the death of Hector, and was killed by Achilles. As with Polixena, various legends described Achilles falling in love with her. See Hammond, 798B.

384 *pequenas quadrilhas*: a reference to the victories in India.

420 *emfuna*: Morais, I, 696A, gives the following definition of *enfunar*, 'encher, entesar' (i.e., of sails), although it can also mean, 'to swell with pride'.

422-23 'An allusion to the legend that places the island of Skyros, where Achilles lived as a girl amongst the daughters of King Lykomedes, on the coast of Portugal' (Michäelis, 202).

stage direction: there are several accounts of Achilles appearing as a ghost. In the *Odyssey* (XI), Odysseus speaks to him in Hades. There was a tradition that he appeared to the Greeks demanding that Polixena be sacrificed upon his tomb (see *The Oxford Companion to Classical Literature*, ed. M. C. Howatson (Oxford: O. U. P., 1989), 4a), and, in the *Life of Appollonius of Tyana*, V, xi-xii, Appollonius talks to Achilles' ghost who offers him advice. See *The Life of Appollonius of Tyana, translated from the Greek of Philostratus*, ed. E. Berwick (London: T. Payne, 1809), 98-99.

431-60 See, on this passage, Luis de Albuquerque, 'A astrologia em Gil Vicente', *Arquivos do Centro Cultural Português*, 3 (1971), 54-75, who points out that Vicente is far from being the rationalist debunker of astrology that critics have made of him on the basis of Mercury in the *Auto da Feira*. Vicente is perfectly happy to use astrological portents in order to praise the monarch.

460 Cp. ll. 422-23.

471 An allusion to the opening of Gómez Manrique's *Decir* entitled *La esclamación e querella de la governación* (Julio Rodríguez Puértolas, ed., *Poesía crítica y satírica del siglo XV*, Clásicos Castalia, 114 (Madrid: Castalia, 1981), 211-5, ll. 1-10 at 211.

Cuando Roma conquistaba	*When Rome conquereed*
Quinto Fabio la regía,	*Quintus Fabius ruled it*
e Çipion guerreaba,	*and Scipio waged war;*
Titus Livius discribía,	*Livy described it all:*
las donzellas e matronas	*the young girls and the matrons*
por la honra de su tierra	*for the honour of their land*
desguarnían sus personas	*unadorned their bodies*
para sostener la guerra.	*to keep the war in hand.*
En un pueblo donde moro	*In a town where I dwell*
al nezio fazen alcalde ...	*they make the fool the mayor ...*

The rest of Manrique's poem is a burlesque characterisation of his 'pueblo'; it would seem to be only his invocation of the classical world that interested the playwright. Generally, in this play, Gil Vicente is keen to stress how superior the Portuguese are when compared with classical times; however, in this example, the Roman women are seen to be superior, for their Portuguese sisters have to be encouraged to copy them by donating jewels to the fighting fund.

487 *Zote*: 'il s'agit avant tout d'un terme péjoratif pour désigner les ecclésiastiques': I. S. Révah, 'Quelques mots du lexique de Gil Vicente', *Revista Brasileira de Filologia*, 2 (1956), 143-54, at 153-54. Bell, *Four Plays*, 78, links *zote* with the Spanish words *zote, zopo, zopenco, zoquete*, a dolt, the low Latin *zottus*, the Dutch *zot*, and the French and English *sot*.

491 *Anibal*: Hannibal (†183 B.C.), Carthaginian leader who crossed into Italy to wage war on Rome in 219 B.C..

492 *Eytor*: Hector, son of Priam, king of Troy, killed, according to the *Illiad*, by Achilles. The *Æneid* (II, 268 *et seq.*) describes Hector appearing to Æneas and instructing him to flee Troy.

Scipiam: Publius Cornelius Scipio (†183 B.C.), known as Scipio Africanus, who waged war against Carthage in Africa. In Cicero's *Somnium Scipionis* (The Dream of Scipio), he appeared to Scipio Æmilianus (†129) in a dream, 'foretold his future, and exhorted him to virtue, patriotism, and disregard of human fame; for those who have served the country well there will be the reward of a heavenly habitation in the afterlife' (Howatson, 531A).

500 Cp. *Auto da Índia*, l. 68.

524 *perra*: see at line 367.

527 *cabeças d'alhos*: according to Morais, I, 310B, these are pine-cones, although another meaning of 'brooch' or 'pin' clearly existed in Vicente's day, as indicted by l. 529.

539 *centum pro uno accipietis*: a Latin phrase, playing with the biblical form of Matthew 19: 29, 'Et omnes qui relinquerit domum, vel fratres, aut sorores, aut patrem, aut uxorem, aut filios, aut agros propter nomen meum, centuplum accipiet, et vitam æternam possidebit' ['And every man that has foresaken home, or brothers or sisters, or father, or mother, or wife, or children, or lands for my name's sake, shall receive his reward a hundred fold, and obtain everlasting life']. As can be seen, Vicente's Latin phrase is not identical with the relevant phrase in the Vulgate; it is a rewording. One should note, however, that the Latin is correct.

ABBREVIATIONS

A   Aurélio Buarque de Holanda, *Novo Dicionário Aurélio da Língua Portuguesa: 2ª edição, revista e aumentada* (Rio de Janeiro: Editora Nova Fronteira, 1986).

Braga   Marquês Braga, ed., *Gil Vicente: obras completas*, Coleção de Clássicos Sá da Costa (6 vols.; Lisboa: Sá da Costa, 1942-44).

GEPB   *Grande Enciclopédia Portuguesa e Brasileira* (40 vols.; Lisboa: Editorial Enciclopédia, 1960).

Morais   António de Moraes Silva, *Diccionario da lingua portugueza* (2nd edn.; 2 vols.; Lisboa: 1813).

OED   Oxford English Dictionary, ed. J. A. Simpson and E. S. C. Weiner (2nd edn.; Oxford: The Clarendon Press, 1989).

PL   *Patrologiæ cursus completus. Series latina*, ed. J.-P. Migne (221 vols.; Paris, 1844-1864).

T   James L. Taylor, *A Portuguese-English Dictionary* (London: Harrap, 1959).

BIBLIOGRAPHY

Albertus Magnus, O. P. (attrib.), *Libellus de natura animalium*, ed. Paola Navone, in *Le proprietà degli animali*, Testi della cultura italiana, 5 (Genova: Costa & Nolan, 1983), 196-346.

Albuquerque, Luis de, 'A astrologia em Gil Vicente', *Arquivos do Centro Cultural Português*, 3 (1971), 54-75.

—, ed., *Crónica do Descobrimento e Conquista da Índia pelos Portugueses* (Lourenço Marquês: Universidade de Lourenço Marquês, 1974).

Alçada, João Nuno, 'Para um novo significado da presença de Todo o Mundo e Ninguém no *Auto da Lusitânia*', *Arquivos do Centro Cultural Português* 21 (1985), 199-271.

Alemán, Mateo, *Guzmán de Alfarache*, ed. Benito Brancaforte, Letras Hispánicas, 86 (2 vols.; Madrid: Cátedra, 1979).

Alfonso X, *Cantigas de Santa Maria*, ed. Walter Mettmann, Clásicos Castalia, 134, 172, 178 (Madrid: Castalia, 1986-89).

Alonso, Martín, *Diccionario medival español: desde la Glosas emilianenses y Silenses (s. X) hasta el siglo XV* (2 vols.; Salamanca: Universidad Pontificia, 1986).

BIBLIOGRAPHY

Amaro de Oliveira, Luís, ed., *Gil Vicente: Farsa chamada Auto da Índia* (Porto-Coimbra-Lisboa: Porto Editora-Livraria Arnado-Emp. Lit. Fluminense, 1977).

Asensio, E., 'Las fuentes de las *Barcas* de Gil Vicente: lógica intelectual e imaginación dramática', *Estudios portugueses* (Paris: Fundação Calouste Gulbenkian-Centro Cultural Português, 1974), 59-77; reprinted from *Bulletin d'Histoire du Théâtre Portugais*, 4 (1953), 207-37.

Bagley, Vimala, and Richard Daniel de Puma, eds., *Rome and India: the ancient sea trade* (Madison, Wisconsin: The University of Wisconsin Press, 1991).

Beda Venerabilis, *De computo dialogus*, PL 90, 647-652.

Bell, Aubrey F. G., *Four Plays of Gil Vicente. Edited from the editio princeps (1562), with translation and notes* (Cambridge: CUP, 1920).

Benedictine Monks of St. Augustine's Abbey, Ramsgate, eds., *The Book of Saints. A dictionary of servants of God canonised by the Catholic Church: extracted from the Roman and other Martyrologies* (3rd edn.; London: A & C Black, 1934).

Berardinelli, Cleonice, ed., *Antologia do teatro de Gil Vicente* (Rio de Janeiro: Grifo, 1971).

Boucquey, Thierry, *Mirages de la Farce: fête des fous, Bruegel et Molière*, Purdue University Monographs in Romance Languages, 33 (Amsterdam-Philadelphia: John Benjamins, 1991).

Braamcamp Freire, Anselmo, *Vida e obras de Gil Vicente, 'trovador, mestre da balança'* (2nd. edn.; Lisboa: Novas Edições 'Ocidente', 1944).

Brundage, James A., 'The crusader's wife: a canonistic quandry', in his *The Crusades, Holy Wars and Canon Law* (Aldershot: Variorum, 1991), XV 427-41.

—, *Medieval Canon Law and the Crusader* (Madison: University of Wisconsin Press, 1969).

Cardoso, José, & Domingos Guimarães de Sá, eds., *Luís de Camões: Teatro (Anfitriões, El-Rei Seleuco e Filodemo)* (Braga, 1980).

Carvalhão Buescu, Maria Leonor, ed., *Copilaçam de todalas obras de Gil Vicente* (2 vols.; Lisboa: Imprensa Nacional - Casa da Moeda, 1984).

Castro, Ivo de, and Maria Ana Ramos, 'Estratégia e táctica da transcrição', in *Critique textuelle portugaise: actes du colloque, Paris, 20-24 octobre 1981* (Paris: Fondation Calouste Gulbenkean, 1986), 99-122.

Clark, Stuart, 'The scientific status of demonology', in *Occult and Scientific Mentalities in the Renaissance* (Cambridge: CUP, 1984), 351-374.

Constable, Giles, *Monastic Tithes from their Origins to the Twelfth Century* (Cambridge: CUP, 1964).

Correas, Gonzalo, *Vocabulario de refranes y frases proverbiales (1625)*, ed. Louis Combet (Bordeaux: Institut d'Études Ibériques et Ibéro-Américaines de l'Université de Bordeaux, 1967).

Costa Ramalho, Américo da, 'A "feia acção" de Gil Vicente', *Estudos sobre a época do Renascimento* (Coimbra: Instituto de Alta Cultura, 1969), 124-129.

—, 'Uma bucólica grega em Gil Vicente', in *Estudos sobre a época do Renascimento* (Coimbra: Instituto de Alta Cultura, 1969), 130-149.

BIBLIOGRAPHY

Cunha Gonçalves, Luiz da, 'Gil Vicente e os homens do fôro', in *Gil Vicente: vida e obra. Série de conferências realizadas na Academia das Ciências de Lisboa* ... (Lisboa: Academia das Ciências de Lisboa, 1939), 205-55

Dante Alighieri, *La Commedia secondo l'Antica Vulgata*, ed. Giorgio Petrocchi (Torino: Einaudi, 1975).

—, *The Inferno of Dante Alighieri*, tr. I. G., The Temple Classics, ed. Israel Gollancz (London: J. M. Dent, 1906).

Diax, Aida Fernanda, ed., *Cancioneiro Geral de Garcia de Resende* (4 vols.; Lisboa: Imprensa Nacional-Casa da Moeda, 1993).

Enciclopeida universal ilustrada europeo-americana (Madrid-Barcelona: Espasa-Calpe, 1927).

Edwards, John, 'Expulsion or indoctrination? The fate of Portugal's Jews in and after 1497', in *Portuguese, Brazilian and African Studies: studies presented to Clive Willis on his Retirement*, ed. T. F. Earle and Nigel Griffin (Warminster, England: Aris & Phillips, 1995), 87-96.

Farmer, D. H., *The Oxford Dictionary of Saints* (Oxford: Clarendon Press, 1978).

Figueira Valverde, J., *La Cantiga CIII: noción del tiempo y gozo eterno en la narrativa medieval* (Santiago de Compostela, 1936; repr. Vigo, 1982).

Figueiredo, Fidelino de, *A Épica Portuguesa no século XVI: subsídios documentares para uma theoria geral da epopêa*, Separata do boletim CI — Letras — n°. 6 (São Paulo: Faculdade de Filosofia, Ciências e Letras da Universidade de São Paulo, 1950).

Fonseca, Quirino da, 'Comentário ao verso, "Ora venha ho caro a ree" do *Auto de Moralidade* de Gil Vicente, edição de 1516 ou 1517 (*Auto da Barca do Inferno*), in *Gil Vicente: vida e obra. Série de conferências realizadas na Academia das Ciências de Lisboa* ... (Lisboa: Academia das Ciências de Lisboa, 1939), 489-547.

Frèches, Claude-Henri, 'L'économie du salut dans la trilogie des "Barques"', in *Mélanges à la mémoire d'André Joucla-Ruau* (2 vols.; Aix-en-Provence: Éditions de l'Université de Provence, 1977), II, 723-736.

—, *Le Théâtre neo-latin au Portugal (1550-1745)* (Paris-Lisbonne: Librairie A. G. Nizet-Librairie Bertrand, 1964).

Garcia da Cruz, Maria Leonor, *Gil Vicente e a sociedade portuguesa de quinhentos: leitura crítica num mundo 'de cara atrás' (as personagens e o palco da sua acção)*, Colecção construir o passado, 21 (Lisboa: Gradiva, 1990).

Geiler, Johannes, *Navicula Penitentie, per excellentissimum sacre pagine doctorem, Joannem Keyserspergium Argentinensium Concionatorem predicata. A Jacobo Otthero collecta* (Augsburg, 1511; repr. Strasbourg, 1512).

Gratianus, *Concordia Discordantia Canonum*, PL 187, 27-1870.

Hammond, N. G. L., and H. H. Scullard, *The Oxford Classical Dictionary* (2nd edn.; Oxford: The Clarendon Press, 1970).

Hart, Thomas R., ed., *Gil Vicente: farces and festival plays* (Eugene, Oregon: University of Oregon, 1972).

Haymo Halberstatensis, *Expositio in D. Pauli epistolas*, PL 117, 361-938.

223

BIBLIOGRAPHY

Herculano, A., ed., *Vita Theotonii*, in *Portugaliæ Monumenta Historica a sæculo octavo post Christum usque ad quintumdecimum, Scriptores I*, (Lisbon, 1856), 79-88.

Hieronymus Stridonensis, *Interpretatio Chronicæ Eusebii Pamphili*, PL 27, 33-674.

—, *Quæstiones Hebraicæ in Genesim*, PL 935-1010.

Hildegard of Bingen, *Physica, seu Subtilitates diversarum naturarum creaturum*, PL 197, 1117-1352

Howatson, M. C., ed., *The Oxford Companion to Classical Literature* (Oxford: O. U. P., 1989).

Juan Ruiz, Arçipreste de Hita, *Libro de Buen Amor*, ed. G. B. Gybbon-Monypenny, Clásicos Castalia, 161 (Madrid: Castalia, 1988).

Kantorowicz, Ernst H., *The King's Two Bodies: a study in mediæval political theology* (Princeton, 1987).

Keen, Maurice, *Chivalry* (New Haven-London: Yale University Press, 1984).

Kelly, J. N. D., ed., *The Oxford Dictionary of Popes* (Oxford: O. U. P., 1986).

Knox, Ronald, tr., *The Holy Bible: a translation from the Latin Vulgate in the light of the Hebrew and Greek originals* (New York: Sheed and Ward, 1956).

Lafer, Celso, 'O judeu em Gil Vicente', in *Gil Vicente e Camões (Dois estudos sobre a cultura portuguesa do século XVI)*, Ensaios, 50 (São Paulo: Ática, 1978), 19-101.

Lewicka, Halina, *Études sur l'ancienne farce française* (Paris-Warszawa, Klincksieck-PWN, 1974).

Ley, Charles David, ed., *Gil Vicente: Auto da Barca do Inferno (según la edición de 1517)*, Biblioteca Hispano-Lusitana, 2 (Madrid: Consejo Superior de Investigaciones Científicas, Patronato Menéndez Pelayo, Instituto Antonio de Nebrija, 1946).

Linehan, Peter, *The Spanish Church and the Papacy in the Thirteenth Century*, Cambridge Studies in Medieval Life and Thought, Third Series, 4 (Cambridge: CUP, 1971).

López Morales, Humberto, 'Parodía y caricatura en los orígenes de la farsa castellana', in *Teatro Comico fra Medio Evo e Rinascimento: la farsa. Convegno di studi del Centro Studi sul Teatro Medioevale e Rinascimentale, Roma, 30 Ottobre – 2 Novembre 1986*, ed. M. Chiabò & F. Doglio (Roma: Centro Studi sul Teatro Medioevale e Rinascimentale, 1987), 211-226.

Lourdes Saraiva, Maria de, *Gil Vicente: Sátiras sociais* (Lisboa: Publicações Europa-América, 1975).

Lynch, John, *Spain under the Habsburgs* (2 vols.; New York: OUP, 1965).

Machado, José Pedro, *Dicionário Onomástico Etimológico da Língua Portuguesa* (3 vols.; Lisboa, Editorial Confluência, 1984).

—, *Influência arábica no vocabulário português* (Lisboa: Álvaro Pinto, 1958).

Marques Esparteiro, António, *Dicionário ilustrado de marinharia* (Lisboa: Livraria Clássica, 1943).

Mateus, Osório, *India*, Vicente: colecção dirigida por Osório Mateus (Lisboa: Quimera, 1988).

McPeeters, Dean W., 'La Celestina en Portugal en el siglo XVI', in *'La Celestina' en su contorno social. Actas del I Congreso Internacional sobre 'La Celestina'*, Colección Summa, 2 (Barcelona: Borras, 1977), 367-76.

224

BIBLIOGRAPHY

Michaëlis de Vasconcellos, Carolina, ed., *Poesias de Francisco de Sá de Miranda* (Halle, 1885).

—, *Notas vicentinas: preliminares duma edição crítica das obras de Gil Vicente. Notas I a V incluindo a introdução à edição facsimilada do centro de estúdios históricos de Madrid* (Lisboa: Edição da Revista 'Ocidente', 1949).

Morgan, Alison, *Dante and the Medieval Other World* (Cambridge, 1990).

Morton, E. D., *Martini A-Z of Fencing* (London: Macdonald, 1988).

Moura, Gilberto, ed., *Teatro de Gil Vicente: Auto da Índia, Auto da Barca do Inferno, Auto da Barca do Purgatório, Farsa de Inês Pereira*, Biblioteca Ulisséia de autores portugueses, 10 (Lisbon: Ulisséia, s.d.).

Murray, Alexander Stuart, *Who's Who in Mythology: classic guide to the ancient world* (2nd edn.; London: Bracken: 1874, repr. 1994).

Nebrija, Antonio de, *Vocabulario de romance en latín: transcripción crítica de la edición revisada por el autor (Sevilla, 1516)*, ed. Gerald J. MacDonald (Madrid: Castalia, 1973).

Novaes Coelho, Nelly, 'As alcoviteiras vicentinas', *Alfa*, 4 (1963), 83-105

Nunes, J. J., 'Uma lenda medieval: o monge e o passarinho', *Boletim da 2ª Classe, Academia das Sciencias de Lisboa*, 12 (1917-18), 389-405.

Ombres, Robert, O. P., 'Images of Healing: the making of the traditions concerning purgatory', *Eastern Churches Review*, 8 (1976), 128-38.

Palla, Maria José, 'O parvo e o mundo às avessas em Gil Vicente — algumas reflexões', in *Temas vicentinos: actas do colóquio em torno da obra de Gil Vicente. Teatro da Cornucópia 1988* (Lisboa: Ministério da Educação. Instituto de Cultura e Língua Portuguesa, 1992), 87-99.

Petrus Alfonsus, *Dialogus*, PL 157, 535-672.

Petrus Comestor, *Historia Scholastica*, PL 198, 1049-1722.

Philostratus, *The Life of Appollonius of Tyana, translated from the Greek of Philostratus*, ed. E. Berwick (London: T. Payne, 1809).

Pimenta Ferro Tavares, Maria José, *Pobreza e morte em Portugal na Idade média* (Lisboa: Presença, 1989).

Pires de Lima, Augusto C., *Os autos das Barcas de Gil Vicente* (Porto, 1985?).

Quintela, Paolo, ed., *Gil Vicente: Auto de Moralidade da Embarcação do Inferno, textos das duas primeiras 'edições avulsas' e das 'Copilações' ... com um apêndice que contém a 'Tragicomedia Alegorica del Parayso y del Infierno'* (Coimbra: Atlântida, 1946).

Rabanus Maurus, *Commentarium in Genesim*, PL 107, 439-670.

Rebello, Luiz Franciso, *O Primitivo Teatro Português* (Lisbon: Biblioteca Breve, 1977).

Reckert, Stephen, *Gil Vicente: espíritu y letra*, Biblioteca Románica Hispánica, IV, 10 (Madrid: Gredos, 1976), 175-78.

Reimerus Sancti Laurentii Leodinensis, *De claris scriptoribus monasterii sui*, PL 204, 15-40.

Révah, I. S., ed., *Gil Vicente: Auto da Moralidade* (Lisboa: O Mundo do Livro, 1959).

—, ed., *Recherches sur les œuvres de Gil Vicente, I: Édition critique du premier 'Auto das Barcas'* (Lisbonne: Bibliothèque du Centre d'Histoire du Théâtre Portugais, 1951).

225

BIBLIOGRAPHY

—, 'Quelques mots du lexique de Gil Vicente', *Revista Brasileira de Filologia*, 2 (1956), 143-54.

Rodrigues Lapa, M., *Vocabulário galego-português* (Coimbra: Galaxia, 1965).

Rodríguez Puértolas, Julio, ed., *Poesía crítica y satírica del siglo XV*, Clásicos Castalia, 114 (Madrid: Castalia, 1981)

Russell, Peter E., ed., *Rojas, Fernando de: Comedia o Tragicomedia de Calisto y Melibea,*, Clásicos Castalia, 191 (Madrid: Castalia, 1991).

Sadie, Stanley, ed., *The New Grove Dictionary of Music and Musicians* (London: Macmillan, 1980).

Santa Rosa de Viterbo, Fr. Joaquim de, *Elucidário das palavras, termos e frases que em Portugal antigamente se usaram e que hoje regularmente se ignoram: obra indispensável para entender sem erro os documentos mais raros e preciosos que entre nós se conservam*, edição crítica por Mário Fiúza (2 vols., Porto: Livraria Civilização, 1966; 1st edn., 1798-1799).

Schevill, Ferdinand, *Medieval and Renaissance Florence*, vol. II: *The coming of Humanism and the age of the Medici* (New York: Harper & Row, 1961); first printed as *History of Florence* (New York: Harcourt, Brace & Co., 1936).

Serjeant, R. B., *The Portuguese off the South Arabian Coast: Hadrami Chronicles with Yemeni and European Accounts of Dutch Pirates off Mocha in the seventeenth century* (Oxford: Clarendon Press, 1963).

Sicardus Cremonensis, *Mitrale seu de officiis ecclesiasticis summa*, PL 213, 13-434.

Spina, Segismundo, ed., *Gil Vicente: O Velho da horta, Auto da Barca do Inferno, A Farsa de Inês Pereira*, (8th edn.; São Paulo: Brasiliense, 1977).

—, ed., *Obras-primas do teatro vicentino* (São Paulo: Difusão Européia do Livro–Editôra da Universidade de São Paulo, 1970).

Stegagno Picchio, Luciana, 'Per una semiologia dell'aldilà: l'idea di purgatorio in Gil Vicente', in *Homenaje a Eugenio Asensio* (Madrid: Gredos, 1988), 447-58.

Suárez, José I., *Vicentine Comedy within the Serio-Comic Mode* (Mississagua, Ontario: Associated University Presses, 1993).

Subrahmanyam, Sanjay, *The Portuguese Empire in Asia, 1500-1700: a political and economic history* (London: Longman, 1993).

Teyssier, Paul, '*Glória* dans Gil Vicente e Camões', *Ibérica*, 1 (1977), 295-311

—, *La langue de Gil Vicente* (Paris: Librairie C. Klincksieck, 1959).

—, 'Le système des deictiques spatiaux en portugais aux XIVe, XVe et XVIe siècles', *Études de littérature et de linguistique* (Paris: Fondation C. Gulbenkian, 1990), 161-98.

—, 'L'envers de l'épopée', *Critique: revue générale des publications françaises et étrangères*, 46 (1988), 676-83.

—, 'L'humanisme portugais et l'Europe', in his *Études de littérature et de linguistique* (Paris: Fondation Calouste Gulbenkian, 1990), 1-26; first published in *L'Humanisme portugais et l'Europe. Actes du XXIe Colloque International d'Études Humanistes, Tours, 3-13 juillet 1978* (Paris: Fondation Calouste Gulbenkian, 1984), 821-45.

—, 'Normes pour une édition des œuvres de Gil Vicente', in *Critique textuelle portugaise: actes du colloque, Paris, 20-24 octobre 1981* (Paris: Fondation Calouste Gulbenkian, 1986), 123-130.

Tillier, Jane Yvonne, *Religious Elements in Fifteenth-Century Spanish Cancioneros* (unpublished PhD. thesis, Cambridge, 1985).

Tirso de Molina, *Marta la piedosa — El burlador de Sevilla*, ed. Antonio Prieto (Madrid: Editorial Magisterio Español, 1974).

Thomaz, Luis Filipe F. R., 'Factions, interests and messianism: the politics of Portuguese expansions in the East, 1500-1521', *The Indian Economic and Social History Review*, 28 (1991), 97-109.

—, 'L'idée impériale manueline', in *La Découverte, le Portugal et l'Europe. Actes du Colloque, Paris, les 26, 27 et 28 mai 1988* (Paris: Fondation Calouste Gulbenkian, 1990), 35-103

Thompson, Stith, *Motif Index of Folk Literature* (6 vols.; Compenhagen: Rosenhilde & Bagger, 1955-1958).

Wallace, Joy E., 'Transposing the Enterprise of Adventure: Malory's "Take the Adventure" and French Tradition', in *Shifts and Transpositions in Medieval Narrative: a festschrift for Dr. Elspeth Kennedy*, ed. Karen Pratt (Cambridge: D. S. Brewer, 1994), 151-167.

Wehr, Hans, *A Dictionary of Modern Written Arabic*, ed. J. M. Cowan (4th edn.; Wiesbaden: Otto Harrassowitz, 1979).

Wickersham Crawford, J. P., 'Echarse pullas:—A popular form of *tenzone*', *Romanic Review*, 6 (1915), 150-164

Wilson, Arnold T., *The Persian Gulf: an historical sketch from the earliest times to the beginning of the twentieth century* (1st. edn., 1928. 2nd. edn.; London: Allen & Unwin, 1954).

A brief guide to pronunciation
of the Portuguese contained in Gil Vicente's plays

Portuguese at the time of Gil Vicente was undergoing a series of changes which eventually led to the evolution of the modern system of pronunciation of European Portuguese. It is impossible to say exactly how Portuguese was pronounced in the first two decades of the sixteenth century, but some basic lines would seem to be clear. In this short 'guide', I intend to produce some few basic ideas concerning contemporary pronunciation.[1]

1. Vowels.

As with modern Portuguese, it would seem that an *-o* at the end of a word was pronounced as a *-u*. However, unlike modern Lisboetan, *-e* at the end of a word would seem to have been pronounced as something close to an *-i*. Thus in Vicente's *Auto de Inês Pereira* we find *vale* being rhymed with the Moorish name, *Ale* (ie., *Ali*), which indicates that, if *-e* was not quite being pronounced as an *-i*, speakers of the period had lost the ability to distinguish between words that ended in *-i* and those which ended in *-e*. A similar inability to distinguish between vowels was found between an unstressed *-o* or *-u* in a word, the pronunciation of both being assimilated to that of a *-u*: *aumir* was also spelt *somir*, and *dormir* as *durmir*. It would seem that all nasal vowels (spelt *-om* or *-am* or *-ão* in the texts) had been regularized to the same pronunciation as the modern Portuguese *-ão*. However, it must be remembered that Gil Vicente probably originated in Guimarães, an area of linguistic conservatism which maintained a distinction between *-om* and *-ão*, and so I have preferred to keep the conventions of the period, lest Vicente be repeating the conventions of his native dialect rather than those of the Lisboetan of the period. The conjunction of vowels *-ou-* was pronounced as [ǫw] and not the modern [ǫ], a pronunciation which occurred in the seventeenth century.

2. Consonants.

In the Portuguese of Vicente's time some differences between the pronunciation of consonants were still maintained in the language although they have since disappeared. The most striking feature of modern Portuguese, the [š] was not nearly as common: it was only pronounced in connection with the letter *x*; *ch-* was pronounced [tš] as Castilian pronounces *ch-* (eg. *macho*) or as Italian pronounces a 'soft' *c* in *ci, ce*. The adoption of [š] for this sound did not occur until the

---

1   I have consulted Paul Teyssier, *Histoire de la langue portugaise* (Paris: Presse Universitaires de France, 1980), 35-75; Thomas R. Hart, Jr., 'Notes on sixteenth-century Portuguese pronunciation', *Word*, 11 (1955), 404-15. I would also like to thank Dr. Stephen Parkinson for his advice on this area.

seventeenth century; the pronunciation of final -*ʃ* and -*z* as [š] similarly did not occur until the late eighteenth century in European Portuguese.

Galician Portuguese had maintained four sounds for the letters *ç/c*, *z*, *ʃʃ* and *ʃ*, namely [tš], [dz], [s] and [ž]. At around the time that Vicente began to write, however, *ç* and *z* had lost their initial element (*t* and *ð*) and were pronounced [š]and [z] respectively. *S* at the beginning of a word, or *ʃʃ* between two vowels) was thus pronounced as [š], as is the *ʃ* in Spanish, eg., *caʃa*; *ç* (or *c* before an *i* or an *e*) was pronounced [s]; -*ʃ*- (ie., a single *ʃ* between vowels) was pronounced as a [ž], and -*z*- was pronounced as [ž]. It is difficult to say, however, whether this feature of speech was spread amongst all levels of society, and it may be that such figures as the fool might have retained the mediæval pronunciation as a rustic feature of their speech. Confusion as to the differences between these consonantal sounds is evident from 1550 onwards. To a certain degree similar to *z* and *ç*, *g* and *j* were pronounced in Galician Portuguese as [dž], but again by Vicente's time, this had probably become [ž], although, again, rustic speech may well have preserved this form.

Printed and bound by CPI Group (UK) Ltd, Croydon, CR0 4YY

09/06/2025

14685957-0002